Women Entrepreneurship in Family Business

There has been growing attention placed on the role of female run and managed business in the global economy due to the increasing emphasis on gender equity. Despite the importance of female entrepreneurship, there has only been recently increased research attention devoted to entrepreneurship in the context of female entrepreneurship dynamics. This edited book examines female entrepreneurship and internationalization from both a practical and policy perspective and looks at the role of female entrepreneurship in the global economy.

Vanessa Ratten is Associate Professor of Entrepreneurship and Innovation at the Department of Entrepreneurship, Innovation and Marketing, La Trobe University, Australia.

Leo-Paul Dana is Professor of Entrepreneurship at Montpellier Business School, Montpellier, France.

Veland Ramadani is Associate Professor of Entrepreneurship and Management at the Faculty of Business and Economics, South East European University, Macedonia.

Routledge Frontiers of Business Management

For a full list of titles in this series, please visit www.routledge.com/series/rfbm

Women Entrepreneurship in Family Business

Edited by
Vanessa Ratten, Leo-Paul Dana
and Veland Ramadani

Routledge
Taylor & Francis Group

LONDON AND NEW YORK

First published 2018 by Routledge

2 Park Square, Milton Park, Abingdon, Oxfordshire OX14 4RN

52 Vanderbilt Avenue, New York, NY 10017

Routledge is an imprint of the Taylor & Francis Group, an informa business

First issued in paperback 2019

British Library Cataloguing-in-Publication Data
A catalogue record for this book is available from the British Library

Library of Congress Cataloging-in-Publication Data
A catalog record for this book has been requested

ISBN: 978-1-138-29861-3 (hbk)
ISBN: 978-0-367-37480-8 (pbk)

Typeset in Galliard
by Apex CoVantage, LLC

In memory of my mum, Kaye Ratten
March 9, 1948–June 23, 2014
—*Vanessa Ratten*

Dedicated to my wife, Teresa Elizabeth Dana
—*Leo-Paul Dana*

To my spouse, Lindita, for making my family happy
—*Veland Ramadani*

Contents

Figures

Tables

Contributors

Leona Achtenhagen is Professor of Entrepreneurship and Business Development at the Jönköping International Business School, Sweden.

Isabel C. Botero is Assistant Professor in Entrepreneurship and Family Business at the Department of Business, Stetson University, United States.

Laura Broccardo is Professor of Management at the Department of Management, University of Turin, Italy.

Andrea Caputo is Assistant Professor at the Department of Management, University of Lincoln, United Kingdom.

Leo-Paul Dana is Professor of Entrepreneurship at Montpellier Business School, Montpellier, France.

Luisa De Vita is Professor of Political Science, Sociology and Communication at the Faculty of Political Science, Sociology and Communication, La Sapienza University of Rome.

Luz Elena Orozco Collazos is Assistant Professor of Business at the Department of Business, Universidad de Los Andes, Colombia.

Kerstin Ettl is Junior Professor of Entrepreneurial Diversity and SME Management at the Department of Business, University of Siegen, Germany.

Alessandra Faraudelleo is Professor of Business at the Department of Management, Eastern Piedmont University, Italy.

Yanav Farja is Professor of Business at the Department of Business, Tel-Hai College, Israel.

Josanco Floreani is Associate Professor of Finance at the Department of Business, University of Udine, Italy.

Johan Gaddefors is Professor at the Department of Economics, Swedish University of Agricultural Sciences, Sweden.

Eli Gimmon is Professor of Business at the Department of Business, Tel-Hai College, Israel.

Luca Gnan is Professor of Entrepreneurship at the Department of Business, University of Rome Tor Vergata, Italy.

Zeevik Greenberg is Professor of Business at the Department of Business, Tel-Hai College, Israel.

Kajsa Haag is Assistant Professor at the Centre of Family Enterprise and Ownership, Jönköping University, Sweden.

Michela Mari is Professor of Management at the Department of Management and Law, University of Rome Tor Vergata.

Michela Mason is Associate Professor of Management at the Department of Business, University of Udine, Italy.

André Pahnke is Senior Researcher at the Institut für Mittelstandsforschung (IfM) Bonn, Germany.

Ramo Palalić is Assistant Professor of Business in the Department of Management, International University of Sarajevo, Bosnia and Herzegovina.

Massimiliano Pellegrini is Assistant Professor of Entrepreneurship at the Department of Business, University of Rome Tor Vergata, Italy.

Sara Poggesi is Professor of Management at the Department of Management and Law, University of Rome Tor Vergata, Italy.

Veland Ramadani is Associate Professor of Entrepreneurship and Management at the Faculty of Business and Economics, South East European University, Macedonia.

Vanessa Ratten is Associate Professor of Entrepreneurship and Innovation at the Department of Entrepreneurship, Innovation and Marketing, La Trobe University, Australia.

Annie Roos is Professor of Entrepreneurship at the Department of Economics, Swedish University of Agricultural Sciences, Sweden.

Lucrezia Songini is Professor of Entrepreneurship at the Department of Business. Eastern Piedmont University, Italy.

Elisa Truant is Professor of Management at the Department of Management, University of Turin, Italy.

Maria Piedad Lopez Vergara is Professor of Management at the Department of Management, Universidad de La Sabana, Colombia.

Friederike Welter is President of IfM Bonn and Professor of SME Management and Entrepreneurship at the Department of Business, University of Siegen, Germany.

1 Women entrepreneurship in family business

An overview

*Vanessa Ratten, Leo-Paul Dana
and Veland Ramadani*

Introduction

To advance economically and be more independent, women entrepreneurs often start their own businesses (Malach-Pines and Schwartz, 2008). This has influenced the growth of women entrepreneurs in family businesses, which are one of the largest types of overall businesses in the global economy. Women are at the forefront of global economic growth but much of the existing research on entrepreneurship has studied male entrepreneurs with less focus on women (Brush, 1992). This is largely due to the social constructions of women entrepreneurs in society. Mirchandani (1999:228) states that there is "recognition that sexual difference (that is, the difference between males and females) is socially constructed". This has led to feminist theories of entrepreneurship suggesting that the focus of research needs to be on the way work is considered gendered (Mirchandani, 1999).

Much of the research on women's entrepreneurship in family business has followed two major paths. The first is that women entrepreneurs face constraints in family businesses because of their gender. This means that there are gender-based characteristics that affect the way a woman behaves in a family business. Despite these differences women entrepreneurship can enhance the diversity of entrepreneurship in the global economy (Jamali, 2009). The second is that women create different types of family businesses that are based on relationships and trust rather than the more economic reasons favoured by men. Typically, men entrepreneurs have had more education, work experience and social networks than women entrepreneurs but this is changing (Carter and Brush, 2005). Women entrepreneurs express themselves differently than do males, which influences their conduct in family business (Chant, 2014). In addition, women usually have different motivations for becoming an entrepreneur including as a way of balancing work and family life (Petridou et al., 2009). Therefore, more recent research about women entrepreneurs in family businesses has focused on the service type of businesses they create in the global economy. For example, Greene et al. (2003) suggests that women-owned businesses typically are smaller, more service-based and grow more slowly than male-owned businesses.

The objective of this chapter is to set the stage for more research into women's entrepreneurship in family business. This will help motivate readers to appraise the role that women in family businesses play in society. This chapter will suggest important contributions towards the study of women's entrepreneurship in family business and how it can inform future research. This will help to build the research about women's entrepreneurship in family businesses by strengthening its role in the overall entrepreneurship literature.

Women's entrepreneurship

Despite the increased number of women starting businesses they generally have a lower level of entrepreneurial activity than males (Langowitz and Minniti, 2007). Despite this there are a variety of opportunities women have when they become entrepreneurs including challenges, independence and initiative (Jamali, 2009). Women entrepreneurs often start businesses to foster social relationships in the community through economic means and family involvement (Galloway et al., 2015). In addition, women entrepreneurs have tended to tap into family support as a way to help develop their businesses. Therefore, critical factors for women entrepreneurs is their self belief and confidence in realizing their business potential through family businesses (Glover, 2014).

There has been a tendency in entrepreneurship research to undervalue the contextual elements and applicability to women (Bruin et al., 2007). This is due to there being both similarities and differences between women and male entrepreneurs in family business. Women are normally considered to focus more on personal enjoyment as part of their reason for being an entrepreneur. Robichaud et al. (2005) supports this view by suggesting that women focus more on intrinsic factors such as self-actualization rather than the male goal of economic performance. Moreover, there is a traditional male stereotype of entrepreneurs that is influenced by societal attitudes towards males in family business.

There are both micro- and macro-level factors affecting women's entrepreneurship in family business. The micro-level factors include opportunity identification, motivation, financing and performance (Jamali, 2009). Opportunity identification for women entrepreneurs includes examining ways they can succeed in involvement in a family business. This may include succession planning or international expansion, depending on the nature of the family business. A motivation might be for women to continue being part of a family through their businesses. Thus, motivations can include maintaining social relationships as well as financial independence (Harrison and Mason, 2007). Financing for women entrepreneurs involves owning part of a family business. This means that women entrepreneurs might have financial considerations as part of their reasons for being involved in a family business. Performance refers to the potential of the family business to grow (Shaw et al., 2009). For many women entrepreneurs the success of a family business is linked to personal goals (Marlow et al., 2009). Macro-level factors include the legal, normative and economic environment (Jamali, 2009). The legal environment in some countries may favour men as business owners due to financial restrictions. The normative environment includes more cultural elements such as ways women are supposed to behave in family businesses. The economic environment refers to the stage of development of a country in terms of productivity and investment with some more developed countries better able to support women entrepreneurs (Sinar, 1975).

There have been social changes over the past decade that have affected traditional sex roles and gender-based vocations (Mueller and Dato-on, 2008). These changes have been linked to the conventional sex roles applied to the involvement of women in business and types of conduct. Feminine behaviours in business include dependency, interpersonal warmth, nurturing and passivity (Sinar, 1975). In comparison, masculine behaviours include aggression, assertiveness and independence. Mueller and Dato-on (2008) refer to masculinity as "instrumentality" in terms of getting the work done whilst femininity is called "expressiveness" as it concerns the harmony of others. These gender stereotypes have been developed through cultural conditioning and socialization (Mueller and Dato-on, 2008). In addition, female behaviour is considered linked to their family in terms of the occupational roles they undertake.

Gender attitudes whilst being a form of stereotype continue to persist in business despite changing social conditions. Increasingly there has been more emphasis on people who possess both feminine and masculine traits called "androgyny". Mueller and Dato-on (2008:10) state "androgynous people have the ability to effectively utilize behaviour that is both instrumental and expressive, both assertive and yielding, and both feminine and masculine". There are less-well-understood explanations for the role of women entrepreneurs in family businesses. Social feminist theory suggests that the differences between males and females are due to socialization processes evident at an early age (Harrison and Mason, 2007). This is evident with males seen as being socialized and educated about entrepreneurship more than are women (Scherer et al., 1990). Women are seen as having lower levels of human, financial and social capital compared to men when engaging in entrepreneurship, which affects their involvement in family businesses.

Family businesses

Family businesses engage in strategic entrepreneurship whilst continuing their pursuit of profit maximization. Increased performance for family businesses results when they focus on strategic entrepreneurship. More literature has stressed the interlinkage between the family business and strategic entrepreneurship literature but there is still a need for further understanding. This chapter seeks to fill the gap by suggesting a theory of women's entrepreneurship in family business that emphasizes its strategic nature. This helps to create new research avenues and opportunities for further research.

The composition of a family depends on the time period. Families can take the form of clan, endogamous, polygamous and tribal (Bettinelli et al., 2014). Moreover, families have been referred to as "organizations" due to their ability to work together for a common goal. The definition of family is open to interpretation based on individual preconceptions. The role of non-blood relations such as husband/wives in family businesses determines their involvement in managerial decisions. Some definitions of family businesses work on the basis that a person will determine its meaning based on their own values. Family businesses can be classified on a continuum from little family involvement to complete family and business linkage (Bettinelli et al., 2014). A commonly applied definition of family businesses is

> a business governed and/or managed with the intention to shape and/or pursue the vision of the business held by a dominate coalition controlled by members of the same family or a small number of families in a manner that is potentially sustainable across generations of the family or families.
>
> (Chua et al., 1999: 25)

A family is defined by its commitment to a shared future and the well-being of a group of people. Bettinelli et al. (2014) further explains how most definitions of a family focus on the interdependence of a group of people that is strengthened by network ties. The difference between a family and a group of people is the long-term nature of their involvement with each other. Long-term Furthermore, Hoy and Verser (1994) suggests that the source of family values is the ethnic backgrounds of family members. This is due to culture being a component of ethnicity, which affects organizational commitment. Hoy and Verser (1994:21) state that "although family businesses are prehistoric in origin, families (and therefore family businesses) are threatened today". Families are changing with different forms of domestic partnerships existing. This is in conjunction with families tending to be more of a hybrid nature combining both biological and emotional bonds. In addition, marriage rates have decreased so there is a changing composition of families over a time period.

Family businesses are an important contribution to society due to their influence in economic growth. Part of the crucial role that families play in the community comes from the way family involvement influences entrepreneurship. Family involvement affects the level of innovation, risk taking and competitiveness in business. Family businesses are complicated by the dynamics existing within the family. Non-economic goals such as family harmony and emotional well-being are important for family business. This means that success in family business is measured by business performance and functionality of the family. The family sometimes is considered an impediment to the success of a business. The problematic aspect of a family business includes children and sibling rivalry. There is also gender dynamics in families with individuals contributing both to the family and business. In addition, the interpersonal dynamics in families means that communication can depend on relationship status within the family.

The anticipation of change is important to family businesses as they transition into new markets. These changes can be in terms of building family security in a business and meeting challenges. In difficult times family businesses survive because of the family rather than because of the business. The functionality integrity of a family is affected by tensions about business issues. Families that manage home-based businesses effectively tend to have an increased business net income. This has resulted in sustainable family business models which are defined as "a model that gives equal recognition to the family and the business and the interplay between the two in achieving sustainability for both" (Olson et al., 2003: 642).

The interaction style between family members affects the family business income. This is due to more engaged communication styles including accessibility for all family business members being important. Some communication in families is routinized but others is individualized depending on the style of each family business member (Olson et al., 2003). Moreover, satisfaction with a family business has been shown to correlate with increased income and health of family members. Family businesses with more non-family employees have lower levels of business success. In a family business, there is ongoing competition balancing the needs of the family versus those of the business.

Family businesses have interpersonal social relationships that influence learning processes (Hall and Nordqvist, 2008). Younger generations of family businesses often learn before joining the business. They do this by sharing experiences and discussing issues about the family business. The learning takes the form of etiquettes, norms and practices that distinguish the family business from non-family businesses.

Family businesses need to think beyond current generations to understand succession issues and participation models. This can be accomplished by family members learning from other family businesses in order to build better capabilities. The awareness of innovation scenarios could help encourage family businesses to engage in more creative processes. However, there is more work to be done on understanding the entrepreneurial process in different types of family businesses. Little research has been conducted on family businesses in the gender context and an effort to study new industries would be helpful.

In family businesses there is an organizational authority in the family that affects decisions. This authority figure can exploit opportunities by deciding on entrepreneurial action. Family relationships are important to economic and entrepreneurial development. Gimeno et al. (2010) suggests that the main categories of family businesses are captain, corporation, emperor, family investment group, family team and professional family. The captain form of family business is managed by the founder who makes all decisions (Ramadani and Hoy, 2015). This means that the founder steers the business towards goals that they want to achieve. Depending on the founders' objectives the goals may relate to business performance or may be non-economic goals like lifestyle decisions. The corporation model has a complex family business structure that is usually older than other family businesses. Often corporation style family businesses develop into new businesses that integrate non-family members. The emperor model links the business and family by a leader who oversees decisions and is the central authority figure. There are normally multiple generations of a family working together in the emperor model as there is a dynastic synergy to business affairs. The family investment group involves family members pooling resources for financial reasons. The distinguishing feature of the family investment model is that usually non-family members manage the financial resources. This enables a separation between the family and business, which helps maintain neutrality. The family team model involves a group of family members working in a business. Most forms of family teams work in small business as they can structure work around a certain activity. The professional family model involves normally service based activities. This means that the level of complexity of the business task is high enabling family members to work together in a professional capacity.

Family business participation can be classified into four main groups: non-family members, inactive family members, the senior generation and the incumbent generation (Venter et al., 2012). Non-family members are those people who assist in the family business but are not part of the family. Examples of non-family members include advisors, and consultants who provide input to the business activities (Ramadani and Hoy, 2015). Inactive family members are individuals who have worked or won part of the business but are not currently involved in the family business. Often inactive family members become active members again when they are needed in the business. The senior generation includes older members of the family business who started the business. They are involved in succession planning for the future of the family business. The senior generations helps to share knowledge about the business in order to achieve sustainable performance. The incumbent generation is comprised of younger family members who are yet to enter the family business. These individuals are still at school or engaged in other professions but might enter the family business.

Family business entrepreneurship

Entrepreneurship involves the discovery of an opportunity and enactment of a resulting entrepreneurial action (Ferreira et al., 2017). There has been overall an increase in entrepreneurship worldwide that has coincided with more people starting their own businesses. The intention and action of entrepreneurial behaviours is important to perceived opportunities (Ferreira, et al., 2016). This change has been the result of organizations downsizing and increased usage of online communication. Entrepreneurship is a product of the environment and can be influenced by different external factors (Ratten, 2011). These include political and technological changes that affect business development. In uncertain economic times entrepreneurship paves the way for more job opportunities to be created. Cardon et al. (2005:24) states "entrepreneurship is often considered mysterious and sometimes even unknowable, the combination of idiosyncratic individuals and random circumstances".

Entrepreneurship has been described as a heroic pursuit in which a previously unattainable goal is achieved. Most definitions of entrepreneurship refer to risk taking and alertness to opportunities. This means that entrepreneurs often act as gap fillers by providing new services that combine resources in novel ways (Cardon et al., 2005). Entrepreneurs generate societal wealth by acting in a creative manner (Ratten, 2015). Entrepreneurship happens everyday through both actual and vicarious processes. Part of the entrepreneurial process involves passion, which inspires business ventures (Ratten, 2016). Passion helps entrepreneurs stay positive in times of hardship.

Webb, Ketchen, and Ireland (2010: 67) define strategic entrepreneurship as "simultaneously exploring for future business domains while exploiting current domains". Strategic entrepreneurship means that a business recognizes that it is important to exploit opportunities that have a long-term effect (Hodge and Ratten, 2015). Most of the research on strategic entrepreneurship is focused on large organizations, with little focus on small to medium-sized entities. Due to the large number of small family businesses, more attention is needed on strategic entrepreneurship.

Family entrepreneurship involves the intersection of two research topics: family business and entrepreneurship (Fayolle and Begin, 2009). This has led to the development of a new field called "family entrepreneurship", which involves enterprising families acting in an innovative manner. There are numerous ways family businesses can act entrepreneurial including adapting entrepreneurial attitudes that are novel in their industry (Nordqvist and Melin, 2010). Chua et al. (2004) suggests that entrepreneurship is the foundation of family businesses as it enables them to grow and develop.

There is increasingly more attention in the literature about the power of entrepreneurship to families. Family business entrepreneurs combine family structures with business ventures in a way that is different to other organizations. Bettinelli et al. (2014: 164) defines family entrepreneurship as "the research field that studies entrepreneurial behaviours of family, family members and family businesses". In family entrepreneurship there are entrepreneurial behaviours that occur at the family, individual and organizational level (Bettinelli et al., 2014). Sometimes it is hard to distinguish a family from a family business due to the interconnections. In family businesses entrepreneurship can occur in an existing business or when new family members enter the business. The changing composition of members in a family business means that when new people join, there can be an adjustment in ideas and vision. In many family businesses the exit of original or older members can mean a transition in thinking and behaviour. This means that it is important for entrepreneurship in family businesses to see the interactions between individuals, family and the organization.

Family businesses are generally defined as the participation and ownership of a family in a business. Strategic entrepreneurship involves a firm exploring future opportunities whilst working on current activities. Family businesses utilize strategic entrepreneurship as a way to foresee future changes in the market in order to predict new trends. A family business may choose to analyse the involvement of competitive environments to see how they can reinvent themselves. This reinvention can involve a process of understanding potential new business opportunities. The founder of a business is important as they include their own values and entrepreneurial attitude. The personality of a founder impacts the management structure of a business. This can impact the way a firm acts entrepreneurially by aligning the vision of the founder to business structure.

The dominant theoretical frameworks in family business are the agency and resource-based views (Chrisman et al., 2005). Hopefully, more theoretical perspectives will develop in the future that integrate changing societal definitions of family business. The addition of related theoretical approaches in other entrepreneurship or management disciplines could be applied to the family business context. The development of new theories about family entrepreneurship would help to further distinguish this field of entrepreneurship. In addition, a more systematic application of existing theories from other disciplines to family entrepreneurship would build the academic rigour of the field.

Family business culture

Most definitions of family business rely on the individual to make their own decision of what is meant when family and business are combined. For most individuals, family businesses imply that younger family members will enter the business once older ones retire. The stability of family businesses, which often rely on unpaid labour of family members in times of economic hardship, are crucial to community well-being. Family businesses have different types of cultures, including charismatic, paranoid and politicized (Ramadani and Hoy, 2015). Charismatic cultures have individuals (usually the founders or leaders of the business) who are passionate. This passion helps entice customers to the business due to the energy of the family business. Paranoid cultures are focused on protecting their assets and ideas at the expense of opening up to new people. This instils a fear of sharing information because of the perceived negative affects to the family business. Politicized cultures are characterized by an atmosphere of competition amongst divisions of the family business. The politics can also be between members of the family business.

Family businesses face succession issues due to the politics of leadership and managing a business.

Family entrepreneurs are found in every inhabited location around the world. Family entrepreneurial activities have a positive social affect on communities and their surrounding environment. Entrepreneurship development involves the process of actualizing a business idea by incorporating capabilities required to enhance the viability of the venture. Entrepreneurs combine or add resources based on new ideas to create new products or services. Family entrepreneurs need to have self-efficacy to be able to make business ideas a reality.

Individuals are embedded in different institutions, including cultural, political and societal, that affect entrepreneurship. The family is also an institution, but it is not often referred to as such because of its influence on everyday life. Bettinelli (2014: 173) states, "as a social institution, the family is historically and culturally positioned: inclusion criteria, the obligations and entitlements of each family member towards the family unit and their roles vary according to culture and/or ethnic group". Kirkwood and Tootell (2008: 285) defines work–family balance as "the extent to which individuals are both equally involved and equally satisfied with their work and family responsibilities". Organizations can help individuals with work–family balance by providing flexible work practices and financial assistance. Flexible work practices take a variety of different forms including compressed work weeks, career breaks and teleworking (Kirkwood and Tootell, 2008). Financial assistance can include childcare allowances, bank loans and workplace nurseries (Kirkwood and Tootell, 2008).

An interesting comparison between family and business systems is that goals, relationships, rules, evaluation and succession are ways to distinguish family from business systems. This is helpful as it acknowledges families have more supportive goals but businesses are interested in profitability. There are personal relationships in families compared to the secondary importance of relationships conducted in a business setting. The rules in families usually comprise an informal structure based on shared norms compared to the written and more formal codes of conduct in business settings. The evaluation of family systems is usually conducted via unconditional love compared to business systems that rely on performance. Succession in family systems is based on position in the family but in businesses it is based on need.

Organizational networks are influenced by the personal reputation of organization members. This helps to explain why human capital and the stability of employees in family businesses contribute to their reputation. The reputation of a family business comes from its level of trustworthiness, which helps build collaborative endeavours. There is likely to be more networking when an organization has a good reputation in the marketplace. Family capital involves the "expectation identity" and obligations that a family business has developed through social networks. "Expectation" refers to the types of products or services sold by a family business, while "identity" indicates how a family business positions itself in the market based on its attributes. Obligations involve a family business maintaining long-term relationships with certain customers and suppliers. Family businesses have an interdependence between family, management and ownership, which can complicate business structures (Howorth and Ali, 2001). In some family businesses it becomes difficult to distinguish between work and family.

Howorth and Ali (2001) suggest that the main forms of ownership structures in family business are controlling owner, cousin consortium and sibling partnership. Family businesses have been characterized as having a more humanistic working environment. This is due to the more relationship-based system existing in family businesses. Family businesses comprise diverse family members from both blood and non-blood relationships, which can sometimes be difficult for consensus building. Often family businesses last for only one generation due to a lack of succession planning and interest of second-generation members. In addition, there may be a conflict between the founder of a family business and the career objectives of subsequent generations. Policymakers should be aware of the entrepreneurship in family businesses and ways to increase innovation. Family businesses need to realize that they will be at an advantage by acting in an entrepreneurial manner by encouraging women to become involved.

Howorth and Ali (2001) suggest the main influence of culture in family business involves 1) size of the business, 2) ideology, 3) attitudes, 4) cognitive biases,

5) traditions and 6) education. First, the size of a family business depends on the amount of family members involved. The structural form that a family business takes influences the complexity and involvement of related family members. Second, the ideology of the family business will be based on its members' religious attitudes or philosophy. This determines the way business and family are linked, which impacts the conditions for relationships. Family members have special relationships that are based on trust and an implicit understanding about appropriate behaviour. Third, the attitudes of family business members towards innovation will be impacted by the founders' original mission. This is due to the belief of the family business towards others in the community. Fourth, cognitive biases are part of family businesses due to certain types of behaviour being evident. These behaviours influence the planning processes of a family business in terms of tactics and strategy. Fifth, the traditions of a family business (such as the way they make products, and how they conduct business) are part of its culture. These traditions might be entrenched based on the family's way of life or they may be based on gender. The selection of leaders in the business will be based on these traditions. Sixth, education is part of culture in terms of the value placed on learning and knowledge within the family. Education influences future generations of a family business by providing exposure to outside ideas.

Family business decision making processes

There are few theoretical approaches to family business that explain regional economic development. Family businesses are unique due to their ability to meld family with economic endeavours. The decision making process of family businesses differs due to the usually controlled ownership structure compared to the disperse ownership of corporations. The decisions that family businesses make are similar to those made by corporations except they might focus more on social objectives due to their link with the community (Block and Wagner, 2014). This is due to the trade-offs family businesses make between profit considerations and stakeholder goals. Hall et al. (2001:193) states "family firms are often characterized as being introverted, burdened by old traditions, inflexible and resistant to change".

The entrepreneurial capacity of family businesses usually lessen as the organization matures (Hall et al., 2001). The original founders of family businesses usually are the more entrepreneurial as they sought an advantage in the marketplace and developed. Subsequent generations in family businesses are said to be less entrepreneurial as they inherit an existing business with established principles. Smircich (1983) proposed two main ways to understand culture: as a tool and as part of an organization. The first approach suggests that culture is dynamic and based on environmental trends. The second approach states that organizations are cultures and this means that they evolve based on people's behaviour within them. Hall et al. (2001:195) defines culture as "beliefs, values, norms, traditions" which depends on the context. Families have their own form of culture as they share beliefs and attitudes towards society. A family's culture is based on its relationships and environment but also its location. In large family businesses the culture involves collective action throughout the organization (Hall et al., 2001).

There is resistance to change in family businesses due to emotions and feelings being more intense within them than non-family businesses. This is influenced by the family values instilled in the business, which can create inertia but are also a strength. A way to overcome stagnation in family businesses is to reinstall an entrepreneurial vision. This helps to re-evaluate current behaviour and affects future strategic capabilities by encouraging entrepreneurship. The entrepreneurial capacity in an organization involves the social relations between employees and stakeholders. Change from entrepreneurial processes comes from rethinking and alternative actions. This means that all members of a family business need to view entrepreneurship as important for long-term performance. This can be conducted by encouraging people in a family business to take risks and be innovative (Hall et al., 2001).

The family business literature has its roots in a variety of disciplines from small business management to organizational behaviour (Heck et al., 2008). Most of the original family business research centred around case studies (Heck et al., 2008). Heck et al. (2008: 320) states "the theme of family business entrepreneurship has provided to be a stimulus for interdisciplinary research addressing issues such as social-capital-based familiness, conflicting family versus business system, and the dark side of entrepreneurship". The link between family business to entrepreneurship is important as it influences societal wealth creation (Heck et al., 2008). The family is an informal way of supporting business that is helpful in the start-up phase. Family capital involves the assets of a family that help to build its wealth. Sorenson and Bierman (2009: 193) defines family capital as the "financial, human and social resources available to the business". Family capital is part of the way women entrepreneurs can be included more in family businesses.

Overview of book chapters

This first chapter of the book has focused on providing an overview of women's entrepreneurship in family business. The second chapter, by Leona Achtenhagen, Kajsa Haag and Friederike Welter, discusses the role of gender in family-business research by providing a systematic overview of the literature. This chapter is useful in providing an guide for the other chapters as to how women in terms of their gender affect the development of family businesses. The third chapter, by André Pahnke, Kerstin Ettl and Friederike Welter, examines the role of women-led enterprises in Germany. Increasingly there are more businesses with women leadership in that country. The fourth chapter, by Laura Broccardo and Elisa Truant, highlights differences between family and non-family firms by analyzing their performance in the Italian and Spanish wine sectors. The fifth chapter, by Alessandra Faraudello, Lucrezia Songini, Massimiliano Pellegrini and Luca Gnan, focuses on the role of women as entrepreneurs by providing a literature review. This is helpful in understanding the contextual factors affecting women as entrepreneurs in family businesses. The sixth chapter, by Annie Roos and Johan

Gaddefors, focuses on sampling issues in research about gender and entrepreneurship. The seventh chapter, by Eli Gimmon, Zeevik Greenberg and Yanav Farja, discusses the role of spouse involvement, which is important in family business. The eighth chapter, by Michela C. Mason and Josanco Floreani, examines the role of gender diversity in top Italian family firms. As there is more attention being placed on the role of women in corporate governance, this chapter is useful in understanding its influence on the performance of family businesses. The ninth chapter, by Luz Elena Orozco Collazos, Isabel C. Botero and Maria Piedad López Vergara, examines the issue of whether women make a difference in family firms. The authors focus on Latin America, which provides an interesting environmental context for the role of women entrepreneurs in family firms. The tenth chapter, by Andrea Caputo, Luisa De Vita, Michela Mari and Sara Poggesi, discusses the role of female entrepreneurship in developing contexts. As women entrepreneurs face different cultural and social barriers in developing countries, this chapter provides a good overview of the challenges and dynamics involved in businesses located in those regions. The eleventh chapter, by Ramo Palalić, Veland Ramadani, Leo-Paul Dana and Vanessa Ratten, discusses how gender affects entrepreneurial leadership in family businesses. This is helpful in understanding how countries such as Bosnia and Herzegovina are implementing women-friendly policies in family businesses. The twelfth chapter, by Laura Broccardo and Elisa Truant, focuses on the role of corporate governance in Italian family firms. This is important in examining the role of women in family business. The last chapter, by Vanessa Ratten, Veland Ramadani and Leo-Paul Dana, concludes the book by highlighting future research directions for women's entrepreneurship in family business.

Conclusion

This chapter is a reference for researchers, practitioners and policymakers interested in women's entrepreneurship and family business. The chapter helped to explain the origins and development of women's entrepreneurship in family business and to predict the research questions that need answering. It provided useful suggestions for scholars already researching women's entrepreneurship and family business and those intending to in the future. As there has been more interest in family business and women's entrepreneurship in general, the growth of family entrepreneurship studies will continue in the future. This chapter helped to identify gaps in current research that will help future research efforts.

References

Bettinelli, C., Fayolle, A., and Randerson, K. (2014). Family entrepreneurship: A developing field. *Foundations and Trends in Entrepreneurship*, 10(3), 161–236.
Block, J.H., and Wagner, M. (2014). The effect of family ownership on different dimensions of corporate social responsibility: Evidence from large US firms. *Business Strategy and the Environment*, 23(7), 475–492.

Bruin, A., Brush, C., and Welter, F. (2007). Advancing a framework for coherent research on women's entrepreneurship. *Entrepreneurship Theory & Practice*, 31(3), 323–339.

Brush, C. (1992). Research on women business owners: Past trends, a new perspective and future directions. *Entrepreneurship Theory and Practice*, 17(4),5–30.

Cardon, M., Zietsma, C., Saparito, P., Matherne, B.P., and Davis, C. (2005). A tale of passion: New insights into entrepreneurship from a parenthood metaphor. *Journal of Business Venturing*, 20(1), 23–45.

Carter, N., and Brush, C. (2005). Gender. In W. Gartner, K. Shaver, N. Carter and P. Reynolds (eds.), *Handbook of entrepreneurial dynamics: The process of business creation* (pp. 12–25). Sage, Thousand Oaks, CA.

Chant, S. (2014). Exploring the feminization of poverty in relation to women's work and home-based enterprise in slums of the Global South. *International Journal of Gender and Entrepreneurship*, 6(3), 296–316.

Chrisman, J.J., Chua, J.H., and Sharma, P. (2005). Trends and directions in the development of a strategic management theory of the family firm. *Entrepreneurship Theory and Practice*, 29(5), 555–575.

Chua, J., Chrisman, J.J., and Chang, E.P. (2004). Are family firms born or made? An exploratory investigation. *Family Business Review*, 17(1), 37–54.

Chua, J., Chrisman, J.J., and Sharma, P. (1999). Defining the family business by behavior. *Entrepreneurship Theory and Practice*, 23(4), 19–39.

Fayolle, A., and Begin, L. (2009). Entrepreneuriat familial: Croisement de deux champs ou nouveau champ issu d'un double croisement? *Management International/Gestion Internacional*, 14(1), 11–23.

Ferreira, J., Fernandes, C.I., and Ratten, V. (2016). A co-citation bibliometric analysis of strategic management research. *Scientometrics*, 109(1),1–32.

Ferreira, J., Fernandes, C.I., and Ratten, V. (2017). Entrepreneurship, innovation and competitiveness: What is the connection? *International Journal of Business and Globalisation*, 18(1), 73–95.

Galloway, L., Kapasi, I., and Sang, K. (2015). Entrepreneurship, leadership and the value of feminist approaches to understanding them. *Journal of Small Business Management*, 54(3), 683–697.

Gimeno, J., Baulenas, G., and Coma-Cros, J. (2010). Family business models. In *Family business models* (pp. 57–77). Palgrave Macmillan.

Glover, J.C. (2014). Gender, power and succession in family farm business. *International Journal of Gender and Entrepreneurship*, 6(3), 276–295.

Greene, P., Hart, M., Gatewood, E., Brush, C., and Carter, N. (2003). *Women entrepreneurs: Moving front and center: An overview of research and theory*. White Paper Series, US Association for Small Business and Entrepreneurship, Boca Raton, Florida.

Hall, A., Melin, L., and Nordqvist, M. (2001). Entrepreneurship as radical change in the family business: Exploring the role of cultural patterns. *Family Business Review*, 14(3), 193–208.

Hall, A., and Nordqvist, M. (2008). Professional management in family businesses: Toward an extended understanding. *Family Business Review*, 21(1), 51–69.

Harrison, R.T., and Mason, C.M. (2007, May). Does gender matter? Women business angels and the supply of entrepreneurial finance. *Entrepreneurship Theory & Practice*, 445–472.

Heck, R.K., Hoy, F., Poutziouris, P.Z., and Steier, L.P. (2008). Emerging paths of family entrepreneurship research. *Journal of Small Business Management*, 46(3), 317–330.

Hodge, J., and Ratten, V. (2015). Time pressure and improvisation: Enhancing creativity, adaption and innovation at high speed. *Development and Learning in Organizations: An International Journal*, 29(6),7–9.

Howorth, C., and Ali, Z.A. (2001). Family business succession in Portugal: An examination of case studies in the furniture industry. *Family Business Review*, 14(3), 231–244.

Hoy, F., and Verser, T.G. (1994). Emerging business, emerging field: Entrepreneurship and the family firm. *Entrepreneurship Theory and Practice*, 19(1),9–24.

Jamali, D. (2009). Constraints and opportunities facing women entrepreneurs in developing countries: A relational perspective. *Gender in Management: An International Journal*, 24(4), 232–251.

Kirkwood, J., and Tootell, B. (2008). Is entrepreneurship the answer to achieving work-family balance? *Journal of Management and Organization*, 14(3), 285.

Langowitz, N., and Minniti, M. (2007). The entrepreneurial propensity of women. *Entrepreneurship Theory & Practice*, 31(3), 341–364.

Malach-Pines, A., and Schwartz, D. (2008). Now you see them, now you don't: Gender differences in entrepreneurship. *Journal of Managerial Psychology*, 23(7), 811–832.

Marlow, S., Henry, C., and Carter, S. (2009). Exploring the impact of gender upon women's business ownership. *International Small Business Journal*, 27(2), 139–148.

Mirchandani, K. (1999). Feminist insight on gendered work: New direction in research on women and entrepreneurship. *Gender, Work and Organization*, 6(4), 224–235.

Mueller, S. L., and Dato-On, M. C. (2008). Gender-role orientation as a determinant of entrepreneurial self-efficacy. Journal of developmental Entrepreneurship, 13(1), 3–20.

Nordqvist, M., and Melin, L. (2010). Entrepreneurial families and family firms. *Entrepreneurship and Regional Development*, 22(3–4), 211–239.

Olson, P., Zuiker, V., Danes, S., Statford, K., Heck, R., and Duncan, K. (2003). The impact of the family and the business on family business sustainability. *Journal of Business Venturing*, 18(5), 639–666.

Petridou, E., Sarri, A., and Kyrgidou, L.P. (2009). Entrepreneurship education in higher education institutions: The gender dimension. *Gender in Management: An International Journal*, 24(4), 286–309.

Ramadani, V., and Hoy, F. (2015). Context and uniqueness of family businesses. In V. Ramadani and F. Hoy (eds.), *In family businesses in transition economies* (pp. 9–37). Heidelberg: Springer.

Ratten, V. (2011). Ethics, entrepreneurship and the adoption of e-book devices. *International Journal of Innovation and Learning*, 10(3), 310–325.

Ratten, V. (2015). International consumer attitudes toward cloud computing: A social cognitive theory and technology acceptance model perspective. *Thunderbird International Business Review*, 57(3), 217–228.

Ratten, V. (2016). The dynamics of sport marketing: Suggestions for marketing intelligence and planning. *Marketing Intelligence & Planning*, 34(2), 162–168.

Robichaud, Y., McGraw, E., and Roger, A. (2005). L'influence des objectifs des entrepreneurs sur la performance des petites enterprises: Une comparison homes/femmes. *Revue de Gestion des Resources Humaines*, 55, 22–35.

Scherer, R.F., Brodzinsky, J.D., and Wiebe, F.A. (1990). Entrepreneur career selection and gender: A socialization approach. *Journal of Small Business Management*, 28(2), 37–43.

Shaw, E., Marlow, S., Lam, W., and Carter, S. (2009). Gender and entrepreneurial capital: Implications for firm performance. *International Journal of Gender and Entrepreneurship*, 1(1), 25–41.

Sinar, E.H. (1975). Sexual stereotypes of occupations. *Journal of Vocational Behavior*, 7, 99–111.

Smircich, L. (1983). Concepts of culture and organizational analysis. *Administrative Science Quarterly*, 1, 339–358.

Sorenson, R.L., and Bierman, L. (2009). Family capital, family business, and free enterprise. *Family Business Review*, 22(3), 193–195.

Venter, E., Van der Merwe, S., and Farrington, S. (2012). The impact of selected stakeholders on family business continuity and family harmony. *Southern African Business Review*, 16(2), 69–96.

Webb, J. W., Ketchen, D. J., and Ireland, R. D. (2010). Strategic entrepreneurship within family-controlled firms: Opportunities and challenges. *Journal of family business strategy*, 1(2), 67–77.

2 The role of gender in family-business research

A systematic review of the literature

Leona Achtenhagen, Kajsa Haag and Friederike Welter

Introduction

In 2009, the *Family Business Review* published a review of research examining women's involvement in family firms (Martinez Jimenez, 2009). The author identified two waves of research findings published since 1985: The first wave centered around analyzing obstacles and difficulties that women encountered when joining their family firms as well as on the lack of recognition for their work. The second wave, mainly consisting of more recent publications, appeared to be more positive towards women's involvement, discussing opportunities and advantages that family businesses can offer women, the pathways of women into leadership positions, and their performance. Despite an apparent increase in interest in women's role in family businesses, Martinez Jimenez (2009) found the research to still be fragmented and few empirical studies, confirming Sharma's (2004: 14) statement that the family business field lacks systematic research about contextual and individual factors related to women in these firms, and especially leadership positions. Martinez Jimenez concluded that no academic work had analyzed the leadership style of women in the family firm in depth and called for more research on "how women run their family firms, what their leadership style is, or how they behave with other members of the firm" (Martinez Jimenez, 2009: 60). However, there appears not only to be a dearth of empirical studies, but also of explicit, gender-based theorizing – for example, Al-Dajani et al. (2014: 218) regret that "despite a growing interest in gender and family business, there is limited literature that explores gender theory within family business research".

Why is a better understanding of the relation between gender and family business relevant? The first, and rather obvious, reason is that women constitute one half of family members, and thus it will be difficult to fully understand family businesses without considering women's roles more explicitly. Second, recent studies propose that family-business successions through daughters outperform those by sons (Ahrens et al., 2015), and the highly educated generation of young women in family businesses increasingly questions the tradition of primogeniture male succession. Also, family businesses are more often run by a female CEO than non-family firms (Jorissen et al., 2005). Thus, a better understanding of women's leadership of family businesses could make an important contribution to family-firm practice. Third, gender issues do not concern women only. Rather, both men and women are increasing traditional family patterns and gender roles – and traversing them – with some people living in patchwork families or with transgender identities. These trends represent a move beyond common images of what constitutes a family and family roles, and they will increasingly have an impact on family businesses and their core questions, such as succession and transgenerational entrepreneurship. Thus, they deserve more focused theorizing.

Almost a decade of research has been published since Martinez Jimenez's (2009) review, which included articles mainly until 2005. The aim of this chapter is to provide an up-to-date, systematic literature review of the research on the intersection between gender and family business published since then, outlining the status quo of the discussion and suggesting a research agenda to move the field forward. The remainder of this chapter is structured as follows. We briefly introduce the method used for our systematic literature review. Then, we present the results along identified themes. We conclude the chapter by outlining gaps in current research and proposing how these could be filled.

Method

In this chapter, we systematically review research published about the link between gender and family firms since 2006 (excluding articles that have been mentioned in Martinez Jimenez's 2009 review). More specifically, the academic database Scopus was searched with the following query: TITLE-ABS-KEY (gender OR son OR daughter OR couple OR wife OR husband OR father OR mother OR brother OR sister OR female OR male OR wom*n OR patriarch OR matriarch OR parent OR sibling) AND ("family firm" OR "family business" OR "family ent*") AND PUBYEAR > 2005. The search was restricted to business, management, and accounting, and works published in the English language, and excluding conference papers. This search led to 408 publications (articles, reviews, books, book chapters, articles in press and editorials). Based on the titles and abstracts, only those publications relevant for the relation between gender and family business were downloaded and reviewed. Sixteen articles that made some reference to male gender issues, such as a link between fathers and sons, were excluded from further analysis, as they did not address gender aspects within this relation.

Surprisingly few articles have been published on gender issues in the two leading family business journals in the field, *Family Business Review* and *Journal of Family Business Strategy*. Only 10 articles in total with a clear focus on gender issues could be found in these journals since 2006. Some publications on the relation of gender and family business can also be found in other established mainstream entrepreneurship and management journals, such as *Entrepreneurship Theory & Practice* or the *Journal of Small Business Management*. More attention to a range of different themes regarding the relation between gender and family business can be found in more niched, lower-impact journals, such as the

International Journal of Gender and Entrepreneurship or the *Journal of Family Business Management*. For example, the former published a special issue on the theme in 2014, exploring the extent to which gendered processes are reinforced (or not) in family-business operations and dynamics (Al-Dajani et al., 2014).

Findings

From our review of published research on the intersection of gender and family business, a number of themes emerged that will be discussed in the following. In addition, literature regarding two focused themes with a large number of publications – succession and copreneurship – is summarized in Tables 2.1 and 2.2.

Succession

The first key theme is that of succession. An overview of selected publications within this theme can be found in Table 2.1.

The articles addressing this theme typically follow one of three paths. The first path refers to articles discussing the choice or comparison between male or female successors, most of which employ gender merely as a variable. For example, Ahrens et al. (2015) study gender preferences for CEO succession in family firms. They find that in family firms with both genders among the predecessor's children, a male family successor is chosen in 82.1 percent of the cases, and the presence of sons significantly increases the probability of family succession. However, they also find that post-succession performance is reduced by 8 percent with male family succession, while it is increased by 7 percent with female family succession. The gender preference is confirmed by Schröder, Schmitt-Rodermund and Arnaud (2011), who find a paternal preference for boys to take over the family firm. In a study of Danish family businesses, Bennedsen Nielsen, Pérez-González, and Wolfenzon (2007) similarly find that the likelihood of deciding to appoint a family successor is significantly higher when the firstborn child is a boy. Haberman and Danes (2007), in one of the few articles using gender as a lens, compare power structures and interactions among family businesses with intergenerational management transition from father to son in one company and father to daughter in another company. They find women in the father–son business to experience feelings of exclusion and incidents of higher conflict among family members, while women in the father–daughter business experience feelings of inclusion, resulting in lower conflict. Koffi et al. (2014) take a different approach and instead investigate how male and female predecessors establish the legitimacy of their successors.

The second path covers articles studying aspects related to women and succession. For example, Overbeke et al. (2013) study factors contributing to daughters' self-assessments regarding succession. They point out daughters' own blindness to the possibility of succession (resulting from automatically activated gender norms), and find that daughters may not deliberately consider succession until a critical event motivates them to do so. Gherardi and Perrotta (2016) and

Table 2.1 Overview of selected publications on succession

Author(s) (year)	Main research question/ aim	Theoretical background	Type of study	Main finding
Gherardi and Perrotta (2016)	Exploring gender and legitimacy in family business (FB) succession	Adding a gender dimension to French pragmatist sociology	Case studies of Italian SMEs with daughters taking over	Shows how daughters' perceived gender inequality in the succession process is justified, how the justification work and the production of legitimacy are accomplished, shifting from one order of worth to the other
Meglio (2016)	Offers alternative understanding of intergenerational transition process through a temporal lens	Time as theoretical focus	Single case of father-daughter succession in small FB	Highlights how one possible source of conflict between father and daughter is their different use of and meanings attached to time
Mathew (2016)	What are the key characteristics and challenges for females in family business succession?	N/A	Case study in Asia	The results reject the general assumption "that selection of successor is based on gender rather than capabilities and skills and women are less competent to take an entrepreneurial role as successor of the family business" (p. 410).
Liu (2015)	Descriptive case study of FB development	N/A	Single case study of development of a family business over time	Due to illness of the founder, his wife takes over and successfully develops the business, and also brings in their son. Reaching retirement age, she needs to decide whether the son should take over.
Cicellin, Mussolino, and Viganò, (2015)	Examines the impact of paternalistic leadership on the gender diversity of family firm succession	Paternalism	Conceptual	Conceptual model that considers different types of paternalistic leadership styles as factors that increase or decrease the likelihood of success of the succession, according to the gender of the successor

(Continued)

Table 2.1 (Continued)

Author(s) (year)	Main research question/ aim	Theoretical background	Type of study	Main finding
Ahrens et al. (2015)	What are the gender preferences for CEO succession in FBs?	Contest theory; agency theory; human capital	Quantitative study of 804 successions in non-publicly listed German family firms between 2002 and 2008	If both genders are represented among predecessors, males are chosen in 81.2% of the cases; presence of sons significantly increases probability of family succession; female family successors equipped with significantly higher levels of human capital; post-succession performance is reduced by 8% in male succession, and increased by 7% after female succession
Tong (2014)	Explore the drawbacks of Asian business networking	Guanxi	Case studies of three Chinese FBs	Shows how family disputes involving wives, second marriages, and daughters-in-law and sibling rivalries can lead to issues of conflicts and inheritance after the demise of the founding patriarch
Glover (2014)	Presents a case example of the power struggles and gender issues one daughter faced when she became a partner, and future successor, in the family business	N/A	Ethnographic study of a small family farm in England	Results shed light on some of the social complexities of small family farms and power struggles within the family exacerbated by perceived gender issues. The work also highlights the potential threat to the daughter's position as a partner, from her father's favoritism of male employees.
Koffi et al. (2014)	How do owner-managers influence the success of the generational transition by facilitating the credibility of the successor in the eyes of the employees?	N/A	Seven case studies of succession	Men and women business owners adopt different behavioral strategies in order to bring credibility to their successors

Author (year)	Research aim	Theory/framework	Method	Findings
Overbeke et al. (2013)	Which factors contribute to daughters' self-assessments of succession?	Theory of planned behavior; gender role theory	Interviews with 21 daughters and sons in the USA	Gender norms make daughters blind to the possibility of succession; daughters may not deliberately consider succession until a critical event motivates them to do so; parental support and mentoring for leadership are seen to facilitate daughter succession
Halkias et al. (2010)	Investigate the trend for daughters in Asian FBs to take over leadership roles from their fathers in the FB and what might hinder or support a daughter's intentions to succeed her father in the FB	N/A	Survey of 30 female students of a university in UAE about their intentions	Females do not feel comfortable working with family members, and are willing to take the risk to pursue a career outside the FB
Haberman and Danes (2007)	Investigate power structures and interactions among father–daughter and father–son family business decision teams experiencing management transfer	Family FIRO model	Two case studies	Women in the father–son business experienced feelings of exclusion and incidents of higher conflict among family members, while women in the father–daughter business experienced feelings of inclusion, resulting in lower conflict.
Pyromalis et al. (2006)	Investigate whether the success of the succession and satisfaction from the process per se depends on the successor's gender	Succession literature	Analytical Hierarchy Process of prior publications	The success of the succession process does not depend on the gender of the successor

Table 2.2 Overview of selected studies on copreneurs

Author(s) (year)	Main research question/aim	Theoretical background	Type of study	Main finding
Belenzon et al. (2016)	How does the social context of owners affect firm strategy and performance?	Embeddedness theory; institutional logics	Quantitative study of large sample of private firms across Europe	Social relationships among owners have a large impact on firm strategy and performance
Kuschel and Lepeley (2016)	Address issues related to women as leaders in copreneurial tech ventures and analyze whether these ventures are growth-oriented or conform to limited partnerships aimed primarily to meet their living standards	N/A	Interviews with three copreneurial women and two divorced copreneurs	Copreneurial teams that work in the technology industry have similar and complementary levels of education and skills development. Working together, each partner becomes well aware of mutual skills and strengths. This allows them to define their respective roles. Both divide work and family, and have developed a level of mutual trust and commitment that is essential to move forward. Commonly they show workaholic tendencies with a high rational underpinning.
Deacon et al. (2014)	Gain insights into the division of labor, capital, and capacities, and gendered identities, within husband and wife heterosexual copreneurial businesses	Gender and entrepreneurship theories	Multiple exploratory interview approach	Entrepreneurial identity and roles and responsibilities within a copreneurial business are shared and complementary, and are dependent upon the unique capacities and capitals of each partner. While there is evidence of duties that could be stereotypically described as either 'men's work' or 'women's work', there was no apparent role tension between the partners. Thus, no partner's contribution was deemed more valuable than the other.
Coad and Timmermans (2014)	Explore the effects of diverse team composition on the survival and growth of new ventures	Team composition literature	Analysis of Danish Linked Employer–Employee database	Family firms have lower employment growth, especially when formed with one's mother.

Brannon, Wiklund, and Haynie (2013)	What are the implications of two types of family relationships (romantic couples versus biologically linked teams) in the formative stages of new venture creation?	Social identity theory	Longitudinal sample of 295 nascent teams	The effects on start-up performance in terms of achieving first sales differ in that couples are more likely than other teams to achieve first sales, while the opposite is true for blood-related teams
Hedberg and Danes (2012)	Examine the dynamic power processes within copreneurial couples as a bridge between entrepreneurship and family firm research	Literature on power processes	Multiple methods (self-reports, observational coding of team interviews, and analytic induction with team and individual interviews)	Findings illustrate the foundational role of an inclusive power structure and suggest that copreneurial businesses where spouses are seen as equal partners engaging in collaborative power interactions are likely to result in a more productive business decision team that has the resilience to creatively solve important business problems
Farrington, Venter, Eybers, and Boshoff (2011)	Empirically assess the influence of selected structural-based factors on the effectiveness of South African copreneurships	Teamwork literature	380 questionnaires completed by individual spouses	Results suggest that the success of a marriage between copreneurs is not influenced by the success of the business, but that the more structural elements such as leadership, needs alignment, and role clarity are in place, the more satisfied the spouses are likely to be with both their business and their marital relationship
Fletcher (2010)	Explore the ways in which venture creation is constructed between co-habiting couples	Family business literature, entrepreneurship	26 copreneurial situations	A typology of copreneurship is developed, using ownership and management structural dimensions. This typology is illustrated with different types of lifestyle businesses to demonstrate the economic assessments and 'market work' that give rise to family entrepreneurship.

(*Continued*)

Table 2.2 (Continued)

Author(s) (year)	Main research question/aim	Theoretical background	Type of study	Main finding
Bensemann and Hall (2010)	Explore the experiences of owners of rural tourism accommodation businesses in New Zealand to examine roles within copreneurial rural tourism businesses	N/A	Mixed method (quantitative survey and qualitative)	Finds the sector to be characterized by lifestylers and copreneurs running their businesses as a 'hobby' and that non-economic, lifestyle motivations are important stimuli to business formation; any perception of copreneurship as a tool for enabling women to become freed from traditional gender roles may not equal the reality as a gendered ideology persists even through copreneurial relationships in rural tourism. Copreneurial couples appear to engage in running their business using traditional gender-based roles mirroring those found in the private home.
Blenkinsopp and Owens (2010)	Aims to develop an expanded conceptualization of copreneurship, locating it within the family embeddedness perspective on entrepreneurship	Entrepreneurship and family business literatures	Conceptual	Copreneurship clearly represents an important phenomenon, and the role of spousal support in entrepreneurship is being identified as particularly significant.
Werbel and Danes (2010)	Investigates the degree that the spouse of the founder of a new venture is a constraint on that process.	Human and social capital	Quantitative study of 110 new ventures	The results suggest that when a spouse experiences work–family conflict, a spouse is likely to be a resource constraint that creates physiological strain on the founder. Furthermore, spousal commitment to the venture is likely to exacerbate this relationship.

Study	Type	Sample	Findings
Wu et al. (2010)	Examine the permeability of work and family domains, and to investigate the relationships of work–family conflict with business and marriage outcomes in copreneurial women	Work–family management strategies	202 Taiwanese copreneurial women	Family boundaries were found to be more permeable than work domains; work–family conflict is found to be negatively related to perceived business success and marriage satisfaction; and work-to-family conflict was found to predict marriage satisfaction, whereas family-to-work conflict predicted perceived business success
Cole and Johnson (2007)	How are separated or divorced copreneurs able to end their marital relationship but maintain their business together?	Copreneurship literature	Nine couples (18 adult men and women), who work together in a first-generation family business after a divorce or separation	Finds that copreneurs who have a great deal of trust in one another can continue to work together post-divorce. Emotional connection, compartmentalization, synergy, commitment to the business, and positive gender issues also contribute to the success of the business and the business relationship.
O'Connor et al. (2006)	Purpose is to discuss the nature of co-entrepreneurs within the ICT sector in Ireland	Literature review	23 copreneurial ventures in Ireland	The findings of the study indicate that the family business or spouse/partner structure represents a major component of mixed gender companies in the ICT sector in Ireland, and that such companies tend to be small, with well-educated and experienced founders.
Muske and Fitzgerald (2006)	Examine continuance in copreneurial business relationships	Literature review	Data from the 1997 and 2000 panels of the National Family Business Survey	Findings indicate that those starting copreneurial business relationships were more likely to be older, more educated, and running larger, more successful businesses. Those who discontinued the copreneurial business relationship during the three years of the survey had lower levels of education and success, both financially and in terms of number of people employed, than the other groups.

(Continued)

Table 2.2 (Continued)

Author(s) (year)	Main research question/aim	Theoretical background	Type of study	Main finding
Larsen (2006)	Provide insights in how vertical and horizontal sex segregation may develop in family businesses	Occupational sex segregation literature	Individual family businesses in American harness horse racing	The findings show how the belief that married couples cannot debate and resolve work-related conflicts without undue strain on their personal relationship leads some of these couples to organize their work into gendered tasks and workspaces, contributing to the maintenance of vertical segregation in the trainer position.
Van Auken and Werbel (2006)	What is the degree to which one's spouse shares a common vision about the goals, risks, and rewards of the business?	Literature review	Conceptual	Models and testable hypotheses are developed to guide empirical research on the antecedents and consequences of spousal commitment to a family business.

Meglio (2016) present case studies of daughters taking over the family business as well as different challenges related to that endeavor. Overall, few studies focus on studying the linkage between women and succession in detail.

Conducting a literature review about the intersection between gender and family business not only captures the role of women in family businesses, but also identifies publications in which the role of men is discussed more explicitly (i.e. beyond taking for granted that family businesses are run by and handed over to males). Thus, the third path of succession articles refers to studies comprising a clear male dimension. For example, in a conceptual paper Cicellin et al. (2015) discuss the impact of a paternalistic leadership style on succession (though without explicitly referring to the gender of successors). They propose that paternalism can intensify success or failure of succession in family firms, spurring a virtuous or vicious circle of behaviors. Zheng et al. (2016) propose that the equal division of assets among sons, typically discussed as diluting the family property, has positive aspects brought about by division and competition. Based on a case study from Hong Kong, where no distinction is made between older and younger sons in the system of an equal division of property among the sons, they show how this practice encourages the (male) members of the family to develop their potential and compete with each other. In result, the authors claim that this practice enhances the drive for self-employment. Based on a sample of Korean family firms, Yoo et al. (2014) find support for the hypothesis that a non-first-son–based succession identity disproportionately better positions successors to take advantage of informational exchange relationships and entrepreneurial opportunities, while simultaneously avoiding the pressures and constraints associated with 'family tradition' aspects of the family business system. Different types of father–son relationships are studied by Joshi and Srivastava (2014), Spraggon et al. (2012), Afghan (2012) and Laakkonen et al. (2011). The performance of blood-related sons versus other successors in Japan is discussed by Mehrotra et al. (2013). Chien (2014) highlights the possession of franchisor and spousal resources, and the importance of entrepreneurial orientation to foster and develop the franchisee performance in a couple-owned franchise outlet.

Copreneurship

Another gender-related theme – that has emerged rather recently – is that of copreneurial couples (for an overview of selected publications, see Table 2.2). For example, Hedberg and Danes (2012) point at the foundational role of an inclusive power structure. In their study of farm-business couples they find that copreneurial businesses, where spouses are seen as equal partners engaging in collaborative power interactions, are likely to result in a more productive business-decision team. Similarly, in a qualitative study of copreneurial teams Deacon et al. (2014) find evidence of duties that could be stereotypically described as either 'men's work' or 'women's work', but no apparent role tension between the partners. Thus, they conclude that no partner's contribution was deemed more valuable than the other.

Drawing on in-depth interviews, Cole and Johnson (2007) study successful post-divorce copreneurs. They identify as driving forces for successful post-divorce copreneurial relationships multiple intangible, emotional factors such as trust, the ability to compartmentalize, emotional connection, synergy, commitment to the business, and positive gender issues. Based on a large-scale quantitative study of European family businesses, Belenzon et al. (2016) find that married-owner family firms are managed more conservatively relative to firms with unrelated owners and even to other family-owned firms. In particular, they find that married-owner family firms invest and grow more slowly and rely less on external finance. However, they also exhibit greater performance stability and higher profitability. Not all studies of copreneurs consider couples; some investigate ventures cofounded with other family members. Coad and Timmermans (2014), for example, find that newly founded family firms have lower employment growth, especially when formed with one's mother.

Performance

Another theme emerging from the literature addresses the performance of family businesses, typically assessing that of women-led firms – though this aspect is often not at the core of the study. For example, in a study of the performance of small family firms, Cruz et al. (2012) find that women-led family businesses outperform other types of firms. Using a comprehensive data set of family-controlled firms in Italy, Amore et al. (2014) find that female directors significantly improve the operating profitability of female-led companies. The authors also show how the positive effect of female interactions on profitability is reduced when the firm is located in geographic areas characterized by gender prejudices and when the firm is large. In a study examining the impact of federal disaster assistance on the survival and success of small family-owned businesses, Haynes et al. (2011) find that women-led family businesses are most likely to succeed. Similarly, for companies facing natural disasters Danes et al. (2009) find higher levels of federal disaster assistance to be associated with lower family-firm resilience for male-owned businesses and higher family-firm resilience for female-owned businesses. Danes et al. (2007) investigate whether the gender of family-business owners moderates the relationship between various business-management practices and performance. Among other things, they find that introducing new production methods has a large positive effect on performance for both genders. Personnel management practices have a nine-times greater effect on performance for female than male owners. Comparing the performance of women-led family firms with women-led non-family firms, however, Kickul et al. (2010) find that being a family business is not a critical factor in the performance of women-led firms. Gill et al. (2014a) investigate factors that affect the growth of family business in Western Canada. They find that male respondents perceive family-business growth to be positively associated with board size, firm size, management skills, and experience. Female respondents, in contrast, perceive family-business growth to be positively associated with CEO duality, management skills, and family size.

Female managers in family firms

The next theme emerging from the literature review addresses female managers, often comparing their management practices and/or performance between family- and non-family firms. Rodríguez-Ariza et al. (2017) compare the role of female directors in family and non-family firms in promoting responsible practices. They find that in family firms, corporate social responsibility (CSR) commitment does not vary significantly with the presence of female directors, as the latter tend to behave in accordance with the family orientation toward CSR. However, Peake et al. (2015) find support that gender moderates the relationship between community duration and satisfaction and measures of CSR. Meroño-Cerdán and López-Nicolás (2017) find that family firms run by women are not smaller, but are concentrated in the services sector like non-family firms. They conclude that gender differences in the type of business and in the manager profile found in general management literature disappear in family firms, and that only a sectoral gender effect persists. Nekhili et al. (2016) find that family firms, which are more conducive to transformational leadership, offer women a more appropriate climate for exercising the function of Chair than that of CEO. In contrast, they find women CEOs to perform better in non-family firms. Vadnjal and Zupan (2011) explore women as managers in family businesses, attempting to explain why women tend to find it attractive and rewarding to work for family businesses, although their contributions to business decisions often remain invisible. They explore attitudes held by men and women regarding the roles of women in relation to managerial and ownership issues and find support for a paradigm of a feminine style of management.

Women on the board of family businesses

The impact of having female members on the board of family businesses is investigated in a number of studies. Sundarasen et al. (2016) examine the effect of board composition on CSR in Malaysia and find that women on the board indicate a positive relationship, and more so in family firms. Bianco et al. (2015) investigate female representation on Italian corporate boards before the introduction of gender-quota legislation in 2012. They identify two different models. In the majority of gender-diverse boards, at least one woman had a family connection to the controlling shareholder. Family-affiliated women are more common in companies that are small, have a concentrated ownership, are in the consumer sector, and have a larger board. Conversely, non-family-affiliated women are more common on the boards of companies that are widely held, have younger and more educated boards, have a higher proportion of independent directors, and have a smaller number of interlocked directors. In addition, the number of board meetings appears to be negatively correlated to both the presence of family members and female directors; moreover, women show lower attendance than men at board meetings. Mínguez-Vera and Martin (2011) analyze the gender diversity of a sample of Spanish small and medium-sized enterprises. For this sample, they find that women's presence on boards generates a negative impact on firm performance, which they attribute to less risky strategies implemented by women directors. This study also finds that family firms and firms with a financial institution as the main shareholder tend to have more women on the board, and that firms with less debt, more assets, and larger boards have more women as directors.

Historical studies of women in family businesses

We found several publications that report on studies of women in family businesses from a historical perspective. Nordlund Edvinsson (2016) investigates the role of wives in the Swedish business elite in the early 1900s. She finds that the corporate wife was expected to perform duties linked to the family business. However, for her to be more directly involved in the firm, the husband had to give his permission. Yet, by offering support, the wife could gain tacit knowledge of her husband's work. Her emotional efforts influenced the achievements of the family business, and sometimes even its survival. Rutterford and Maltby (2006) summarize the evidence for women as financial investors in the UK before the twentieth century –investing for income, capital growth, or a share in the family business –and discuss why their participation until recently has been largely ignored by scholars. Using data on self-employment as an indicator of entrepreneurship, Honeyman (2009) argues that for centuries women in Britain have been instrumental as partners in or originators of business, but that the nature and impact of their commercial acumen has been seriously under-reported. She identifies and explores three dimensions of women's interaction with 20th-century businesses, namely their specific contribution to business activity, the barriers to such activity, and the way in which business historians have understood or interpreted women's commercial engagement. She concludes that through their business activities women made a significant contribution to the expansion of the commercial sector in Britain during the second half of the 20th century.

Tweedale (2013) explores the development of the cutlery industry in Sheffield, UK during the 19th century, where the family was largely synonymous with the firm. The author proposes that businesses drew their strength mainly from individual family skills within the essentially craft-based industry. The backstreet nature of most cutlery enterprises enabled women (and children) to play a key role in both the home and factory – sometimes providing additional support through their involvement in the beer houses and shops that many families operated as a second enterprise. Companies often formed miniature family dynasties, reflecting a father-to-son nature of the trade and the connectedness (sometimes through marriage) with other families. Muñoz) discuss how structural changes during the past two centuries shaped Spanish women's economic activity in firms, family businesses, and self-employment, reflecting women's adaptation to a social system that assigned gender-specific roles and rights. They explain how especially the shift to a democratic system in Spain during the 1970s paved the way for women to enter public and private firms as professionals. As a result, more women became self-employed or helped to run family businesses – mainly related to tourism, the hotel and restaurant industries, design, fashion, and the arts.

Gender as a side aspect of family business studies

In several publications, gender issues are not really in focus, but appear as side aspects (e.g. Gill, 2013; Gill et al., 2014; Smith, 2009; Van Der Merwe, 2009a, 2009b, 2010), for example as "attitude variable "in Fahed-Sreih and Djoundou-rian's (2006) study of Lebanese family firms. In their study, more than 75 percent of the family firms considered female ownership acceptable and 67.9 percent state that they would consider a female as a potential CEO. Other studies include gender as a control variable or as one of several variables forming a construct (Vandebeek et al., 2016). Rubino et al. (2016) compare board characteristics in family and non-family firms and find that gender diversity has a negative impact on the firm value when a member of the family leads a family firm. Studying the influence of CEOs on family firms' internationalization, Ramón-Llorens et al. (2017) find that gender does not significantly predict the propensity to export.

Gender as variable in studies assessing a family-business background

Ten publications report on studies in which a family-business background and gender are included as variables. Typically, these studies investigate (social) entre-preneurial intentions or more generally career intentions of students or adoles-cents (Hadjimanolis and Poutziouris, 2011; Harris and Gibson, 2008; Levie and Hart, 2011; Mohamad et al., 2014; Schröder et al., 2011; Shirokova et al., 2016; White et al., 2007). For example, Hoffmann et al. (2015) study reasons for the likelihood that children of self-employed parents are more likely to become self-employed themselves, and find that the effect of a self-employed father (mother) is much higher for males (females), even if they do not take over the family business. In an international comparative study, Robinson and Stubberud (2012) find that that in several countries more women than men state that a family business background was a motive for entrepreneurship. An interesting variation of these studies is provided by Block et al. (2016), who explore who prefers to work for family businesses rather than non-family firms, and find that a preference to work in family firms correlates positively with being female.

Studies with a focus on the link between gender and family business

We also identified a number of studies in which the link between gender and fam-ily business was the main topic of the research. Aygören and Nordqvist (2015) provide a framework of identity work in family businesses, with particular focus on two specific habitats of meaning: gender and ethnicity. They show that the distinctive forms of formation and management of plural identities in family firms, and the two habitats of meaning – gender and ethnicity – prove to be fundamental in organizing and performing in the family business context. Identities of women in family businesses are also in focus in Smith's (2014) work. Based on the sociological theory of matriarchy, she suggests a theoretical framework that is tested against narratives of matriarchical figures written up using retrospective ethnography. These stories illustrate how gender differences impact entrepreneurial identities and the everyday practicalities of doing business. While the male head of the family may be the titular business owner, many privately defer to the matriarchal voice, which acts as a positive driving force in business, binding a family together. This study can help to explain how gendered relationships influence entrepreneurial identities and open our eyes as to how we narrate stories of women in family business. Bjursell and Melin (2011) offer a perspective on entrepreneurial identity as a narrative construction emerging in stories about entering the family business. Based on an interpretative analysis of narrative interviews with women from Swedish family businesses, they present two distinct narratives: The 'Pippi Longstocking' narrative illustrates conscious choices, drive, and motivation based on an entrepreneurial identification, while the 'Alice in Wonderland' narrative illustrates women who happen to become entrepreneurs or business persons because the family business was there. The contrasting and complementing narratives illustrate ambiguities in the identity process. Also drawing on narratives, Hamilton (2006) illuminates complex relationships in a family-business context, putting the family at the heart of the research (as opposed to an individual owner-manager), and drawing on narrative accounts as told by the founders and by the succeeding generation in three family businesses. While some literature conceptualizes women in family business as marginalized through the forces of patriarchy or paternalism, the narratives presented in this study point to alternative gender discourses and practices, and to evidence of clear resistance to patriarchy. In so doing it identifies conditions under which patriarchy might be challenged in family businesses.

Based on a social constructivist analysis of the accounts of women regarding their influence in family businesses, Heinonen and Stenholm (2011) aim to gain a deeper understanding of the contribution of women to family business from the perspective of the women themselves. They find that women perceive themselves to be vital for the functioning of the family business. Their closeness to the business and contribution seem to go hand in hand, independent of formal ownership. The authors discuss how formal and visible ownership remain in the background when women define their contribution, indicating that psychological ownership is important for understanding women's contribution to the family business. Their results suggest that the woman herself does not belittle her contribution and recognizes her own ways of exerting influence.

A critical assessment of the complexity inherent in gendering processes in family businesses is provided by Katila (2010), who explores how Chinese business families in the Chinese catering sector in Helsinki articulate gendered and ethnicized moral orders. The study suggests that families do not necessarily adhere to patriarchal arrangements of gender in their everyday life and that commitment or resistance to the gendered familial moral orders can be seen as an act of ethnic identification. Barrett and Moores (2009) explore how women exercise leadership and entrepreneurship in family firms. Using frameworks that avoid essentialist assumptions about women's and men's approach to leadership, they suggest that there are some characteristic ways in which women leaders learn family-business leadership and entrepreneurship roles. The authors label these ways as "stumbling into the spotlight", "building your own stage", "directing the spotlight elsewhere", and "coping with shadows". The journey of those who had failed to attain leadership was labelled "becoming invisible". The same authors (Barrett and Moores, 2009b) also wrote a somewhat more practitioner-oriented book about leadership roles of women in family businesses.

While most studies in this theme use qualitative methods, some quantitative studies can be found that investigate the link between gender and family businesses. In a study of the role played by culture and gender differences in family business across 10 countries based on Global Entrepreneurship Monitor (GEM) data, Lerner and Malach-Pines (2011) consistently find big cross-cultural differences between the owners of family businesses in the 10 countries and far smaller and less consistent differences between male and female owners of family businesses. These findings offer a strong support for the usefulness of social theories of gender to better understand gender aspects related to family firms. In a six-country study, Sonfield and Lussier (2009) similarly find no significant relationships between the gender of family business owner-managers and 10 management characteristic variables in a sample of 593 family businesses. Another quantitative study by Movahedi et al. (2016) identifies barriers associated with the development of rural women's family businesses in Iran. The most pressing barriers faced by rural women's family businesses are low ability of the women in creativity and innovation as well as low income-generating of the family businesses. The authors categorize the barriers into five groups, including supportive and logistic barriers, managerial and monitoring barriers, individual and family barriers, skill and expertise barriers, and communication and information barriers.

While studies depicting male owner-managers as 'heroes' are common in family-business studies (see Pauli, 2015), while corresponding studies illustrating women's achievements are rare. Carvalho and Williams (2014) explore the case of the growth and internationalization of a traditional family business in Portugal, originally producing cork but facing an industry crisis. Then a young woman entrepreneur introduces significant changes to the business to modernize it, develops a brand, and focuses on product diversification and innovation, paving the road to growth. Refreshingly, the business-related achievements of this woman in the family firm, rather than her personal attributes, are brought to the fore.

Finally, one theme emerging in this literature represents examples of women in family firms in different types of country contexts – to name but a few, Welsh (2016) discusses women-owned family businesses in sub-Saharan Africa;

Yuldinawati and Oktadanio (2016), Indonesian family businesses; and Byrne and Fattoum (2014), case studies from France. Welsh et al. (2014) investigate the characteristics of Japanese women entrepreneurs and their family firms, and identify barriers and resources that affect their success. They find a customized long-term support system with strong connections between family business supporters and women business owners by both the governmental and private agencies to be important for further growth of Japanese women entrepreneurs. Vadnjal and Zupan (2013) study women in family firms in Slovenia, arguing that as women in Slovenia have reached a high level of equality in education as well as employment it could be expected that they also play a crucial role in family firms. Instead, the authors find that women's contribution seems to be underestimated and undervalued due to the conservative, more patriarchic tradition in these firms, and thus the full potential of women is still not well utilized. The key drivers for women's active involvement in family businesses in Turkey, their contributions, and the challenges they face are studied by Karataş-Özkan et al. (2011), highlighting the importance of cultural dynamics. Investigating the influences of Colombian women's participation in family businesses, Vergara et al. (2011) identify a range of internal factors (namely protection of personal wealth, professional development, and the conservation of family unity), and transcendent factors (namely contribution to the growth of the business, and generation of opportunities for family communication) as most important for motivating women's participation. In contrast, external factors (such as family conflict, work–family imbalances and the definition of a career plan) discourage participation. The authors conclude that family firms must improve their work with these external factors to avoid the loss of talent and professional commitment of women. Finally, Jones (2008) argues that many Indian companies have to cope with the problem of incompetent family members at the top of businesses. Due to increasing competitive pressures, the insight is emerging that company success depends on their attitude towards men and women of high ability and advanced training. The author notes that women have often found more potential in Indian family businesses, and that more women have gained prominence in family-run businesses as compared to non-family firms.

Gender theories and family business

Only a few studies explicitly theorize about the gender dimension in relation to family business studies, some of these have already been mentioned. For example, Barrett (2014) discusses women's entrepreneurship in the family-firm context based on radical subjectivist economics and suggests that the elements of entrepreneurial imagination, empathy, modularity, and self-organization generate new research questions that contest previous apparently settled views about women entrepreneurs. Therefore, protocols for investigating these questions are suggested by the author, touching also on the potential for women entrepreneurs to create new industries. Another noteworthy exception is Rothausen (2009), who discusses the gendering of family and work roles in family businesses. Bjursell and Bäckvall (2011) analyze the role ascribed to women in family businesses in Swedish print media. They find a tension between women's roles as mothers and in business. While the role of mothers is largely unproblematic as such, their role in business is seen as more ambivalent, requiring them to make sense of what a businesswoman is and as an expression of that women are not the norm in family business. Here, it is interesting to note that whilst these questions have not yet been systematically explored in family-business research, they are currently discussed in women's entrepreneurship research.

Discussion and ways forward

Our literature review has shown that a link between gender and family business can be found in a substantial number of studies. Categorizing this literature into different themes, however, makes evident that the family-business field is in dire need of more research that questions our taken-for-granted assumptions on the role of gender in family business, and in particular of work that goes beyond considering gender as a (control) variable for biological sex, or as a problem that concerns women only.

Earlier research had centered around obstacles and difficulties as well as on opportunities and advantages of women in family business (Martinez Jimenez, 2009), and our literature review shows that additional themes have emerged to complement this earlier research. Yet, a number of gaps remain. In the following, we propose different approaches that could advance research on the interface between gender and family firms.

Gender theories

Although the relevance of women for family businesses is gaining increasing scholarly attention, surprisingly few studies make use of gender theories to better understand the social construction of gendering in family businesses. Both work and family roles in our society are predicated on gender expectations (Rothausen, 2009): The particularly strong gendering associated with family pertains to the social ideals of 'femininity' as mother, daughter, and wife and the social ideals of 'masculinity' are reflected in the ideal father, husband, or brother. The expectations of the 'ideal worker' follow these norms and are described by 'masculine' characteristics, such as being assertive, competitive, and rational, while 'feminine' characteristics match expectations for the ideal 'caregiver' as being emphatic, sensitive, and a good listener. Gender theories could help explain the gendered nature of family businesses and the dynamics between a family and its business, which might hinder women from progressing, and force them to assimilate to a predominately male organization (cf. Acker, 1992), but even support them in their roles. In family businesses, where family and business systems overlap, a better understanding of gender-role dynamics across generations could be achieved by applying a gender-theory lens.

Socialization theory

Gender roles are deeply rooted in societal structures, which makes them difficult to change. Moreover, their taken-for-granted nature makes them difficult to identify. Socialization theory can help explicate their invisible nature. Socialization is "the process whereby the helpless infant gradually becomes a self-aware, knowledgeable person, skilled in the ways of the culture into which she or he is born"(Giddens, 1993: 60). It begins with the infant assimilating the world of its closest caregivers (Berger and Luckmann, 1966). As the child interacts with family members, it unconsciously adopts the values, norms, and doings of the family. Our socialization forms the basis from which we make sense of our lives, and it constitutes our background coping skills that we automatically draw on to deal with unfamiliar situations (Chia, 2004). At later stages in life other socializing agents, such as colleagues at work, play important roles in the further shaping of our identity. A fundamental part of socialization, ingrained since infancy, is the learning of gender roles (Suar and Gochhayat, 2016). These roles have been segmented over centuries into what is considered as appropriate 'male' versus 'female' behavior.

An example of fruitfully employing this perspective to family-business research is Iannarelli (1992), who explores the socialization of leaders in family business from a gender perspective. Her research shows that family firms are unique settings where family and business socialization coincide and constitute lifelong learning processes where the business values are learned since early childhood. Different expectations are put on children depending on their sex. She finds that sons in business families generally get to spend more time at the business, developing 'natural abilities' and are seen as 'leadership material', while daughters are expected to take on more domestic chores and develop caregiving abilities (Iannarelli, 1992). Creating awareness of these unintentional patterns is important for family-business management and succession to advance. Socialization theory can help explain inequality in the working life as stemming from deeply ingrained practices that are unconsciously transmitted over generations and embedded in local context.

Interpretivist methodologies

Increased awareness of gendering behavior and gendered systems is an important step towards achieving change. The implicit nature of how gender roles are socially constructed, however, causes some challenges for researching them. The difficulty in explicating gender dynamics calls for methods that acknowledge the indirect and inconspicuous nature of everyday practice. Such methods are found in interpretivist methodologies. In family-business research, interpretivism remain largely underutilized and are rarely published in the leading family-business journals (cf. Nordqvist et al., 2009). Even case studies are often based on positivist assumptions, according to a recent review (Leppäaho et al., 2016). Hence, acknowledging that gender is socially constructed implies the need to choose suitable research methods. Other methodologies can eventually contribute, but a priori a solid explorative building of theory is needed. It is not until concepts have been developed that constructs can be validated (Gioia et al., 2013). To this end, interpretivism holds great promise to contribute to the *why* and *how* questions of the link between gender and family business. Among appropriate methods for theory building from interpretive fieldwork we particularly suggest longitudinal, in-depth single-case studies (Stake, 1995), the 'Gioia methodology' for grounded-theory development (Gioia et al., 2013), ethnography (van Maanen, 1988,2011), and theorizing from process data (Langley, 1999). Moreover, the implicit nature of gender roles require researchers to go beyond interviews as the sole data-collection technique. Here, narratives (Dawson and Hjort, 2012), shadowing (Czarniawska, 2007), and other observation-based techniques hold merit to capture the implicit nature of family-business life.

Context

Gender roles are culturally defined and hence differ between societies (Acker, 1992). Research acknowledging contextual differences is therefore important for advancing knowledge about the link between gender and family businesses. Gender has different meanings in different settings and is thus ideally studied with research designs that account for context. The methods proposed earlier are well suited for that task.

Context refers to "circumstances, conditions, situations, or environments that are external to the respective phenomenon and enable or constrain it"(Welter, 2011: 167). The business, social, spatial, and institutional dimensions of context all affect the meaning of gender in family business. Context includes both distal contexts – such as countries, political systems, or society – and more proximate contexts, such as the social environment or the local neighborhood of the family business (cf. Welter, 2011). Particular to the family-business context is the inevitable interplay between family and business realms. The impact of place on the role of gender in family businesses could be captured through a feminist-geography perspective that draws on feminist theories to explore how gender and geographies are mutually structured and transformed (Berg, 1997). A contextualized view of the interplay between gender and family business can contribute to developing a deeper and more fine-grained understanding of the phenomenon.

A call for a gendered view of family businesses

There is still a dearth of studies that apply a gender lens to family-business dynamics or investigate how gender orders in societies impact family businesses. Most publications do not make explicit use of gender theories to explain these issues. We conclude this review by suggesting that research on gender and family businesses needs to pay more attention to gendered structures instead of interpreting gender as an individualistic – good or bad – characteristic of women alone. In other words, we replicate a call that has been made for research on women's entrepreneurship (Ahl, 2006; Hughes et al., 2012) and encourage research that moves towards a focus on social and other contextualized gendered structures that explain gendered outcomes. Relevant research could, for example, take a closer look into how the gender of both men and women is constructed and legitimized by families and family businesses, and whether and how this can be changed through individual or family agency. Such research would be of great value not only to the family business research field, but to entrepreneurship research in general (see Baker and Welter, 2017).

References

Acker, J. (1992). From sex roles to gendered institutions. *Contemporary Sociology*, 21, 565–569.

Afghan, N. (2012). Avari group: Organizational values and crisis leadership. *Asian Journal of Management Cases*, 9(1), 59–78.

Ahl, H. (2006). Why research on women entrepreneurs needs new directions. *Entrepreneurship: Theory & Practice*, 30(5), 595–621.

Ahrens, J.-P., Landmann, A., and Woywode, M. (2015). Gender preferences in the CEO successions of family firms: Family characteristics and human capital of the successor. *Journal of Family Business Strategy*, 6, 86–103.

Al-Dajani, H., Bika, Z., Collins, L., and Swail, J. (2014). Gender and family business: New theoretical directions, guest editorial. *International Journal of Gender and Entrepreneurship*, 6(3), 218–230.

Amore, M. D., Garofalo, O., and Minichilli, A. (2014). Gender interactions within the family firm. *Management Science*, 60(5), 1083–1097.

Aygören, H., and Nordqvist, M. (2015). Gender, ethnicity and identity work in the family business. *European Journal of International Management*, 9(2), 160–178.

Baker, T., and Welter, F. (2017). Come on out of the ghetto, please! – Building the future of entrepreneurship research. *International Journal of Entrepreneurial Behavior & Research*, 23(2),170–184.

Barrett, M. (2014). Revisiting women's entrepreneurship: Insights from the family-firm context and radical subjectivist economics. *International Journal of Gender and Entrepreneurship*, 6(3), 231–254.

Barrett, M., and Moores, K. (2009). Spotlights and shadows: Preliminary findings about the experiences of women in family business leadership roles. *Journal of Management and Organization*, 15(3), 363–377.

Barrett, M., and Moores, K. (2009b). *Women in family business leadership roles: Daughters on the stage*. Cheltenham: Edward Elgar.

Belenzon, S., Patacconi, A., and Zarutskie, R. (2016). Married to the firm? A large-scale investigation of the social context of ownership. *Strategic Management Journal*, 37(13), 2611–2638.

Bennedsen, M., Nielsen, K. M., Pérez-González, F., and Wolfenzon, D. (2007). Inside the family firm: The role of families in succession decisions and performance. *The Quarterly Journal of Economics*, 122(2), 647–691.

Bensemann, J., and Hall, C. M. (2010). Copreneurship in rural tourism: Exploring women's experiences. *International Journal of Gender and Entrepreneurship*, 2(3), 228–244.

Berg, N. (1997). Gender, place and entrepreneurship. *Entrepreneurship & Regional Development*, 9(3), 259–268.

Berger, P., and Luckmann, T. (1966). *The social construction of reality: A treatise in the sociology of knowledge*. London: Penguin Books.

Bianco, M., Ciavarella, A., and Signoretti, R. (2015). Women on corporate boards in Italy: The role of family connections. *Corporate Governance*, 23(2), 129–144.

Bjursell, C., and Bäckvall, L. (2011). Family business women in media discourse: The business role and the mother role. *Journal of Family Business Management*, 1(2), 154–173.

Bjursell, C., and Melin, L. (2011). Proactive and reactive plots: Narratives in entrepreneurial identity construction. *International Journal of Gender and Entrepreneurship*, 3(3), 218–235.

Blenkinsopp, J., and Owens, G. (2010). At the heart of things: The role of the "married" couple in entrepreneurship and family business. *International Journal of Entrepreneurial Behaviour & Research*, 16(5), 357–369.

Block, J. H., Fisch, C. O., Lau, J., Obschonka, M., and Presse, A. (2016). Who prefers working in family firms? An exploratory study of individuals' organizational preferences across 40 countries. *Journal of Family Business Strategy*, 7(2), 65–74.

Brannon, D. L., Wiklund, J., and Haynie, J. M. (2013). The varying effects of family relationships in entrepreneurial teams. *Entrepreneurship: Theory & Practice*, 37(1), 107–132.

Byrne, J., and Fattoum, S. (2014). A gender perspective on family business succession: Case studies from France. In K. V. Lewis, C. Henry, E. J. Gatewood and J. Watson (eds.), *Women's entrepreneurship in the 21st century: An international multi-level research analysis* (pp. 138–164). Cheltenham: Edward Elgar.

Carvalho, L., and Williams, B. (2014). Let the cork fly: Creativity and innovation in a family business. *International Journal of Entrepreneurship and Innovation*, 15(2), 127–133.

Chia, R. (2004). Strategy-as-practice: Reflections on the research agenda. *European Management Review*, 1, 29–34.

Chien, S.-Y. (2014). Franchisor resources, spousal resources, entrepreneurial orientation, and performance in a couple-owned franchise outlet. *Management Decision*, 52(5), 916–933.

Cicellin, M., Mussolino, D., and Viganò, R. (2015). Gender diversity and father-daughter relationships: Understanding the role of paternalistic leadership in family firm succession. *International Journal of Business Governance and Ethics*, 10(1), 97–118.

Coad, A., and Timmermans, B. (2014). Two's company: Composition, structure and performance of entrepreneurial pairs. *European Management Review*, 11(2), 117–138.

Cole, P. M., and Johnson, K. (2007). An exploration of successful copreneurial relationships postdivorce. *Family Business Review*, 10(3), 185–198.

Cruz, C., Justo, R., and De Castro, J. O. (2012). Does family employment enhance MSEs performance? Integrating socioemotional wealth and family embeddedness perspectives. *Journal of Business Venturing*, 27(1), 62–76.

Czarniawska, B. (2007). *Shadowing and other techniques for doing fieldwork in modern societies*. Malmö: Liber.

Danes, S. M., Lee, J., Amarapurkar, S., Stafford, K., Haynes, G., and Brewton, K. E. (2009). Determinants of family business resilience after a natural disaster by gender of business owner. *Journal of Developmental Entrepreneurship*, 14(4), 333–354.

Danes, S. M., Stafford, K., and Loy, J. T.-C. (2007). Family business performance: The effects of gender and management. *Journal of Business Research*, 60(10), 1058–1069.

Dawson, A., and Hjorth, D. (2012). Advancing family business research through narrative analysis. *Family Business Review*, 25(3), 339–355.

Deacon, J. H., Harris, J. A., and Worth, L. (2014). Who leads? Fresh insights into roles and responsibilities in a heterosexual copreneurial business. *International Journal of Gender and Entrepreneurship*, 6(3), 317–335.

Fahed-Sreih, J., and Djoundourian, S. (2006). Determinants of longevity and success in Lebanese family businesses: An exploratory study. *Family Business Review*, 9(3), 225–234.

Farrington, S. M., Venter, E., Eybers, C., and Boshoff, C. (2011). Structuring effective copreneurial teams. *South African Journal of Business Management*, 42(3), 1–16.

Fletcher, D. (2010). 'Life-making or risk taking'? Co-preneurship and family business start-ups. *International Small Business Journal*, 28(5), 452–469.

Gherardi, S., and Perrotta, M. (2016). Daughters taking over the family business: Their justification work within a dual regime of engagement. *International Journal of Gender and Entrepreneurship*, 8(1), 28–47.

Giddens, A. (1993). *Sociology* (2nd ed.). Cambridge: Polity Press.

Gill, A. (2013). Financial policy and the value of family businesses in Canada. *International Journal of Entrepreneurship and Small Business*, 20(3), 310–325.

Gill, A., Biger, N., Sharma, S. P., and Shah, C. (2014a). Gender differences and the factors that affect family business growth in Canada. *International Journal of Entrepreneurship and Small Business*, 21(1), 115–131.

Gill, A., Flaschner, A. B., Mann, S., and Dana, L. -P. (2014). Types of governance, financial policy and the financial performance of micro-family-owned businesses in Canada. *International Journal of Business and Globalisation*, 13(4), 542–558.

Gioia, D., Corley, K., and Hamilton, A. (2013). Seeking qualitative rigor in inductive research notes on the gioia methodology. *Organizational Research Methods*,16(1), 15–31.

Glover, J. L. (2014). Gender, power and succession in family farm business. *International Journal of Gender and Entrepreneurship*, 6(3), 276–295.

Haberman, H., and Danes, S. M. (2007). Father-daughter and father-son family business management transfer comparison: Family FIRO model application. *Family Business Review*, 20(2), 163–184.

Hadjimanolis, A., and Poutziouris, P. (2011). Family business background, perceptions of barriers, and entrepreneurial intentions in Cyprus. *International Journal of Entrepreneurial Venturing*, 3(2), 168–182.

Halkias, D., Thurman, P. W., Harkiolakis, N., Katsioloudes, M., Stavrou, E. T., Swiercz, P. M., and Fragoudakis, M. (2010). Father-daughter succession issues in family business among regional economies of Asia. *International Journal of Entrepreneurial Venturing*, 2(3–4), 320–346.

Hamilton, E. (2006). Whose story is it anyway? Narrative accounts of the role of women in founding and establishing family businesses. *International Small Business Journal*, 24(3), 253–271.

Harris, M. L., and Gibson, S. G. (2008). Examining the entrepreneurial attitudes of US business students. *Education and Training*, 50(7), 568–581.

Haynes, G. W., Danes, S. M., and Stafford, K. (2011). Influence of federal disaster assistance on family business survival and success. *Journal of Contingencies and Crisis Management*, 19(2), 86–98.

Hedberg, P. R., and Danes, S. M. (2012). Explorations of dynamic power processes within copreneurial couples. *Journal of Family Business Strategy*, 3, 228–238.

Heinonen, J., and Stenholm, P. (2011). The contribution of women in family business. *International Journal of Entrepreneurship and Innovation Management*, 13(1), 62–79.

Hoffmann, A., Junge, M., and Malchow-Møller, N. (2015). Running in the family: Parental role models in entrepreneurship. *Small Business Economics*, 44(1), 79–104.

Honeyman, K. (2009). Invisible entrepreneurs? Women and business in twentieth century Britain. In R. Cooper and P. Lyth (eds.), *Business in Britain in the twentieth century: Decline and renaissance?* Oxford: Oxford University Press, Chapter 5.

Hughes, K. D., Jennings, J. E., Brush, C., Carter, S., and Welter, F. (2012, May). Extending women's entrepreneurship research in new directions. *Entrepreneurship Theory & Practice*, 429–442.

Iannarelli, C. (1992). *The socialization of leaders in family business: An exploratory study of gender*. Doctoral Dissertation, University of Pittsburgh.

Jones, N. (2008). Governance in the family, the family business and family trusts. In L. S. Spedding (eds.) *Due diligence handbook: Corporate governance, risk management and business planning* (pp. 657–681). Amsterdam: Elsevier.

Jorissen, A., Laveren, E., Martens, R., and Reheul, A.-M. (2005). Real versus sample-based differences in comparative family business research. *Family Business Review*, 18(3), 229–246.

Joshi, M., and Srivastava, A. (2014). Family business in transition: A case of PAL. *Journal of Entrepreneurship in Emerging Economies*, 6(1), 72–96.

Karataş-Özkan, M., Erdogan, A., and Nicolopoulou, K. (2011). Women in Turkish family businesses: Drivers, contributions and challenges. *International Journal of Cross Cultural Management*, 11(2), 203–219.

Katila, S. (2010). Negotiating moral orders in Chinese business families in Finland: Constructing family, gender and ethnicity in a research situation. *Gender, Work and Organization*, 17(3), 297–319.

Kickul, J., Liao, J., Gundry, L., and Iakovleva, T. (2010). Firm resources, opportunity recognition, entrepreneurial orientation and performance: The case of Russian women-led family businesses. *International Journal of Entrepreneurship and Innovation Management*, 12(1), 52–69.

Koffi, V., Guihur, I., Morris, T., and Fillion, G. (2014). Family business succession: How men and women predecessors can bring credibility to their successors? *Entrepreneurial Executive*, 19, 67–85.

Kuschel, K., and Lepeley, M.-T. (2016). Copreneurial women in start-ups: Growth-oriented or lifestyle? An aid for technology industry investors. *Academia*, 29(2), 181–197.

Laakkonen, A., Kansikas, J., and Valtonen, H. (2011). In search of family business continuity: The case of transgenerational family entrepreneurship. *International Journal of Entrepreneurship and Small Business*, 13(2), 193–207.

Langley, A. (1999). Strategies for theorizing from process data. *Academy of Management Review*, 24, 691–710.

Larsen, E. A. (2006). The impact of occupational sex segregation on family businesses: The case of American harness racing. *Gender, Work and Organization*, 13(4), 359–382.

Leppäaho, T., Plakoyiannaki, E., and Dimitratos, P. (2016). The case study in family business: An analysis of current research practices and recommendations. *Family Business Review*, 29(2), 159–173.

Lerner, M., and Malach-Pines, A. (2011). Gender and culture in family business: A ten-nation study. *International Journal of Cross Cultural Management*, 11(2), 113–131.

Levie, J., and Hart, M. (2011). Business and social entrepreneurs in the UK: Gender, context and commitment. *International Journal of Gender and Entrepreneurship*, 3(3), 200–217.

Liu, Y. (2015). Alloy Construction Service Inc. In J. Ofori-Dankwa (ed.), *Comparative case studies on entrepreneurship in developed and developing countries* (pp. 200–211). Hershey, PA: IGI Global.

Martinez Jimenez, R. (2009). Research on women in family firms: Current status and future directions. *Family Business Review*, 22(1), 53–64.

Mathew, V. (2016). Women and family business succession in Asia – characteristics, challenges and chauvinism. *International Journal of Entrepreneurship and Small Business*, 27(2–3), 410–424.

Meglio, O. (2016). Father-daughter intergenerational transition in a small family business: A temporal perspective. In H. D. Syna and C.-E. Costea (eds.), *Women's voices in management: Identifying innovative and responsible solutions* (pp. 254–271). Heidelberg: Springer.

Mehrotra, V., Morck, R., Shim, J., and Wiwattanakantang, Y. (2013). Adoptive expectations: Rising sons in Japanese family firms. *Journal of Financial Economics*, 108(3), 840–854.

Meroño-Cerdán, A. L., and López-Nicolás, C. (2017). Women in management: Are family firms somehow special? *Journal of Management and Organization*, 23(2), 224–240.

Mínguez-Vera, A., and Martin, A. (2011). Gender and management on Spanish SMEs: An empirical analysis. *International Journal of Human Resource Management*, 22(14), 2852–2873.

Mohamad, N., Lim, H.-E., Yusof, N., Kassim, M., and Abdullah, H. (2014). Estimating the choice of entrepreneurship as a career: The case of Universiti Utara Malaysia. *International Journal of Business and Society*, 15(1), 65–80.

Movahedi, R., Mantashloo, M., Heydari, F., and Shirkhani, M. (2016). Identifying the barriers of developing rural women's family businesses. *International Journal of Globalisation and Small Business*, 8(4), 355–368.

Muñoz, L. G., and Pérez, P. F. (2007). Female entrepreneurship in Spain during the nineteenth and twentieth centuries. *Business History Review*, 81(3), 495–515.

Muske, G., and Fitzgerald, M. A. (2006). A panel study of copreneurs in business: Who enters, continues, and exits? *Family Business Review*, 19(3), 193–205.

Nekhili, M., Chakroun, H., and Chtioui, T. (2016). Women's leadership and firm performance: Family versus nonfamily firms. *Journal of Business Ethics*, 1(1), 1–26.

Nordlund Edvinsson, T. (2016). Standing in the shadow of the corporation: Women's contribution to Swedish family business in the early twentieth century. *Business History*, 58(4), 532–546.

Nordqvist, L., Hall, A., and Melin, L. (2009). Qualitative research on family businesses: The relevance and usefulness of the qualitative approach. *Journal of Management & Organization*, 15, 294–308.

O'Connor, V., Hamouda, A., McKeon, H., Henry, C., and Johnston, K. (2006). Co-entrepreneurial ventures: A study of mixed gender founders of ICT companies in Ireland. *Journal of Small Business and Enterprise Development*, 13(4), 600–619.

Overbeke, K. K., Bilimoria, D., and Perelli, S. (2013). The dearth of daughter successors in family businesses: Gendered norms, blindness to possibility, and invisibility. *Journal of Family Business Strategy*, 4(3), 201–212.

Pauli, K. S. (2015). Gender theory and the family business. In M. Nordqvist, L. Melin, M. Waldkirch and G. Kumeto (eds.), *Theoretical perspectives on family businesses* (pp. 191–210). Cheltenham: Edward Elgar.

Peake, W. O., Cooper, D., Fitzgerald, M. A., and Muske, G. (2015). Family business Participation in community social responsibility: The moderating effect of gender. *Journal of Business Ethics*, 19 p.

Pyromalis, V. D., Vozikis, G. S., Kalkanteras, T. A., Rogdaki, M. E., and Sigalas, G. P. (2006). An integrated framework for testing the success of the family business succession process according to gender specificity. In P. Z. Poutziouris, K. X. Smyrnios and S. B. Klein (eds.), *Handbook of research on family business* (pp. 422–442). Cheltenham: Edward Elgar.

Ramón-Llorens, M. C., García-Meca, E., and Duréndez, A. (2017). Influence of CEO characteristics in family firms' internationalization. *International Business Review*.

Robinson, S., and Stubberud, H. A. (2012). All in the family: Entrepreneurship as a family tradition. *International Journal of Entrepreneurship*, 16(APLISS), 19–30.

Rodríguez-Ariza, L., Cuadrado-Ballesteros, B., Martínez-Ferrero, J., and García-Sánchez, I.-M. (2017). The role of female directors in promoting CSR practices: An international comparison between family and non-family businesses. *Business Ethics*, 26(2), 162–174.

Rothausen, T. R. (2009). Management work-family research and work-family fit: Implications for building family capital in family business. *Family Business Review*, 22(3), 220–234.

Rubino, F. E., Tenuta, P., and Cambrea, D. R. (2016). Board characteristics effects on performance in family and non-family business: A multi-theoretical approach. *Journal of Management and Governance*, 1–36.

Rutterford, J., and Maltby, J. (2006). 'The widow, the clergyman and the reckless': Women investors in England, 1830–1914. *Feminist Economics*, 12(1–2), 111–138.

Schröder, E., Schmitt-Rodermund, E., and Arnaud, N. (2011). Career choice intentions of adolescents with a family business background. *Family Business Review*, 24(4), 305–321.

Sharma, P. (2004). An overview of the field of family business studies: Current status and directions for the future. *Family Business Review*, 17(1), 1–36.

Shirokova, G., Osiyevskyy, O., and Bogatyreva, K. (2016). Exploring the intention – behavior link in student entrepreneurship: Moderating effects of individual and environmental characteristics. *European Management Journal*, 34(4), 386–399.

Smith, G. D. (2009). East Africa: Extended families with many rights. *Entrepreneurship: Theory and Practice*, 33(6), 1239–1244.

Smith, R. (2014). Assessing the contribution of the 'theory of matriarchy' to the entrepreneurship and family business literatures. *International Journal of Gender and Entrepreneurship*, 6(3), 255–275.

Sonfield, M. C., and Lussier, R. N. (2009). Gender in family business ownership and management: A six-country analysis. *International Journal of Gender and Entrepreneurship*, 1(2), 96–117.

Spraggon, M., Bodolica, V., and Manoussifar, M. (2012). Succession management challenges: The case of a family business in the UAE. *Asian Journal of Management Cases*, 9(2), 115–126.

Stake, R. (1995). *The art of case study research*. Thousand Oaks, CA: Sage.

Suar, D., and Gochhayat, J. (2016). Influence of biological sex and gender roles on ethicality. *Journal of Business Ethics*, 137(2), 199–208.

Sundarasen, S. D., Je-Yen, T., and Rajangam, N. (2016). Board composition and corporate social responsibility in an emerging market. *Corporate Governance*, 16(1), 35–53.

Tong, C. K. (2014). Feuds and legacies: Conflict and inheritance in Chinese family business. In *Chinese business: Rethinking Guanxi and trust in Chinese business networks* (pp. 77–95). Berlin: Springer.

Tweedale, G. (2013). Backstreet capitalism: An analysis of the family firm in the nineteenth-century Sheffield cutlery industry. *Business History*, 55(6), 875–891.

Vadnjal, J., and Zupan, B. (2011). Family business as a career opportunity for women. *South East European Journal of Economics and Business*, 6(2), 23–32.

Vadnjal, J., and Zupan, B. (2013). The role of women in family businesses: The case of Slovenia. In V. Ramadani and R. C. Schneider (eds.), *Entrepreneurship in the Balkans: Diversity, support and prospects* (pp. 133–150). Berlin, New York: Springer.

Van Auken, H. E., and Werbel, J. D. (2006). Family dynamic and family business financial performance: Spousal commitment. *Family Business Review*, 19(1), 49–63.

Van Der Merwe, S. (2010). The determinants of the readiness to let go among senior generation owner-managers of small and medium-sized family businesses. *South African Journal of Economic and Management Sciences*, 13(3), 293–315.

Van Der Merwe, S. P. (2009a). An investigation of the determinants of estate and retirement planning in intergenerational family businesses. *South African Journal of Business Management*, 40(3), 51–63.

Van Der Merwe, S. P. (2009b). Determinants of family employee work performance and compensation in family businesses. *South African Journal of Business Management*, 40(1), 51–63.

Van Maanen, J. (1988). *Tales of the field: On writing ethnography*. Chicago: University of Chicago Press.

Van Maanen, J. (2011). Ethnography as work: Some rules of engagements. *Journal of Management Studies*, 48(1), 218–234.

Vandebeek, A., Voordeckers, W., Lambrechts, F., and Huybrechts, J. (2016). Board role performance and faultlines in family firms: The moderating role of formal board evaluation. *Journal of Family Business Strategy*, 7(4), 249–259.

Vergara, M. P. L., Gómez-Betancourt, G., and Ramírez, J. B. B. (2011). Factors that influence the participation of women in management positions and organs of government in Colombian family businesses [Factores que influyen en la participación de la mujer en cargos directivos y órganos de gobierno de la empresa familiar Colombiana]. *Cuadernos de Administracion*, 24(42), 253–274.

Welsh, D. H. B. (2016). Women-owned family businesses in Africa: Entrepreneurs changing the face of progress. In M. Acquaah (ed.), *Family businesses in sub-Saharan Africa: Behavioral and strategic perspectives* (pp. 155–173). Berlin, New York: Springer.

Welsh, D. H. B., Memili, E., Kaciak, E., and Ochi, M. (2014). Japanese women entrepreneurs: Implications for family firms. *Journal of Small Business Management*, 52(2), 286–305.

Welter, F. (2011). Contextualizing entrepreneurship-conceptual challenges and ways forward. *Entrepreneurship: Theory & Practice*, 35(1), 165–184.

Werbel, J. D., and Danes, S. M. (2010). Work family conflict in new business ventures: The moderating effects of spousal commitment to the new business venture. *Journal of Small Business Management*, 48(3), 421–440.

White, R. E., Thornhill, S., and Hampson, E. (2007). A biosocial model of entrepreneurship: The combined effects of nurture and nature. *Journal of Organizational Behavior*, 28(4), 451–466.

Wu, M., Chang, C.-C., and Zhuang, W.-L. (2010). Relationships of work-family conflict with business and marriage outcomes in Taiwanese copreneurial women. *International Journal of Human Resource Management*, 21(5), 742–753.

Yoo, S. S., Schenkel, M. T., and Kim, J. (2014). Examining the impact of inherited succession identity on family firm performance. *Journal of Small Business Management*, 52(2), 246–265.

Yuldinawati, L., and Oktadanio, M. Y. (2016). Small family business development from three dimension of family business model. *International Journal of Economics and Management*, 10(Special Issue), 197–210.

Zheng, V., Wan, P.-S., and Wong, S.-L. (2016). Succession, division, and the drive for self-employment: The case of the renowned Hong Kong restaurant 'Yung Kee'. *International Journal of Management Practice*, 9(4), 344–364.

3 Women-led enterprises in Germany

The more social, ecological, and corporate responsible businesses?

André Pahnke, Kerstin Ettl
and Friederike Welter

Introduction

Firm performance and growth are prominent research topics with regard to women's entrepreneurship (De Bruin et al., 2007). However, existing findings are confusing. While the results of Joecks et al. (2013) or Lindstädt et al. (2011), for example, suggest a positive relation between gender diversity and performance, Laible (2013), Minguez-Vera and Martin (2011), and Du Rietz and Henrekson (2000) identify a negative link. Several other studies also show that gender-specific differences in organizational performance may result less from the particular sex of the business owner and more from environmental influences, such as the embeddedness of the business or the entrepreneur (Thornton, 1999), the location (Mirchandani, 1999), industry differences, and the size of the business (e.g., Anna et al., 2000; Du Rietz and Henrekson, 2000; Rosa et al., 1996), with the individual characteristics of the entrepreneur representing an additional layer (Cowling and Taylor, 2001; Kalleberg and Leicht, 1991).

Since the extent of performance differences between male-led and female-led businesses also depends on the measurement categories used, more broadly defined performance measures should be used in addition to (pure) financial measures, whereby interdependencies between performance, success, and goals also have to be taken into account (Brush and Hisrich, 2000). Some studies already complement research based on "objective" (in many cases financial) measures by both using more "subjective" measures such as self-stated growth intentions and paying attention to the overall attitude of society towards business growth (Diaz-Garcia, 2006). In addition, Ettl and Welter (2012) conclude in line with previous studies (e.g., Moser and Schuler, 1999) that success of women entrepreneurs' business ventures should not be measured in economic terms alone. Non-monetary factors (such as creativity, self-realization, contentment with less ambitious growth objectives or the combination of business and family responsibilities) must be taken into account, in order to explain women's entrepreneurial behavior more comprehensively. Goals and motives, strategies and attitudes play a role for entrepreneurial success. These findings stress the strong need to take structural differences of enterprises and different characteristics of entrepreneurs or managers into account when gender related aspects of firm development are analyzed. However, it is still largely unclear to what extent men-led and women-led enterprises differ not only with regard to their entrepreneurial strategies and aims but also with respect to the individual attitudes and motives pursued by their managing directors.

Against this background, based on a sample of 518 German enterprises, we seek to identify possible differences between women-led and men-led enterprises particularly with regard to strategies and attitudes of the managers. Our goal is to investigate whether possible differences in the performance of men- and women-led enterprises can be explained by different entrepreneurial aims and strategies as well as by diverging individual attitudes among managing directors. Our chapter deals with the following questions: What can we learn from our sample about women-leadership in general? Are there performance differences between men- and women-led enterprises? If so, can these differences be explained by gendered different entrepreneurial aims and strategies as well as by diverging individual attitudes among managing directors? Are women-led enterprises maybe even different due to a relatively stronger focus on social, ecological, or corporate responsibility issues rather than on profit maximization?

The chapter is structured as follows: In the next section, we explain our data collection and methodological approach, before we turn to present our findings related to structural characteristics of women-led enterprises (in Germany), their entrepreneurial aims, and strategies as well as the attitudes of their managers. We conclude with implications for future research.

Data and methods

Our empirical analysis is based on a recent online survey that was conducted on behalf of the German Institut für Mittelstandsforschung (IfM) Bonn in 2014. Drawn from the largest available German firm database of Creditreform, the final representative sample contains 541 observations and covers firms of all sizes and industries of the private sector; the response rate was 3.8 per cent. However, the maximum sample size for this paper has been reduced to those 518 observations for which we could determine whether these enterprises are (mainly) led by women or not.

Our data comprises information about the total size of a firms' executive board and the total number of women working as business executives. In order to identify women-led enterprises, we focus on the proportion of women on the firms' executive boards and apply a 50 per cent threshold. Similar to Haunschild and Wolter (2010), we define women-led enterprises as such companies in which at least 50 per cent of the business executives are female. Regarding majority decisions of the executive boards, this means, on the one hand, that female business executives will not always be able to preserve their interests. On the other hand, this applies to male business executives as well. Hence, we distinguish between men-led and women-led enterprises exactly at the point where neither male nor female business executives will prevail – assuming that there are gender specific differences with respect to the management of a firm. As a result, our sample is split into 393 men-led and 125 women-led enterprises.

However, there is obviously no commonly used or widely accepted definition of women-led enterprises in prior studies, so we extend our analyses for further robustness checks by using two additional measures of gender diversity in the executive boards:

1. The proportion of women in the executive board as a metric measure.
2. A set of four dummy variables dividing the sample into enterprises in which executive boards either consist of women by less than 25 per cent, 25–49 per cent, 50–74 per cent, or 75–100 per cent.

These possibilities to identify women-led enterprises are illustrated in Figure 3.1, which shows the results of a smoothed Epanechnikov-Kernel-Density estimation of the proportion of women in executive boards.

The data also provides detailed information on firm objectives, strategies and attitudes of managing directors. Regarding the firms' objectives and strategies,

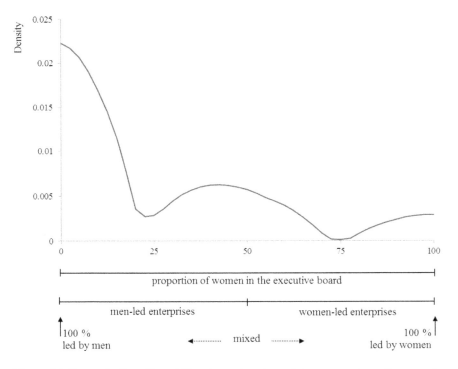

Figure 3.1 Epanechnikov-Kernel-Density estimation of the proportion of women in executive boards

Source: Survey data of IfM Bonn, 2014. Own calculations. $n = 518$.

the enterprises had to assess the importance of 10strategies and objectives using a 5-point Likert scale that varies from "unimportant" to "very important". In particular, the strategies and objectives cover short-term profit maximization, company growth/increase of market shares, independence/autonomy of the enterprise, prestige/influence, customer satisfaction, employees' job satisfaction, increase of enterprise value, social/societal objectives, ecological objectives, and maintenance/creation of jobs.

Moreover, information about strategies regarding market positioning of the enterprises is available. The data cover different ways to face competition whereas multiple answers were permitted. The survey specifically refers to competition via the quality of products, price competition, the supply of individual products or services, the supplement of the main product by additional services, competition via innovative products and services, aiming at a leading position in a market niche or finally adjustments to the market without pursuing a certain competitive strategy.

The personal motives and attitudes of the members of the executive board were prompted by a set of eight items. In detail, they had to state how important their job is in order to secure personal income, to secure personal wealth, to realize their full potential, to receive societal recognition, to take societal responsibility, to improve family–work balance, and to use their own (professional) expertise the best possible way. Our results are limited due to the fact, that in each case only one member of the executive board was a respondent in our study and answered the question about the personal motives and attitudes regarding his or her job. However, it is possible to investigate whether the personal motives of business executives differ with respect to the gender-specific composition of the executive board.

Additional information about the ownership structure allows us also to decide whether an enterprise belongs to the so-called German Mittelstand and therefore can be defined as a family business, too. Following the definition of Wolter and Hauser (2001), we assign enterprises to the German Mittelstand if and only if at least 50 per cent of the shares of the enterprise are owned by up to two members of the executive board. Hence, the main characteristic of the German Mittelstand is the unity of owner- and leadership of an enterprise, so that family businesses are often also associated with the German Mittelstand (Welter et al., 2014). From a technical point of view, our data allow the identification and analyses of women-led enterprises that belong to the German Mittelstand, and thus to family businesses. However, given the actual size of our sample, a sole focus on women-led enterprises of the German Mittelstand is unrewarding. Strategies of family businesses and the German Mittelstand may be similar – and differ from the strategies of other enterprises because of interweaving structures of ownership and leadership. Therefore, this additional (control) variable is central for our analysis. Finally, with our data set we were able to control for variables such as size, industry, region, and the age or legal form of the firm. However, more detailed data on the composition of management boards (apart from number and sex of managing directors) or on the characteristics of company owners are not available.

Structural characteristics of women-led enterprises in Germany

Ambiguous results of existing research on the performance of women-led enterprises already stress the importance of structural characteristics of the surveyed enterprises. The underlying assumption is that (special) characteristics of the firm are more likely to drive performance than the sex of the decision makers within the executive boards. However, it seems obvious that structural differences between women-led and men-led enterprises may not only be linked to performance but also to other aspects of women-led enterprises.

In this regard, our data show some distinct structural differences between women-led and men-led enterprises. At first, the average proportion of women in executive boards is 19.4 per cent in our sample whereas about every fourth enterprise can be regarded as a women-led enterprise. However, the proportion of women in executive boards does not exceed one third in 75 per cent of the observed enterprises. In addition, two thirds of the enterprises are solely led by men while the proportion of enterprises being completely managed by women is only 8.9 per cent. These numbers indicate that women in executive positions and therefore women-led enterprises are not the norm in Germany. This finding is in line with comparable research on gender diversity in (top) management of German firms. For example, Pahnke et al. (2017) report that 19.7 per cent of all German establishments (with at least one employee covered by social security insurance) are led by women. They use weighted data of the largest German panel survey of the Institute for Employment Research, the IAB Establishment Panel, but do not include the whole private sector in their analyses. Likewise based on the IAB Establishment panel, but covering the whole private sector, Kohaut and Möller (2016) show that about every fourth top-manager in Germany is a woman and that this has not changed since 2004. An investigation of gender diversity in top management positions of large German family firms with an annual turnover of at least 50 million euros highlights that 6.5 per cent of all top management positions in these large enterprises are occupied by women, albeit that the proportion of women in the top management in large family firms is somewhat higher than in large non-family firms (Kay and Schlömer-Laufen, 2016). Hence, about every fifth of the large German family firms have at least one female executive director while this one applies to roughly every 10th large non-family firm (Kay and Schlömer-Laufen, 2016). In conjunction with the results of Haunschild and Wolter (2010), referring to women-led enterprises of the German Mittelstand in the year 2006, the available data and research obviously point towards quite persistent structural differences between women-led and men-led enterprises in Germany.

Looking at the differences in our sample in more detail, we observe the lowest proportions of women in executive boards in manufacturing (9.0 per cent) and in business services (17.6 per cent) while the proportion of women in executive boards is above average in commerce (22.8 per cent) and other services (28.0 per cent). Nearly two thirds of all women-led enterprises in our sample either belong to the trade sector or to other services (see Figure 3.2). The smallest proportion of women-led enterprises can be found in manufacturing while most of the men-led enterprises are located in this industry. Moreover, the proportion of men-led enterprises in the trade sector and other services is about 10 percentage points lower than compared to the distribution of women-led enterprises by industry.

Besides differences regarding industry, women-led enterprises are likely to differ in terms of size, too. Every third member of executive boards in enterprises with one to nine employees is female, on average. However, the average proportion of women in executive boards is lower in larger firms. In very large firms with more than 500 employees the average proportion of women in executive boards in our sample drops to 10.3 per cent. Therefore, it is not surprising that nearly 40 per cent of women-led enterprises have one to nine employees while less than 3 per cent of women-led enterprises are large firms with 500 and more employees (see Figure 3.3). In contrast, about 14 per cent of all men-led enterprises have at least 500 employees.

As similar pattern can be observed when we compare the age of women-led and men-led enterprises (see Figure 3.4). While nearly two thirds of all women-led enterprises are between 10 and 49 years old, this applies to (only) every second men-led enterprise. This difference can be explained by the fact that there are relatively fewer women-led enterprises older than 50 years or more specifically older than 75 years. Actually, the proportion of men-led enterprises that are 75–99 years old is twice as high as the corresponding proportion of women-led enterprises in this category. This difference between men-led and women-led enterprises triples with respect to firms that are at least 100 years old.

This result implies that women are not likely to be on the executive boards of second- or third-generation family businesses. Looking at the German Mittelstand

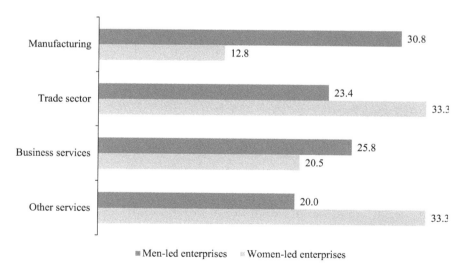

■ Men-led enterprises　▨ Women-led enterprises

Figure 3.2 Distribution of women-led and men-led enterprises by industry (in percentage terms)

Source: Survey data of IfM Bonn, 2014. Own calculations. *n* = 497.

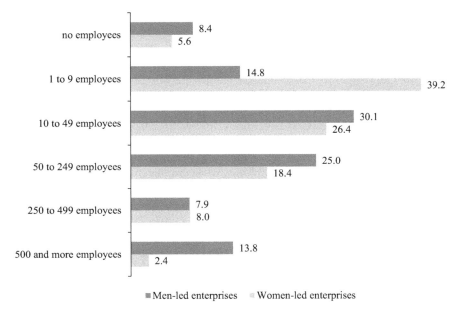

Figure 3.3 Distribution of women-led and men-led enterprises by firm size (in percentage terms)

Source: Survey data of IfM Bonn, 2014. Own calculations. n = 517.

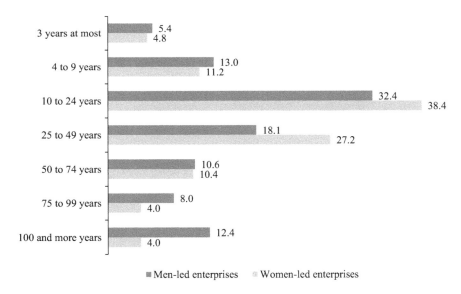

Figure 3.4 Distribution of women-led and men-led enterprises by firm age (in percentage terms)

Source: Survey data of IfM Bonn, 2014. Own calculations. *n* = 517.

only, the average proportion of women on executive boards is significant higher compared to enterprises that do not belong to the German Mittelstand (22.0 vs. 15.5 per cent) while 75.0 per cent of all women-led and 61.9 per cent of all men-led enterprises are affiliated with the German Mittelstand.

However, this broad distinction between "German Mittelstand" and "Non-Mittelstand" does not contradict the findings on firm size and age. In conjunction with our findings related to the distribution of women-led enterprises by industry, size, and age, it is apparent that structural differences may affect the firm performance, too. Finally, descriptive statistics indicate that the smaller the average proportion of women in executive boards, the more turnover the enterprise obtains. Specifically, the average proportion of women in executive boards with a yearly turnover of less than 2 million euros is roughly three times bigger (27.9 per cent) in comparison with enterprises that obtain a yearly turnover of at least 50 million euros (10.7per cent).

Similar to the average proportion of women in executive boards, the proportion of women-led enterprises is quite small regarding enterprises with a high annual turnover (see Figure 3.5). Since the proportion of men-led enterprises is more or less the same in every size group, the proportion of women-led enterprises with an annual turnover of at least 10 million euros is only half of the corresponding proportion of men led-enterprises. With a value of 26.9 per cent, the proportion of men-led enterprises that obtain at least 50 million euros in sales is more than three times higher than the proportion of women-led enterprises in this category (8.9 per cent).

Now, using the definition of small and medium-sized enterprises (SME) provided by the European Commission (2003), we are able to combine the available

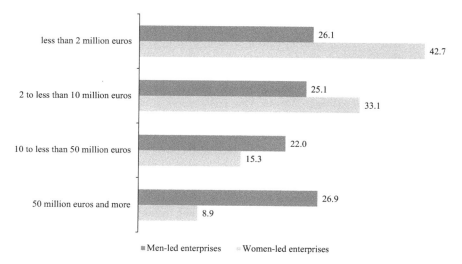

Figure 3.5 Distribution of women-led and men-led enterprises by annual turnover (in percentage terms)

Source: Survey data of IfM Bonn, 2014. Own calculations. *n* = 497.

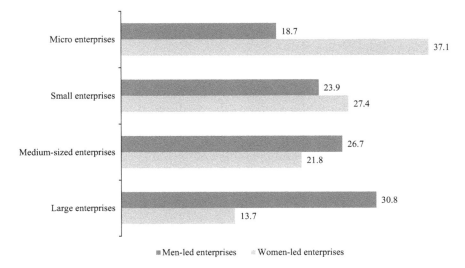

Micro enterprises   18.7   37.1

Small enterprises   23.9   27.4

Medium-sized enterprises   26.7   21.8

Large enterprises   30.8   13.7

■ Men-led enterprises   ▨ Women-led enterprises

Figure 3.6 Distribution of women- and men-led enterprises by SME size-classes according to the European Commission (in percentage terms)

Source: Survey data of IfM Bonn, 2014. Own calculations. *n* = 497.

information on firm size (measured by the total number of employees) and annual turnover in order to obtain further insights into the structural differences between women-led and men-led enterprises. Splitting our sample into different types of SMEs and large enterprises, we again observe major differences between women-led and men-led enterprises that are likely to drive performance differences (see Figure 3.6).

Actually, 37.1 per cent of all women-led enterprises are micro enterprises with less than 10 employees and less than 2 million euros annual turnover, whereas only 18.7 per cent of all men-led enterprises are also this small. Investigating the other tail of the distribution, this ratio reverses, while the distribution of women-led and men-led enterprises that either belong to the group of small or medium-sized enterprises is interestingly very similar:30.8 per cent of all men-led enterprises are large enterprises with at least 250 employees and at least 50 million euros in sales while this applies to only 13.7 per cent of all women-led enterprises. Hence, nearly two thirds of all women-led enterprises are either micro or small enterprises while about every sixth men-led enterprise is at least medium-sized.

Although the very obvious differences regarding industry and firm size between women-led and men-led enterprises are important when outcomes of these two firm types are being compared, there may also be other relevant firm characteristics that have a more-or-less indirect impact. For example, in Germany the most common legal form of an enterprise is the so-called *Einzelunternehmen* (sole proprietorship), which involves an unlimited personal liability of the owner/entrepreneur. Now, an unlimited liability with all personal and business assets can theoretically influence business decisions. Regarding simple investments, for example, an unlimited liability may *ceteris paribus* yield a lower (expected) net present value of an investment in comparison to a situation with a limited liability because the payment or loss, respectively, of the decision maker can be relatively higher if the project fails.

Combining information on the legal form of the enterprises and additional information on the (personal) liability of the owner(s) and family members, respectively, we actually find some differences between women-led and men-led enterprises. While 61.5 per cent of men-led enterprises have a limited liability of the owner(s), this applies to only 49.6 per cent of all women-led enterprises. Hence, women-led enterprises are to some extent more likely to have an owner who is also legally liable for all personal and business assets. Of course, the legal form and liability is related to the size of an enterprise, too. However, these differences between women-led and men-led enterprises show that there may also be additional (indirect) structural differences that are not very obvious.

Our descriptive analyses support existing research on women-led enterprises in Germany and confirm that German women-led enterprises more often operate in the trade sector or other services, compared to men-led enterprises. They are also more likely to be smaller and to generate less turnover.

Strategies of women-led enterprises and attitudes of their executive managers

Despite the structural differences outlined in the previous section, our further (econometric) results show that men- and women-led enterprises are obviously very similar with respect to the pursued entrepreneurial aims. This result also holds when different approaches to identify women-led enterprises are used.

In order to get a first impression of the importance of several (competitive) strategies, Figure 3.7 shows the proportion of women-led and men-led enterprises that rate the corresponding global firm strategy/entrepreneurial aim as important and very important, respectively. Women-led as well as men-led enterprises stress the importance of customer satisfaction and employee job satisfaction. Only few of the women-led and men-led enterprises state short-term profit maximization is an important strategic goal of the company. However, and to some extent surprisingly, this applies to a relatively larger proportion of women-led enterprises than to men-led enterprises. The results also reveal a different evaluation regarding both the preservation and creation of jobs, which seems to be more important in women-led enterprises. Apart from that, we do not find evidence for other major differences.

Table 3.1 summarizes the regression results regarding the effect of female leadership on the importance for each entrepreneurial aim and the impact of the affiliation to the German Mittelstand and the group of family businesses. In general, the regression results confirm the descriptive statistics shown in Figure 3.7. For the majority of entrepreneurial aims, we do not observe statistically significant differences between women-led and men-led enterprises. However, women-led enterprises are actually more likely to pursue short-term profit maximization. Nevertheless, this is obviously only the case if the proportion of women

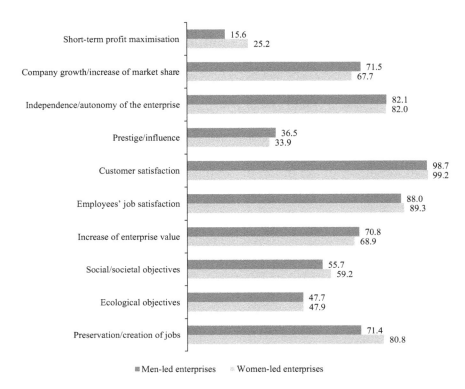

Short-term profit maximisation	15.6		
		25.2	
Company growth/increase of market share		71.5	
		67.7	
Independence/autonomy of the enterprise		82.1	
		82.0	
Prestige/influence		36.5	
		33.9	
Customer satisfaction		98.7	
		99.2	
Employees' job satisfaction		88.0	
		89.3	
Increase of enterprise value		70.8	
		68.9	
Social/societal objectives		55.7	
		59.2	
Ecological objectives		47.7	
		47.9	
Preservation/creation of jobs		71.4	
		80.8	

■ Men-led enterprises   ▪ Women-led enterprises

Figure 3.7 Importance of different entrepreneurial aims in women-led and men-led enterprises (in percentage terms)

Source: Survey data of IfM Bonn, 2014. Own calculations. The number of observations per item varies from 492 to 515.

Table 3.1 Logistic regression results on the differences between women-led and men-led enterprises with respect to the importance of entrepreneurial aims

	Identification of women-led enterprises					German Mittelstand	n
	Proportion	Dummy	Intervals				
			25–49 %	50–74%	75–100%		
Short-term profit maximisation	+**	n.s.	n.s.	n.s.	+**	n.s.	413
Company growth	n.s.	n.s.	n.s.	n.s.	+**	n.s.	418
Autonomy of the enterprise	n.s.	n.s.	n.s.	n.s.	n.s.	+***	418
Prestige/Influence	n.s.	n.s.	n.s.	−*	n.s.	n.s.	411
Employees' job satisfaction	n.s.	n.s.	n.s.	n.s.	n.s.	+**	381
Increase of enterprise value	n.s.	n.s.	n.s.	n.s.	n.s.	n.s.	416

	Identification of women-led enterprises						German Mittelstand	n
	Proportion	Dummy	Intervals					
				25–49 %	50–74%	75–100%		
Social/societal objectives	n.s.	n.s.	n.s.	n.s.	n.s.	n.s.	n.s.	419
Ecological objectives	n.s.	n.s.	n.s.	n.s.	n.s.	n.s.	n.s.	405
Maintenance/ creation of jobs	+**	+**	n.s.	+*	n.s.		+**	418

Notes: Coefficients are significant on the *** 1%, ** 5% and * 10level; estimation of robust standard errors. Additional control variables are: firm size according to the SME definition of the European Commission (three dummy variables), affiliation to the German Mittelstand (a dummy variable which can also be regarded as a proxy for family businesses), personal liability of the firm owner(s), age of the firm (six dummy variables), region (a dummy variable for West Germany) and industry (three dummy variables). Results regarding "customer satisfaction" are not included because of insufficient variance of the dependent variable (see Figure 3.7). The statistical significance of the coefficient of the variable "German Mittelstand" is always the same in every single set of logistic regressions so that the corresponding results are summarized in a single column. A complete set of results is available upon request from the authors.
Source: Survey data of IfM Bonn, 2014. Own calculations.

in executive boards is very high, or women exclusively lead the enterprise. Since we do not have any additional data at the individual level of the enterprise owners and managers, our interpretation of this result is limited. Additional estimations show that this finding is even more pronounced when micro enterprises are excluded from the regression sample. Short-term profit maximization therefore seems to be important in larger enterprises with a very high proportion of women in the executive board.

Moreover, the results show that the preservation and creation of jobs is more important in women-led enterprises even if structural characteristics of women-led enterprises are taken into account. All three specifications reveal a positive statistical significant effect of gender diversity in management on job preservation and job creation.

Finally, preservation and creation of jobs is also more important in enterprises that are affiliated with the German Mittelstand. The same applies with respect to employee job satisfaction and the autonomy of the enterprise. Since women-led enterprises belong more often to the German Mittelstand and the group of family businesses than men-led enterprises, these differences in the ownership structure may also impact their (economic) behavior and evaluation, respectively.

In addition to the importance of certain entrepreneurial aims of women-led and men-led enterprises, we investigate different ways of market positioning in a comparable way. Similar to the regression results on the entrepreneurial aims, we neither observe any considerable difference between women-led and men-led enterprises with respect to market positioning (see Table 3.2). There is only weak evidence for women-led enterprises to be less likely to compete via individual or

Table 3.2 Logistic regression results on the differences between women-led and men-led enterprises with respect to market positioning

	Identification of women-led enterprises						German Mittelstand	n
	Proportion	Dummy	Intervals					
			25–49%	50–7%	75–10%			
Quality of products	n.s.	n.s.	n.s.	n.s.	n.s.		n.s.	427
Prices	n.s.	n.s.	n.s.	n.s.	n.s.		n.s.	427
Individual products	n.s.	−*	+*	n.s.	n.s.		n.s.	427
Supplementation of main product(s)	n.s.	n.s.	n.s.	n.s.	n.s.		n.s.	427
Innovations	n.s.	n.s.	n.s.	n.s.	n.s.		n.s.	427
Leader in market niche	n.s	n.s.	n.s.	−*	n.s.		−*	427

Notes: Coefficients are significant on the *** 1%, ** 5% and * 10% level; estimation of robust standard errors. Additional control variables are: firm size according to the SME definition of the European Commission (three dummy variables), affiliation to the German Mittelstand (a dummy variable which can also be regarded as a proxy for family businesses), personal liability of the firm owner(s), age of the firm (six dummy variables), region (a dummy variable for West Germany) and industry (three dummy variables). The statistical significance of the coefficient of the variable "German Mittelstand" is always the same in every single set of logistic regressions so that the corresponding results are summarized in a single column. A complete set of results is available upon request from the authors.

Source: Survey data of IfM Bonn, 2014. Own calculations.

a customization of their products. In general, these results on market positioning support the findings on entrepreneurial aims if a certain type of market positioning is regarded as one possibility (next to others) for achieving the more global entrepreneurial aims or strategic goals of the enterprise.

Finally, we investigate the personal motives for working as an entrepreneur or manager and – in this regard – possible differences between women-led and men-led enterprises. We thereby assume that – at least to some extent – managers sort themselves into such enterprises that match with their attitudes and motives the best possible way. Looking again at the importance of certain motives, the results indicate that there no big differences between women-led and men-led enterprises (see Figure 3.8). Income support and the best possible use of (professional) experience are obviously the two most important motives of managers in both women-led and men-led enterprises.

Nevertheless, a larger proportion of managers in women-led enterprises state that a good balance between family and work is (very) important. However, this finding does not sustain our corresponding logistic regressions that take structural differences between women-led and men-led enterprises into account. As shown in Table 3.3, there are no considerable differences between women-led and men-led enterprises regarding work–life balance and also regarding other prompted motives and attitudes.

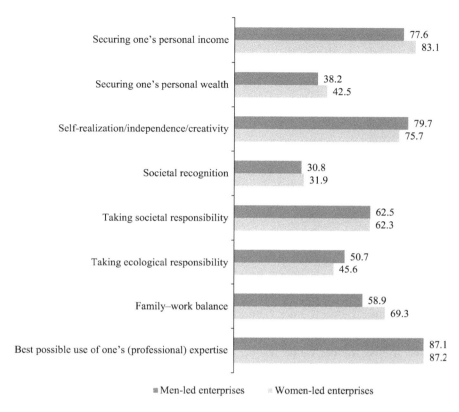

Securing one's personal income — 77.6 / 83.1
Securing one's personal wealth — 38.2 / 42.5
Self-realization/independence/creativity — 79.7 / 75.7
Societal recognition — 30.8 / 31.9
Taking societal responsibility — 62.5 / 62.3
Taking ecological responsibility — 50.7 / 45.6
Family–work balance — 58.9 / 69.3
Best possible use of one's (professional) expertise — 87.1 / 87.2

■ Men-led enterprises   ▨ Women-led enterprises

Figure 3.8 Importance of different personal motives for working as an entrepreneur or manager in women-led and men-led enterprises (in percentage terms)

Source: Survey data of IfM Bonn, 2014. Own calculations. The number of observations per item varies from 464 to 480.

Table 3.3 Logistic regression results on the differences between women-led and men-led enterprises with respect to motives and attitudes of their managers

	Identification of women-led enterprises					German Mittelstand	n
	Proportion	Dummy	Intervals				
			25–49%	50–74%	75–100%		
Securing one's personal income	n.s.	n.s.	n.s.	n.s.	n.s.	n.s.	399
Securing one's personal wealth	n.s.	n.s.	n.s.	n.s.	n.s.	n.s.	389
Self-realisation	n.s.	n.s.	n.s.	n.s.	n.s.	n.s.	395
Societal recognition	n.s.	n.s.	n.s.	n.s.	n.s.	n.s.	397

(*Continued*)

Table 3.3 (Continued)

	Identification of women-led enterprises						German Mittelstand	n
	Proportion	Dummy	Intervals					
			25–49%	50–74%	75–100%			
Taking societal responsibility	n.s.	n.s.	n.s.	n.s.	n.s.		n.s.	393
Taking ecological responsibility	–*	n.s.	n.s.	n.s.	n.s.		n.s.	384
Family-work-balance	n.s.	n.s.	n.s.	n.s.	n.s.		n.s.	390
Best possible use of one's (professional) expertise	n.s.	n.s.	n.s.	n.s.	n.s.		n.s.	398

Notes: Coefficients are significant on the *** 1%, ** 5% and * 10%level; estimation of robust standard errors. Additional control variables are: firm size according to the SME definition of the European Commission (three dummy variables), affiliation to the German Mittelstand (a dummy variable which can also be regarded as a proxy for family businesses), personal liability of the firm owner(s), age of the firm (six dummy variables), region (a dummy variable for West Germany) and industry (three dummy variables). The statistical significance of the coefficient of the variable "German Mittelstand" is always the same in every single set of logistic regressions so that the corresponding results are summarized in a single column. A complete set of results is available upon request from the authors.

Source: Survey data of IfM Bonn, 2014. Own calculations.

Discussion and implications

Although there are distinct structural differences between women-led and men-led enterprises in Germany in terms of their characteristics, we find no (systematic) differences between women-led and men-led enterprises with respect to the enterprises 'objectives or the motives/attitudes of the managers. Moreover, our data do not give evidence for a significant impact of the proportion of women in the executive board on the importance of the enterprises objectives. Interestingly, the public image of women-owned businesses differs in this regard and seems to be more stereotyped than based on facts.

However, we found some differences regarding profit maximization in the short run as well as creation and preservation of jobs. Both of these objectives are more important in women-led enterprises than in men-led enterprises. The results on profit maximization may be driven by a certain type of women-led enterprise with a relatively high proportion of women in the executive board. However, we find no further explanation in our dataset for the importance of "preservation of jobs". Summing up our research, we can conclude: The manager's sex and his or her motives and attitudes are less important for an enterprise's objectives than are the business environment and competitive conditions. Hence, our findings support other current studies that stress environmental and contextual factors of women-led enterprises, respectively, over the sex of the business owner or members of the executive board. All in all, our findings do not support the thesis that women-owned businesses are more responsible socially or ecologically, or exhibit greater corporate responsibility, than do other businesses.

We were not able to investigate the impact of different management styles (which may differ between male and female managers) due to data restrictions. Besides this, our study faces several other limitations. The sample size limits analyses of certain subpopulations. Additional personal data for managers in the executive board were not available. Therefore, the identification and analysis of women-owned businesses is limited. We could identify only the sex of the interviewee in case of executive boards consisting of only men or women.

To summarize the results of our study, we can state: Women-led enterprises are not likely to have a stronger focus on social, ecological or corporate responsibility issues that are men-led enterprises. Hence, our initial results with regard to the differences between men- and women-led enterprises provide additional support for previous research that stresses the impact of economic and environmental factors on company performance rather than the particular sex of the business owner or manager. In which way this influences different types of businesses is an ongoing question for future research.

References

Anna, A., Chandler, G., Jansen, E., and Mero, N. (2000). Women business owners in traditional and non-traditional industries. *Journal of Business Venturing*, 15(3), 279–303.

Brush, C. G., and Hisrich, R. (2000). *Women-owned businesses: An exploratory study comparing factors affecting performance.* Working Paper Series 00-02, RSIE business, Washington, DC.

Cowling, M., and Taylor, M. (2001). Entrepreneurial men and women: Two different species? *Small Business Economics*, 18(3), 167–175.

De Bruin, A., Brush, C. G., and Welter, F. (2007): Advancing a framework for coherent research on women's entrepreneurship: Introduction to the second special issue on women's entrepreneurship. *Entrepreneurship Theory and Practice*, 31(3), 323–339.

Diaz-Garcia, C. (2006). *The influence of gender on small firm's resources and performance.* Dissertation, Universidad de Castilla La Mancha, Albacete, Spain.

Du Rietz, A., and Henrekson, M. (2000). Testing the female underperformance hypothesis. *Small Business Economics*, 14(1), 1–10.

Ettl, K., and Welter, F. (2012). Women entrepreneurs and success. In M.-A. Galindo and D. Ribeiro (eds.), *Women's entrepreneurship and economics. International Studies in Entrepreneurship*, 1000, 73–88.

European Commission (2003). *Commission recommendation of 6 May 2003 concerning the definition of micro, small and medium-sized enterprises* (Text with EEA relevance, notified under document number C(2003) 1422. http://data.europa.eu/eli/reco/2003/361/oj

Haunschild, L., and Wolter, H.-J. (2010). *Volkswirtschaftliche Bedeutung von Familien- und Frauenunternehmen.* IfM-Materialien Nr. 199, Bonn.

Joecks, J., Pull, K., and Vetter, K. (2013): Gender diversity in the boardroom and firm performance: What exactly constitutes a "critical mass?" *Journal of Business Ethics*, 118(1), 61–72.

Kalleberg, A. L., and Leicht, K. T. (1991). Gender and organizational performance: Determinants of small business survival and success. *Academy of Management Journal*, 34(1), 136–161.

Kay, R., and Schlömer-Laufen, N. (2016). *Gender diversity in top-management positions in large family and nonfamily businesses.* IfM Bonn Working Paper 02/2016, Bonn.

Kohaut, S., and Möller, I. (2016). *Führungspositionen in der Privatwirtschaft: Im Osten sind Frauen öfter an der Spitze.* IAB-Kurzbericht 2/2016, Nürnberg.

Laible, M.-C. (2013). *Gender diversity in top management and firm performance: An analysis with the IAB-Establishment Panel.* CAED Conference Paper, Atlanta, September 18–20, 2013.

Lindstädt, H., Wolff, M., and Fehre, K. (2011). *Frauen in Führungspositionen: Auswirkungen auf den Unternehmenserfolg.* Berlin: Bundesministerium für Familie, Senioren, Frauen und Jugend.

Minguez-Vera, A., and Martin, A. (2011): Gender and management of Spanish SMEs: An empirical analysis. *Journal of Human Resource Management*, 22(14), 2583–2873.

Mirchandani, K. (1999). Feminist insight on gendered work: New directions in research on women and entrepreneurship. *Gender, Work and Organization*, 6(4), 224–235.

Moser, K., and Schuler, H. (1999). Die Heterogenität der Kriterien unternehmerischen Erfolgs. In K. Moser, B. Batinic and J. Zempel (eds.), *Unternehmerisch erfolgreiches Handelns*. Göttingen: Verlag für Angewandte Psychologie.

Pahnke, A., Kay, R., and Schlepphorst, S. (2017). *Unternehmerisches Verhalten im Zuge der Unternehmensnachfolge.* IfM-Materialien Nr. 254, Bonn.

Rosa, P., Carter, S., and Hamilton, D. (1996). Gender as a determinant of small business performance: Insights from a British study. *Small Business Economics*, 8(6), 463–478.

Thornton, P. (1999). The sociology of entrepreneurship. *Annual Review of Sociology*, 25(1), 19–46.

Welter, F., May-Strobl, E., and Wolter, H.-J. assisted by Günterberg, B. (2014). *Mittelstand im Wandel.* IfM-Materialien Nr. 232, Bonn.

Wolter, H.-J., and Hauser, H.-E. (2001). Die Bedeutung des Eigentümerunternehmens in Deutschland – Eine Auseinandersetzung mit der qualitativen und quantitativen Definition des Mittelstands. In IfM Bonn (eds.), *Jahrbuch zur Mittelstandsforschung 1/2001, Schriften zur Mittelstandsforschung Nr. 90 NF* (pp. 25–77). Wiesbaden: Deutscher Universitätsverlag.

4 Family firms and non-family firms

A survey in Italian and Spanish wine sector performance

Laura Broccardo and Elisa Truant

1. Introduction

The influence of ownership structures on business performance has been researched extensively in the theoretical and empirical literature. The relevant literature suggests that ownership structure is one of the main corporate governance mechanisms influencing the scope of a firm's agency cost (Arosa, Iturralde and Maseda, 2010).

Identifying differences between family firms and non-family firms and understanding the medium and long-term consequences of the family firms' strategic behaviour constitute two of the basic fields of family business research. Recent research has taken important steps toward these ends. However, in some cases, the differences between family firms and non-family firms have not been sufficiently explained (Gallo, Tàpies and Cappuyns, 2004).

This study compares family and non-family firms in two different countries, Italy and Spain, considering a particular sector where these countries excel, the manufacture of wine from grape, to have a better understanding where the most value is created.

Gallo, Tàpies and Cappuyns (2004) study the field of financial structure and policies, as well as the economic results of family firms. The following research is worth noting.

First, Daily and Dollinger (1993), analysed a sample of 186 manufacturing businesses in Indiana (USA), with fewer than 500 employees and sales levels of less than $30 million per year. They compared family firms and non-family firms, between 1986 and 1988, and they found that family firms surpassed non-family firms in rate of sales and profit margins.

Second, Gallo and Vilaseca (1998), using a sample of 104 Spanish family firms having an average sales figure of €33.7 million, found that smaller family firms used less complex financial practices and had very low debt ratios, but the research failed to identify statistically significant differences in resource profitability.

This chapter tries to identify any significant differences between family firms and non-family firms in general and also determine if there are significant differences or analogies in these two different countries. It is organised as follows. Firstly, it analyses the theoretical background concerning the family firms and non-family firms. Secondly, it outlines the research method and presents the sample analysed. Finally, it discusses the results and the main conclusions, along with the limitations of the study.

Theoretical background

Defining family firms

In the last years family firms have received increased attention and several recent studies have reported that in continental Europe, Asia, and Latin America, the vast majority of publicly traded firms are family controlled (La Porta et al., 1999; Claessens et al., 2000; European Corporate Governance Network, 2001; Faccio and Lang, 2002). Research also suggests that family firms play an important role in economic activity worldwide. In fact, two-thirds of private businesses in many countries are considered to be family firms (Neubauer and Lank, 1998). They contribute to wealth creation and job generation with reference to narrow and broad family firm definitions (Astrachan and Shanker, 2003).

However, how is it possible to define the meaning of "family firm"? It is not so easy to give a definition of family firm; in fact, ambiguities in the literature persist. Kraiczy (2013, p. 7) affirms that:

> although many researchers have tried to develop a satisfactory definition, there is still no consensus about a widely accepted definition. Although some studies in the finance literature identify any public company where a family or a founder owns more than 5 percent as a family firm, other studies define firms only as family firms if the first succession into the second generation has taken place. However, in most studies a family firm has been characterized as a firm that is controlled and usually managed by multiple family members, sometimes from multiple generations. The use of different definitions is a major problem in family firm research. Although studies analyse related topics, the use of different family firm definitions makes the comparability of these results difficult. One of the biggest challenges of developing a general definition is the heterogeneity of family firms.

The main definitions are the following. Chua) define "family business" as a business governed and/or managed on a sustainable, potentially cross-generational, basis to shape and perhaps pursue the formal or implicit vision of the business held by members of the same family or a small number of families.

La Porta, Lopez-de-Silanes, and Shleifer (1999) define "family business" as a firm that is partly owned by one or more family members, who control together at least 20 per cent of the total votes outstanding.

Astrachan and Kolenko (1994) suggest that a family has to own more than 50 per cent of the business in a private company or more than 10 per cent of a public company in order to qualify as a family business.

Le Breton-Miller, Miller, and Steier (2004) do not explicitly define a family firm but they assume that management succession means firm leadership will pass from one family member to another or, in the absence of a competent family contender in the short-term, a bridge manager between family tenures.

Zahra, Hayton, and Salvato (2004) define family firms according to the presence of both a family member with some identifiable share of the ownership of the firm and multiple generations of family members in leadership positions within that firm.

Morck and Yeung (2004) use the following criteria of family control to distinguish family firms: (1) the largest group of shareholders in a firm is a specific family, and (2) the stake of that family is greater than either a 10 per cent or 20 per cent control of the voting shares.

Astrachan and Kolenko (1994) specify that a family has to own more than 50 per cent of the business in a private company or more than 10 per cent of a public company in order to qualify as a family business.

Family versus non-family firms

After defining "family firm", it is important to examine the "family effect" on firm performance.

Jensen and Meckling (1976) suggested that ownership concentration has a positive effect on performance because it alleviates any conflict of interest between owners and managers. The opposite view of the ownership structure directs attention towards the effects of the agency problem resulting from the combination of concentrated ownership and owner control (Fama and Jensen, 1983).

In the literature, there are studies that underline that family firms are better than non-family firms and they report that controlled family ownership positively influences firm performance (Anderson and Reeb, 2003;Burkart et al., 2003; Wang, 2006).

Anderson and Reeb (2003, p. 1316) found that family firms outperformed non-family firms in the S&P 500, noting "family firms are significantly better performers than non-family firms".

Another study, conducted by Arosa, Iturralde, and Maseda (2010), underlines that the distinctive features of family firms have a positive effect on their corporate behaviour. The family's interest in the long-term survival of the business as well as its concern for maintaining the reputation of the firm and the family, lead the family to avoid acting opportunistically with regard to the earnings obtained (Burkart, Panunzi and Shleifer, 2003; Wang,2006). Families have concerns and interests of their own, such as stability and capital preservation, that may not be aligned with the interests of other firm investors.

However, in general, the empirical evidence is not conclusive.

Arosa et al. (2010) also underline that some empirical findings indicate that firms with concentrated ownership structure, such as founding families, show lower profitability than those firms with a dispersed ownership structure

(DeAngelo and DeAngelo, 2000; Fama and Jensen, 1983; Gomez-Mejia et al., 2001).

Furthermore, there are also many studies that highlight that family firms under-perform if compared with non-family firms.

Daily and Dollinger (1993) write that family-run firms appear to achieve performance advantages whether performance is measured in terms of financially oriented growth rates or perceived measures of performance.

Faccio, Lang, and Young (2001) have noted that family firms are relatively poor performers due to conflicts that arise as a family attempts to manage an enterprise.

Despite the different positions in the literature, the study described in this chapter seeks to determine if the most value is created in family or in non-family firms.

2. Methodology

The sample

This study is based on a sample of 274 companies operating in the Manufacture Sector of wine from grape, where the two considered countries, Italy, and Spain, are historical producers (see Table 4.1).

The sample includes only large firms and data were extracted from the Amadeus database.

The sample comprises 140 companies from Italy and 134 from Spain.

In this study a firm is classified as a family firm if family owns more than 50 per cent of the business in a private company or more than 10 per cent of a public company (Astrachan and Kolenko, 1994).

The sample includes 136 family firms (50 per cent) and 138 non-family firms (50 per cent). The details for each country are included in Table 4.2.

Table 4.1 The sample

	n. company	*% n. of companies*
Italy	140	51%
Spain	134	49%
Total	274	100%

Source: Own elaboration

Table 4.2 Family firms and family firms sample

	family firms	*% family firms*	*Non-family firms*	*% non-family firms*	*Total*	*% Total*
Italy	65	46%	75	54%	140	100%
Spain	71	53%	63	47%	134	100%
Total	136	50%	138	50%	274	100%

Source: Own elaboration

Research question and method

The main goal of this study is to analyse the impact of the variable "family" on performance. The main research question (RQ1) is: Does the family variable have a positive impact on financial performance? To answer this research question, the most relevant financial and economic ratio between family and non-family firms were compared, for each country.

3. Findings

To analyse performance, both in Italy and Spain, we considered the mean for each ratio, in particular the return on equity (ROE), return on assets (ROA), and liquidity ratio, in the years 2013, 2014, and 2015.

Italy

Analysing Italy, the mean of each ratio has been calculated on 65 family firms and 75 non-family firms.

   In regard to Italian family firms, the data show that family firms outperform in ROE, and non-family firms outperform in ROA, how shown in Table 4.3.

   The ROA shows that the assets in non-family firms are more profitable in generating revenue; in particular, this ratio shows how many euro of earnings they derive from each euro of assets they control.

   On the contrary, family firms outperform in ROE, which measures the rate of return on the ownership interest of the common stock owners. Italian family firms seem more efficient at generating profits from every unit of shareholders' equity.

   About the liquidity ratio (see Table 4.4), the index that measures the ability of a company to meet its short term debt obligations and the ability of a company to pay off its short-term liabilities when they fall due, it emerges that non-family firms outperform family firms.

Spain

Analysing Spain, the mean of each ratio includes for family firms 71 companies and for non-family firms 63 companies.

Table 4.3 Economic performance in Italian family firms and non-family firms

	Italian family firms	Italian non-family firms	Outperformance classification – Italy
ROE mean 2013–2015	4.73	4.07	family firms
ROA mean 2013–2015	1.41	1.83	Non-family firms

Source: Own elaboration

Table 4.4 Financial performance in Italian family firms and non-family firms

	Italian family firms	Italian non-family firms	Outperformance classification – Italy
Liquidity ratio mean 2013–2015	0.72	0.80	Non-family firms

Source: Own elaboration

Table 4.5 Economic performance in Spanish family firms and non-family firms

	Spanish family firms	Spanish non-family firms	Outperformance classification – Spain
ROE mean 2013–2015	–0.83	1.03	non-family firms
ROA mean 2013–2015	1.36	0.97	family firms

Source: Own elaboration

Table 4.6 Financial performance in Spanish family firms and non-family firms

	Spanish family firms	Spanish non-family firms	outperformance classification – Spain
Liquidity ratio mean 2013–2015	1.60	1.41	family firms

Source: Own elaboration

About Spanish family firms the data show that, in this case, non-family firms outperform in ROE, and family firms outperform in ROA, how underlined in Table 4.5.

The ROA shows that the assets in family firms are more profitable in generating revenue; in particular, this ratio shows how many euro of earnings they derive from each euro of assets they control.

Spanish non-family firms outperform in ROE, which measures the rate of return on the ownership interest of the common stock owners. Spanish non-family firms seem more efficient in generating profits from every unit of shareholders' equity.

About the liquidity ratio (see Table 4.6), Spanish family firms seem more able, than non-family firms, to meet its short-term debt obligations, if we consider the mean, also if non-family firms outperform for two year in this index.

Italy and Spain

In addition, to summarize the evidence collected, Table 4.7 gathers the results for both Italian and Spanish family firms and non-family firms.

Table 4.7 Financial performance in Italian and Spanish family firms and non-family firms

	Italian family firms	Italian non-family firms	Outper-formance in Italy	Spanish family firms	Spanish non-family firms	Outper-formance in Spain	Outperformance classification Italy and Spain
ROE mean 2013–2015	4.73	4.07	family firms	–0.83	1.03	NFFs	Italian family firms
ROA mean 2013–2015	1.41	1.83	Non-family firms	1.36	0.97	FFs	Italian Non-family firms
Liquidity ratio mean 2013–2015	0.72	0.80	Non. family firms	1.60	1.41	FFs	Spanish family firms

Source: Own elaboration

4. Conclusion, contribution and future research

The purpose of this study is to scrutinize the relationship between ownership structure and the performance in Italian and Spanish non-family firms and family firms that manufacture wine from grape.

Firstly, the analysis reveals that Italian non-family firms outperform Italian family firms in ROA; consequently, Italian non-family firms are more profitable in generating value.

On the contrary, it emerged that the behaviour of Spanish family firms and non-family firms is opposite, compared to Italian companies. Indeed Spanish family firms outperform in ROA, compared to Spanish non-family firms.

Regarding ROE, observing Italy, it emerged that FFs outperform non-family firms, appearing to be more efficient in generating profits from every unit of shareholder equity. In Spain, observing the ROE ratio, non-family firms outperform family firms.

Regarding the liquidity ratio, Italian non-family firms outperform, and in Spain the family firms outperform.

Observing Italy, it emerged that non-family firms outperform family firms, due to ROA and the liquidity ratio. On the contrary, observing Spain, it emerged that family firms outperform, due to ROA and the liquidity ratio.

Some evidence emerges from this research:

- Firstly, about the variable "family" it is possible to affirm that the "family" affects performance;
- Secondly, it emerged that Italian Firms present opposite features than Spanish firms.

The Italian family firms' results confirm the literature that emphasizes that firms with concentrated ownership structure, such as founding families, show lower profitability than firms with a dispersed ownership structure (DeAngelo and DeAngelo, 2000; Fama and Jensen, 1983; Gomez-Mejia et al., 2001).

On the contrary, the Spanish findings are in line with the literature that considers family firms to be better performers than non-family firms (Anderson and Reeb, 2003;Burkart et al., 2003; Wang, 2006).

To explain these controversial results in the literature (Arosa, Iturralde and Maseda, 2010), it has been underlined that the distinctive features of family firms could affect a company's corporate behaviour and consequently its performance.

In conclusion, this research confirms what it is possible to find in the literature: the family is a relevant variable in performance evaluation, but it is not easy to determine whether it positively affects performance or not.

Based on this discussion, the research contributes theoretically to enrich the debate about the performance of family firms and non-family firms. Empirically it contributes to the investigation that seeks to identify the valuable internal features of family firms and non-family firms that should be managed to address performance.

Future developments in the research could focus on the size variable, and on different numbers of ratios investigating the internal reasons behind different performance results in family firms and non-family firms in Italy and Spain, considering that it is surprising to discover opposite results for companies operating in the same sector.

References

Anderson, R. C., and Reeb, D. M. (2003). Founding-family ownership and firm performance: Evidence from the S&P 500. *Journal of Finance*, 58(3), 1301–1328.

Arosa, B., Iturralde, T., and Maseda, A. (2010). Ownership structure and firm performance in non-listed firms: Evidence from Spain. *Journal of Family Business Strategy*, 1, 88–96.

Astrachan, J. H., and Kolenko, T. A. (1994). A neglected factor explaining family business success: Human resource practices. *Family Business Review*, 7(3), 251–262.

Astrachan, J. H., and Shanker, M. C. (2003). Family businesses' contribution to the US economy: A closer look. *Family Business Review*, 16, 211–219.

Burkart, M., Panunzi, F., and Shleifer, A. (2003). Family firms. *The Journal of Finance*, 58(5), 2167–2202.

Chua, J. H., Chrisman, J. J., and Sharma, P. (1999). Defining the family business by behaviour, entrepreneurship. *Theory and Practice*, 23(4), 19–39.

Claessens, S., Djankov, S., and Lang, L. H. P. (2000). The separation of ownership and control in East Asian Corporations. *Journal of Financial Economics*, 58(1), 81–112.

Daily, C. M., and Dollinger, M. J. (1993). Alternative methodologies for identifying family versus non-family businesses. *Journal of Small Business Management*, 31(2), 79.

DeAngelo, H., and DeAngelo, L. (2000). Controlling stockholders and the disciplinary role of corporate payout policy: A study of the Times Mirror Company. *Journal of Financial Economics*, 56(2), 153–207.

Faccio, M., Lang, L. H. P., and Young, L. (2001). Dividends and expropriation. *American Economic Review*, 91(1), 54–78.

Faccio, M., and Lang, L. H. P. (2002). The ultimate ownership of Western corporations. *Journal of Financial Economics*, 65, 365–395.

Fama, E. F., and Jensen, M. C. (1983). Separation of ownership and control. *Journal of Law and Economics*, 26, 301–325.

Gallo, M. Á., Tàpies, J., and Cappuyns, K. (2004, December). Comparison of family and nonfamily business: Financial logic and personal preferences. *Family Business Review*, XVII(4).

Gallo, M. A., and Vilaseca, A. (1998). A financial perspective on structure, conduct, and performance in the family firm: An empirical study. *Family Business Review*, 11(1), 35–47.

Gomez-Mejia, L. R., Nunez-Nickel, M., and Gutierrez, I. (2001). The role of family ties in agency contracts. *Academy of Management Journal*, 44(1), 81–95.

Jensen, M. C., and Meckling, W. H. (1976). Theory of the firm: Managerial behaviour, agency cost and ownership structure. *Journal of Financial Economics*, 3, 305–360.

Kraiczy, N. (2013). Innovations in small and medium-sized family firms, Familienunternehmen und KMU. doi:10.1007/978-3-658-00063-9_2, © Wiesbaden: Springer Fachmedien.

La Porta, R., Lopez-de-Silanes, F., and Shleifer, A. (1999). Corporate ownership around the world. *The Journal of Finance*, 54(2), 471–517.

Le Breton-Miller I. L., Miller D., and Steiner L. P. (2004), Toward an integrative model of effective FOB succession, *Entrepreneurship theory and practice*, 28(4), 305–328.

Morck, R., and Yeung, B. (2004). Family control and the rent-seeking society. *Entrepreneurship Theory and Practice*, 28(4), 391–409.

Neubauer, F. F., and Lank, A. G. (1998). *The family business: Its governance for sustainability*. New York: Routledge.

Neubauer, F., and Lank, A. G. (1998). *The family business: Its governance for sustainability*. London: Palgrave Macmillan.

Wang, D. (2006). Founding family ownership and earnings quality. *Journal of Accounting Research*, 44(3), 619–656.

Zahra, S. A., Hayton, J. C., and Salvato, C. (2004). Entrepreneurship in family vs. non-family firms: A resource-based analysis of the effect of organizational culture. *Entrepreneurship Theory & Practice*, 28(4), 363–379.

5 The role of women as entrepreneurs in family business

A literature review

Alessandra Faraudello, Lucrezia Songini, Massimiliano Pellegrini and Luca Gnan

1. Introduction

Especially in the past, woman's professional capabilities and competencies were mostly ignored both in family and nonfamily businesses. Many wives, daughters and women in general played several central roles in companies; however, in general their work is invisible, with no recognition and no monetary gain with few chances to show their true abilities. Due to this 'invisibility', studies on gender in family business and the role of women are quite recent. Considering the recent literature, it is possible to identify an evolution in women's representation in ownership and governance bodies and their key role in shaping the founding process and the development of many private family firms. Taking into account previous contributions, the current work aims for a better understanding of the state of the art in research in this field and future directions. This review identifies an evolution in women's involvement in family firms.

Discussions about supporting women's participation in the business world is only a part of a much wider debate about the role of women in society (Carter et al., 2015). Women have been economically active since 11th century. At that time, they played roles such as agents who sold textiles for merchants or even brokers who dealt in books (Goitein, 1967). However, especially in the past, women's professional capabilities and competencies were mostly ignored, both in family and nonfamily businesses. Many wives, daughters, and women in general, played several roles within an organization, but often they were invisible, with no consideration and no monetary gain. Women commonly were not respected and had no opportunities to show their capabilities (Dumas, 1998). Historically speaking, family businesses commonly had 'no women' and 'no wives' rules (whether formal or informal), in contrast, in today's world of family ambition and increasing gender neutrality, women's roles can be placed at the top of the organizational hierarchy (Aronoff, 1998; Terjesen and Ratten, 2007). Particularly in the last decades, great advancements in involvement of women in entrepreneurial and managerial roles, especially in family-owned businesses, has been achieved, and the situation is further developing. Women have a strong presence in family-owned firms, particularly in those founded since the 1950s (Dumas, 1998). More and more, wives and daughters are rising to the leadership of family firms – even in some of the most male-dominated industries. The paradigm is changing from "invisible to invincible" (Nelton, 1999, pp. 48–51). Moreover, it is forecasted that in 10 years more than a third of family firms will be owned and run by women (Nelton, 1998). Due to the historical 'invisibility' of women, studies on gender in family business and the role of women are relatively recent (Cole, 1997; Harveston et al., 1997). In the 1980s, articles about women in family firms focused mostly on barriers and resistance, and compared female accomplishments to those of businessmen. As time passed, women have been recognized also as stakeholders, successors, managers, policy makers, and owners in family business (Frishkoff and Brown, 1993). However, in relation to developing or transitional economies, the situation is still lacks behind (e.g. Ramadani et al., 2013; Ramadani, 2015, Ramadani, Danaet al., 2015; Caputo et al., 2016; Mehtap et al., 2016).

Contrary to the general stereotype, family businesses are rich in opportunities for women in many ways. Modern women are more comfortable discussing their wealth openly with their families and advisers (Almallah and Schwartz, 2008). However, despite the great advancement made by women in such organizations, many issues are still stressed in recent literature on women role in family and nonfamily firms. According to research by Sánchez-Sellero and Sánchez-Sellero (2013), conducted in Spain, the probability of men to work for a family firm is equal regardless the size, whereas for women the odds are lower when the size gets bigger. Yet women are less likely to have linear careers, and they tend to not receive mentorship even in small firms; however, they admit feeling less pressure than their male counterparts in large firms.

Women have played key roles in founding and shaping the development of many private family firms, both behind the scenes and in the front lines (Howorth et al., 2010). Even though women CEOs and founders are an emerging phenomenon (Dumas, 1998), gender stereotypes are still quite strong when we look at the possibility of women occupying top management positions, despite a steady increase of their number over the last few decades (Chirikova and Krichevskaia, 2002). Specifically, the number of women opting to work in family-owned businesses has largely increased. Unfortunately, however, they still have lower status and face more operational challenges in running the business (Anshu, 2012). This is confirmed by an analysis of survey data studying the multidimensional nature of gender inequality in entrepreneurship from 24 countries, over the span of eight years: women are substantially underrepresented in entrepreneurship across countries and have lower probability of being an entrepreneur in high-childcare-spending contexts than in low-childcare-spending contexts (Thébaud, 2015). In 2009, based on a deep analysis of literature including 48 articles and other research materials, Martinez-Jimenez proposed a categorization of obstacles and propelling aspects that can influence women involvement in family firms.

The three identified obstacles are: women's invisibility and the glass ceiling, emotional leadership, and succession and primogeniture. Promoting aspects include: development of a professional career and running the company. Martinez-Jimenez (2009) analyzed factors that can help or hinder daughters' involvement in top management positions in family firms. He found that wives played an important role for the continuity and growth of family firms. This is confirmed in the general literature (e.g. Pellegrini et al., 2012).

Taking into account previous contributions (Sharma, 2004; Sharma et al., 2005; Martinez-Jimenez, 2009), the current work aims to reach a better understanding of the state of the art in research exploring the role of women in family businesses to identify future research directions. The chapter is based on the framework proposed by Martinez-Jimenez (2009). It pursues the aim of updating that 2009 article and identifying changes and trends in the literature that have occurred in recent years. The updated literature review on the role of women in family firms will allow the authors to identify relevant current issues and to propose future research directions. The literature was analyzed according to categories proposed by Martinez-Jimenez (2009): obstacles (women's invisibility, glass ceiling, emotional leadership, succession and primogeniture) and opportunities (professional career and running a company). Based on the critical analysis of previous literature, a research framework is proposed from previous literature, on the role of women in family firms, main drivers, and obstacles. Both situations of 'women-entrepreneurs', who have established their own company, and 'women-managers', who run a family business, are considered. To critically compare different articles, a list of relevant topics, concerning drivers for and obstacles to women's involvement in family business, as well as their leadership styles and impacts on the firm (strategy, organization, 'managerialization', and performance), was developed.

Each quadrant/variable of our research framework represents a specific research stream that can be tackled using different theories and methods. This can also be used to give a clearer picture of family businesses and relations inside them to family business owners, managers, consultants, and policy makers interested in the topic of "women in family business".

This chapter is organized as follows. The introduction described the research aim and design so in Section 2 we directly presented the methodology used to review previous literature. In Section 3, main findings of literature analysis are provided first in a quantitative fashion and then in the analysis of the papers. Finally, Section 4 discusses the research findings, suggests a research framework to be used for future research directions, and offers practical insights for family business scholars and practitioners.

2. Research methodology

To integrate the framework presented in the introduction, a total of 121 sources were analyzed. Computer-based information searches were first conducted using the keywords 'women' or 'woman' and 'businesswomen' paired with terms such

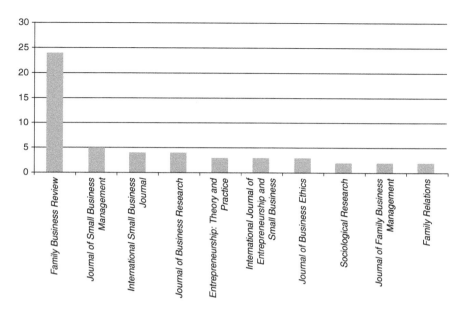

Figure 5.1 Top 10 sources

as 'family business', 'family firms', 'succession', 'invisibility', 'glass ceiling', 'wife', and 'entrepreneur'. These keywords were searched using the following databases: Business Source Premier (EBSCO), Wiley Online Library, American Psychological Association Database (PsycArticles), ResearchGate, SAGE Journals Database, Elsevier Database. Sixty-two sources, containing papers and literature on the topic "women in family business" were identified.

The top 10 of the sources (Figure 5.1) where papers concerning the topic have been identified, are: *Family Business Review, Journal of Small Business Management, International Small Business Journal, Journal of Business Research, Entrepreneurship: Theory and Practice, International Journal of Entrepreneurship and Small Business, Journal of Business Ethics, Sociological Research, Journal of Family Business Management,* and *Family Relations.* Other papers were added to give consistency to the findings; these contributions were conference papers, books and book chapters, dissertations, practitioners' reports, etc.

3. Main findings

Since 1967 the number of articles published about women in family business constantly increased, reaching 10 papers in 2015 and 16 papers in July 2016 (Figure 5.2).

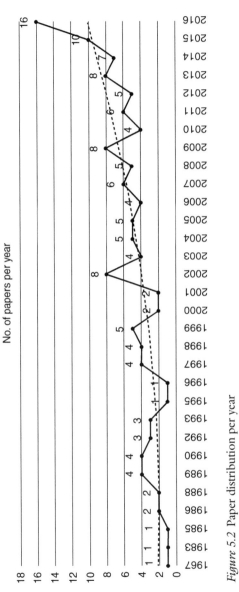

No. of papers per year

Figure 5.2 Paper distribution per year

The trend presented in Figure 5.2 shows us that the attention to the topic has increased as the time pass. Since 1967, 61 percent of articles analyzed were published before 2009 while the remaining 39 percent appeared after Martinez-Jimenez's contribution.

Since 1967, *Family Business Review* has published 24 papers on the topic (Table 5.1). Other journals interested in the topic are *Journal of Small Business Management* and *International Small Business Journal,* with totals of five and four papers respectively in the same period.

It is quite interesting to observe that women in family businesses are also the object of research for Big 4 Research consulting firms such as Ernst & Young and McKinsey.

The literature that has been analyzed contains studies made at least in 36 countries, with 26 percent of all the cases in the USA, 10 percent in Canada and 8 percent in Italy (Figure 5.3).

A total of 141 publications were selected, divided into different topics. The most frequent topics, organized according to Martinez-Jimenez's framework (2009), are women's invisibility (23 percent) and professional careers of women in family firms (21 percent) (Table 5.2).

Women's invisibility remains one of the most important topics, and it always becomes more significant with time; however, there is a clear trend in the emergence of some topics and the disappearance of others (Figure 5.4). For example, the emotional leadership of women is a topic much less discussed. In the selected publications, 68 percent of papers are empirical while 32 percent are theoretical. Almost 40 percent of all the empirical articles that were analyzed are based on case studies and the remaining 60 percent are based on quantitative analysis.

Table 5.1 Most relevant journals

Source title	No. of papers
Family Business Review	24
Journal of Small Business Management	5
International Small Business Journal	4
Journal of Business Research	4
Entrepreneurship: Theory and Practice	3
Big 4 Research	3
International Journal of Entrepreneurship and Small Business	3
Journal of Business Ethics	3
Sociological Research	2
The Leadership Quarterly Journal	2
Chapter in a book	2
Critical Sociology	2
Journal of Family Business Management	2
Family Relations	2
International Journal of Business Governance and Ethics	2

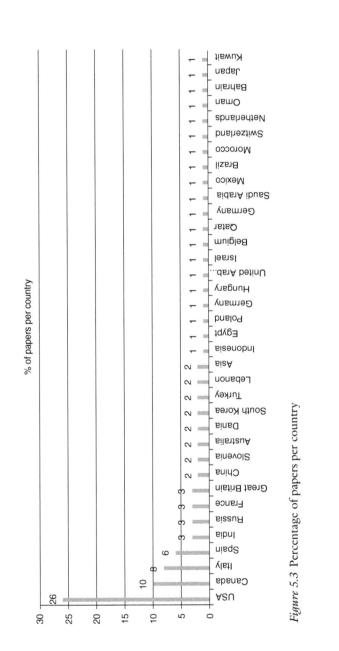

% of papers per country

Figure 5.3 Percentage of papers per country

Table 5.2 Most frequent topic distribution among the selected publications.

Topics	N. papers	%
Women's invisibility	32	23%
Emotional leadership	25	18%
Succession	26	18%
Professional career in family firms	30	21%
Running the family firms	28	20%
Total	141	100%

Considering all the papers analyzed, 63 percent of them concern family firms only, 13 percent are on nonfamily firms and 19 percent analyze both family and nonfamily firms. The remaining 5 percent analyze individuals rather than firms. The most common empirical approach is the case study approach. Analysis based on case studies contains from one (McManus, 1999) to 14,000 interviews with the use of quality methodology and in-depth interviews (Fitzgerald and Muske, 2002). Case studies include several types of industries: grocery stores, automotive dealerships, the food industry, communications businesses, commercial real estate, marketing consultants, industrial or commercial distribution and manufacturing, and so on. These analyses are equally distributed between small and medium family firms and large family firms while there is a prevalence of case studies related to one generation of family owners only; however, for the succession topic naturally more than one generation is included (Hamilton, 2006).

3.1. Qualitative interpretation of results

This section presents a review of literature on women in family business. It begins by presenting the main contributions to obstacles that hinder women from being involved in family businesses' top management and governance roles; then it explores the drivers that favor such women participation.

3.1.1 Obstacles

The main factors that prevent women involvement in top leadership positions in family business have been classified by Martinez-Jimenez (2009) into three main categories: women's invisibility and the glass ceiling, emotional leadership, and succession and primogeniture.

GLASS CEILING AND WOMEN'S INVISIBILITY

The glass ceiling
The glass ceiling is an invisible barrier "so subtle that it is transparent, yet so strong that it prevents women from moving up higher professional position" (Morrison et al., 1994). Thus, women can see high-level corporate positions

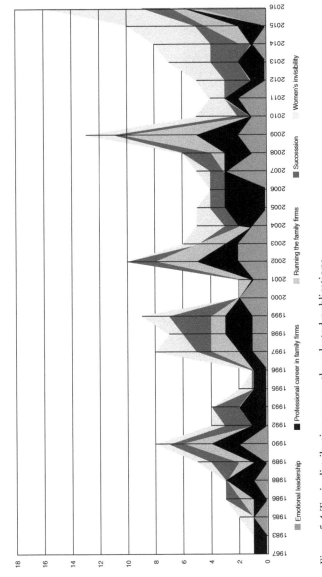

Figure 5.4 Topic distribution among the selected publications

but are kept from 'reaching the summit' of the corporation. The glass ceiling "is not simply a barrier for an individual, based on the person's inability to handle a higher-level job. Rather, the glass ceiling applies to women as a group who are kept from advancing higher because they are women" (Morrison et al., 1994). The glass ceiling can refer to ownership, management and governance alike. There has been much research and conjecture concerning the barriers women face in trying to climb the corporate ladder. First, there is still evidence of the glass ceiling situation; second, even if this situation does not occur, women may experience a 'glass escalator' effect where men are more likely to benefit in terms of career progression (Ryan and Haslam, 2005).

Compared to men, women who assume leadership roles may be differentially exposed to criticism; they are in greater danger of being blamed for negative outcomes that were set in train well before they assumed their new roles. Moreover, it is apparent that even if they arrive in top positions, women are likely to receive greater scrutiny and criticism than men, and to secure less positive evaluations, even when performing exactly the same leadership roles (Eagly et al., 1992). It now seems apparent that in addition to these obstacles, the leadership positions that women occupy are likely to be less promising than those of their male counterparts. Thus, in addition to confronting a glass ceiling and not having access to a glass elevator, they are also likely to be placed on a "glass cliff" (Ryan and Haslam, 2005). In relation to board and governance, Sealy and colleagues (2009) reveals three levels of diversity for women: personal, interpersonal and appointment processes. In terms of personal factors, women do not lack in qualifications or aspirations to sit in boards, but there is persistent bias in assessing their competence and ability. At the interpersonal level, informal and relational factors are essential in gaining access to boards; successfully integrating board dynamics tend to put under-represented groups at a disadvantage. In addition, the appointment process to boards remains subject to personal bias due to a lack of transparency of openings and unclear selection criteria, particularly in the private sector. Livingstone et al. (2014) show that women's representation in top-level jobs remains very restricted, and most women still manage only women, i.e. female-dominated sectors. Greater employment experience and higher educational qualifications are generally significant factors for promotion of women as well as men. But the stereotype of women's primary responsibility for household work remains the major obstacle to equitable promotion (Dana and Dana, 2008; Caputo et al., 2016; Mehtap et al., forthcoming). Indeed, women seem face to a double glass-ceiling problem, according to Nekhili and Gatfaoui (2013) who focused on French large-and mid-capitalized companies from 2000 to 2004. Although women have the necessary education and skills to hold top jobs, they face the glass-ceiling effect, which prevents them from being as competitive as their male counterparts once they reach a certain hierarchical level. Yet, even if a few women succeed in breaking through this glass ceiling, they face a second glass ceiling once they reach the board level. The opaqueness and closed nature of the appointment process for corporate board positions stem from a restrictive view of the appropriateness of the applicants' profiles as well as the traditional bias illustrated by gender stereotyping.

If we consider family firms, the literature and evidence reveal that the presence of women in ownership does not assure a significant influence on the company's operations and performance as an active role of women in governance and management can do. However, a presence of women in governance bodies and managerial positions does not automatically translate into an effective removal of the glass ceiling by definition, even in the family-owned businesses that are expected to be a more favorable context (Songini and Dubini, 2003). Indeed, for women, breaking the glass ceiling is relatively easier in family firms with regards to ownership and governance roles, while it is more difficult for managerial roles, with the exception of the posts of CFO/administrative director and purchase director. There is a tendency for women to be in charge of mostly operational, clerical and support roles in small and medium-sized enterprises (SMEs; Songini and Gnan, 2004). As far as managerial roles are concerned, a larger number of women can be found in charge of the functional director position only (Songini and Gnan, 2014). In family-owned firms a wider presence of women in ownership and operational management is revealed, but only few of them are in charge of top management roles. This confirms those theories and researches which have pointed out the ambiguous role of family in supporting women entrepreneurship (Salganicoff, 1990). These results are also consistent with theories and evidences that explain the presence of women in operational and support roles in family businesses as a consequence of the replication inside the firm of the same process of functional specialization of activities and the authority model typical of the family (Grant and Tancred, 1992).

The literature and case studies on women in management point out similar evidence with regard to big companies, where only few women are in charge of managerial positions. It is necessary to stress that not all the women in business want to reach managerial and leadership positions; their reasons are simply because they do not want to be in this position or because they want to take care of their family. According to Cole (1997) a differentiation must be made between a glass ceiling that is transparent or mirrored. A transparent glass ceiling may create a barrier when women can see advancements that lie beyond their reach simply because they are women. A mirrored ceiling may give women the opportunity to reflect on why they do not want to reach upper management positions. Ideally, this ceiling should be 'Mylar' (both flexible and mirrored), so that women can reach the top and experience the responsibility but, if needed, return to a lesser position and reflect on their decision in order to balance their professional and personal needs (Cole, 1997).

Women's invisibility
Gender stereotypes, discrimination against women and occupational segregation experienced in the general business world (Terjesen and Ratten, 2007; Welsh et al., 2014; Ramadani, 2015; Ramadani, Hisrich et al., 2015; Caputo et al., 2016) also affect family firms (Jaffe, 1990; Salganicoff, 1990). In this case, in addition

to problems related to the business, women also have to face problems connected to the family: conflict over roles, relationship with parents and relatives, consideration, and esteem gained from nonfamily members and stakeholders (Dumas, 1992; Rosenblatt et al., 1985).

Commonly, the main women's tasks are seen as related to managing the house and the social life of the family, and taking care of the children; all the other responsibilities connected with a business are secondary. These cultural traditions are the basis of the woman's invisibility in family firms (Rowe and Hong, 2000; Ramadani, Hisrich et al., 2015; Mehtap et al., 2016).

Invisibility means a role created for a woman in which family members and others ignore the woman's professional capabilities (Cole, 1997). Sometimes women are referred to as 'invisible' because they work in the family firm and supporting male family members but do not have any role and remuneration. In this case, support provided by sister-wife-mother-daughter to the work of brother-husband-son-father is included in traditional family care that is considered unpaid and not formalized work (Rowe and Hong, 2000; Voydanoff, 1990). For women, reaching visibility is much more difficult unless they are supported by a male family member 'mentor' (Caputo et al., 2016; Mehtap et al., forthcoming). Moreover, many women take on roles as assistant, informal advisor or mediator between the members of the family who run the business (Gillis-Donovan and Moynihan-Bradt, 1990; Francis, 1999; Martinez-Jimenez, 2009). Traditional gender stereotypes also impact on different roles and tasks that every member assumes in the firm. In general, women are in charge of areas deemed as 'feminine', such as human resources, sales support, customer care and so on (Galiano and Vinturella, 1995). This means that women are victims of occupational segregation. Women are less often integrated into certain industries, for instance in the manufacturing, government or military sectors. Research shows that in collectivist and informal societies, success is dependent on personal contacts and relationships, with key individuals who facilitate the start-up (Baum et al., 1993). Moreover, in general women are not paid for all of their work in family firms. Women's roles in family firms are highly important because they manage family conflict and support other family member, and their work is often unpaid. This unpaid work contributes, directly and indirectly, to the economic well-being of the family and, consequently, that of the firm (Martinez-Jimenez, 2009).

EMOTIONAL LEADERSHIP

The overlapping of women's roles in family business might be difficult to manage: saying 'no' to your boss means also that you are saying 'no' to your husband or father, and work problems are frequently discussed at the dinner table. For example, quite often women in family business, can play multiple roles: they are wives, mothers, daughters and female in-laws; they are involved in the business and they are represented in family trees but without job titles and salaries next to their names (Lyman et al., 1985). Thus women play several roles while maintaining stability in personal and business relationships. According to Cole (1997), "nurturing" and "peacekeeping" roles are examples of what is considered normal behavior for women in family business. These roles, which may include behaviors such as listening and mediating, are assets to any business, especially in management. Another women's important role is the transmission of values to new generations both in the family and in the business (Dugan et al., 2011). This role is vital for business continuity and some authors refer to this situation with the term "emotional leadership" (Ward, 1987; Salganicoff, 1990; Lyman, 1998). An interesting study from Poza and Messer (2001) considers that spouses assume different leadership functions depending on their relationship to the CEO, their knowledge and interest in the business, and their commitment to a vision that includes continuity of the business in family members' hands. From this research, six functional or role types emerged: (a) the 'Jealous Spouse', who on the one hand 'shares her husband' with business as far as he is too involved in it, but on the other hand provides motivation for greater delegation and professionalization of the business; (b) the 'Chief Trust Officer', who acts as 'healer', 'mediator' and 'facilitator' for the family; (c) the 'Business Partner' or 'Copreneur', a role in which spouses begin as partners or coprenuers during the start-up and early stages of business development and then move on to different roles; (d) the 'Vice President of Human Resources, Finance and Facilities', who is often critical to running the family-owned business; (e) the 'Senior Advisor and Values Keeper', who helps children to grow with a sense of the business and its customers; and (f) the 'Free Agent', who is often very aware of both family and business matters, having perhaps served the family-owned business in some capacity earlier in life (Poza and Messer, 2001). In this classification, emotional leadership is clearly identified in at least two of the six roles (i.e. Chief Trust Officer and Senior Advisor and Values Keeper). Women also manage the social capital of a family firm, which according to Lesser (2000) better than any other construct may capture the unique characteristic of a family business and may also describe the vital contributions that women 'donate' to family firms. The essential characteristic of social capital is that interpersonal connections among members of a group, in this case the family, create value for an organization. Family businesses should recognize the importance of social capital and look more to women as 'experts' in its creation, even when women act in peripheral roles in the business. (Folker 2008). Several authors (e.g. Lipman, 1984; Gilligan, 1987) have argued for women's special psychological characteristics that better suit their different roles ('peacemakers', 'conflict solvers', 'value savers'); such characteristics are also vital for the success of the business and the family at the same time.

SUCCESSION AND PRIMOGENITURE

Succession is a crucial moment in every family firm and vital for survival of family business (Stavrou, 1999; Pellegrini et al., 2012). Especially in the past, women rarely were considered potential successors to leadership due to the primogeniture criterion (Llano and Olguin, 1986; D'Arquer, 1992). The literature suggests that women in family businesses still have a slim chance of running the company because of the primogeniture rule (i.e. the first-born son usually inherits the business; see Cole, 1997). Studies considering the impact of family firms' culture on women's professional opportunities have shown that primogeniture was implicit in the decision-making process (Hollander and Bukowitz, 1990). No later than 30 years ago, Keating and Little (1997) demonstrated that gender was the most important factor in the choice of successor: this implicit rule required, and still requires today, that daughters cannot succeed in a family firm. Women in family-owned firms have often been invisible successors; they are rarely considered serious contenders for succession, but that daughter successors were the most visible in terms of full-time involvement and ownership in the family firm. These women seemed to take leadership roles even in families that had more sons than daughters (Dumas, 1998). Most women in one of Dumas' studies (1992) revealed that, even though many females had previous work experience as businesswomen, after joining the family business they found themselves reduced to the role of 'daddy's little girl' in spite of their best intentions. Many of these women were not included in major business decisions that affected their jobs or informed of facts that were pertinent to their jobs. Due to the primogeniture rule, it is possible to identify a related phenomenon: many women do not take into consideration the possibility of joining the family business as a career opportunity (Dumas, 1992; Vera and Dean, 2005). However, in more recent times, according to a later study from Dumas (1998), something has changed: the process of choosing a successor varies depending on the family and the business. Sometimes parents need to evaluate their daughter by her interest in the business, her skills, her education, her leadership ability and prior experience. This evaluation process could be 'colored' by biases that parents may have about the daughter's capabilities and potential. However, on the bright side, more and more women are taken into consideration for succession, although thee process is still biased.

In addition to a change of attitude from parents, it is possible to identify a new trend in education trend: nowadays in general women have a higher level of formal education than men. Thus, in teams of potential successors, daughters look more appealing than sons (García-Álvarez et al., 2002). Although Cole (1997) points out that jobs held by women in family businesses are not the most important positions and that women generally hold positions with lower levels of responsibility, other research contradicts Cole's findings. Due to ongoing changes in educational trends (García-Álvarez et al., 2002), female successors join firms and find that they can fulfill positions not previously handled by other family members. The differences in education along gender lines highlight paradoxical consequences, with men handling areas representing the foundation for building and developing the business in the past and women assuming responsibilities that are strategically key for the future, e.g. design, marketing and information technology (García-Álvarez et al., 2002). It has also emerged that greater employment experience and higher education qualifications are significant factors for promotion for both genders; moreover, when women are 'visible', they introduce innovations, take risks, and are active in commercialization and competition (Khan, 2015). In research conducted by Vera and Dean

(2005), almost all daughters report they have had previous work experience outside the family business as well as inside (part time and full time) prior to taking over the family firm. Notably, 60 percent of the interviewees never assumed that they would one day take control of the family business. All women reported having difficulties dealing with nonfamily members of the firm, most of whom doubted the daughters' ability to run the business. This means that women not only have to face distrust from their own families but also from others not in the family.

Women also have to face a personal conflict between their expected family role and the expected business role (Mehtap et al., forthcoming). Unfortunately as a result of this, women have to choose which role to sacrifice to be fully satisfied with the other (Martinez-Jimenez, 2009). In addition, daughters also have to face the 'queen bee' phenomenon in family business. Mother-owners tend to be very connected to their companies and try to control business decisions even after their retirement (Cadieux et al., 2002; Vera and Dean, 2005). However, recent studies are illustrating a new direction: women are trying to overcome the 'queen bee' phenomenon and giving more responsibility to their successors. The results of research conducted by Koffi et al. (2014) show that women try to establish good relationships with their successor. The fact that women have confidence in them automatically drives employees to have confidence in the successor too, giving credibility to the successor. Women-owners understand their children and their potential, thereby giving them more credit. Moreover, they spontaneously offer their support.

The shifting landscape of women's roles in family businesses is evident in the experiences of daughters who have taken over top leadership positions in their family firms. Skill and commitment override gender in successor selection. The women were intrinsically motivated to take over their family businesses and owned significant shares in their firms (Humphreys, 2013). From this emerges the centrality of the successor–incumbent relationship; it also reveals mentoring, frequently by the incumbent, as the principal vehicle for the transfer of business leadership. Emotional competence emerged as a key successor quality (Humphreys, 2013). Overbeke et al. (2013) examined factors that may contribute to daughters' self-assessments of succession. Findings reveal that daughters' own blindness – i.e. self-bias toward an entrepreneurial career (Dana and Dana, 2008; Ramadani, 2015; Ramadani, Dana et al., 2015; Mehtap et al., forthcoming) – to the possibility of succession often resulted in an automatically activated gender norm that impeded their ascendancy. Daughters may not deliberately consider succession until a critical event motivates them to do so. In addition, parental support and mentoring for leadership seem to facilitate daughter succession. Some authors affirm that father–daughter succession is less competitive and conflictive than father–son succession (Bork, 1993; Danes et al., 2007). In contrast, a quantitative study conducted of father/mother–daughter successions showed that mother–daughter succession is much more difficult and conflictive because the daughter has the sensation of being in the shadow of her mother; her capabilities, leadership style, etc. are always compared with those of her mother (Vera and Dean, 2005). So it seems that cross-gender successions can be much easier than same-gender successions. However, because few empirical studies are available, it is not possible to define the best way to manage the succession process.

3.1.2 Opportunities

Opportunities represent positive aspects that can favor women involvement in top leadership roles. They can be categorized into two main aspects: professional career and running the company.

PROFESSIONAL CAREER

According to Aronoff (1998), in more and more families and in family businesses in general, gender is becoming a nonissue as it relates to leadership, ownership and participation. It is no longer unusual to find daughters and wives rising to leadership positions in family firms (Nelton, 1998), even though fewer male than female owners of family businesses look to their spouse for chief executive leadership (Allen and Langowitz, 2003). Perhaps more importantly, women are more active in a wider range of roles.

In terms of the professional career of women in family firms, the previous literature has highlighted the following three main issues:

a.   Women's personal motivations

Social structures, work, family and organized social life are likely to affect motivations of women entrepreneurs and family businesses, particularly in countries with transition economies (Hisrich and Fülöp, 1997; Dana and Dana, 2008; Ramadani et al., 2013; Ramadani, 2015; Mehtap et al., 2016; Mehtap et al., forthcoming). Dumas (1989a, 1989b) proposed that, in general, women do not plan a career in their family business, they do not aspire to ownership and see their work as a job rather than a career. But in his research, which studies the effect that women have on family businesses and increases the knowledge and understanding of women's participation and leadership in family-owned firms (Dumas, 1998), he admits that women always see family business as a potential place of work. Women who chose to pursue the family business early on and who follow that pursuit with a variety of training and education expressed this career choice in positive, affirming terms. They described the paths they took in such terms as "challenging", "my future", "a family dream", "a chance to prove myself" and "giving back to the family". Still others saw the chance to take over the family business as an opportunity that was "too good to pass up" and "the best thing to come along", and "it's more satisfying to work for yourself than for someone else" (Dumas, 1998, 226).

b.   Family firm context

Some elements of the family firm environment can favor the involvement of women in the firm, such as: the possibility of balancing family and work, the better conditions that characterize a job in the family firm (career opportunities, flexibility of tasks etc.) and some families' values.

b.1. Balancing family and work

Because of the increasing participation of women in the labor force (especially in North America), work–family integration has become a key interest for family scholars (Jennings et al., 2013). In addition, European women may be showing a trend towards seeking leadership positions in the workplace, gradually working their way into the business arena through the family business (Stavrou, 1999). However, balancing work and family is gradually becoming a gender-neutral concern. More than one-third of both men and women ascribed high importance to both work and family roles, indicating significant deviation from traditional gender-based attitudes toward life's roles. Family is an important domain for many men, and work is an important domain for many women (Cinamon and Rich, 2002). Women are more likely to take unfinished work home and to juggle family and work responsibilities at home. Despite greater family obligations, women cannot be remiss in their work responsibilities (Cinamon and Rich, 2002). Eddleston and Powell (2012) concluded that women's satisfaction with work–family balance is especially nurtured by their experience of a higher level of instrumental family-to-business enrichment than men do. Men's satisfaction with work–family balance is especially nurtured by their receiving a higher level of instrumental support at home than women do. The flexibility in a family firm allows women to combine career and child-rearing duties, but several women resent having to perform the child-caring role.

b.2. Career opportunities and flexibility in doing job tasks

Nonfamily women managers perceive themselves as competitive and independent people; in addition, they have better academic qualifications and are less likely to be married and have children (Cromie and O'Sullivan, 1999). However, they are unenthusiastic about their training, mentors and personal contacts, and consider career progress to be easier for men. In general, women managers feel a lack power and opportunities to make progress. Instead, women seem to achieve more advancement in their family businesses (Cole, 1997). Working in a family business offers a freedom that is unavailable elsewhere. This condition, coupled with greater opportunities, allows women in family businesses to achieve and find personal fulfilment (Cromie and O'Sullivan, 1999). Women family managers enjoy increased status, job security and flexibility. Many of them are able to take advantage of this flexibility to combine childcare and career roles. However, as prem-ised in the previous sections, family membership can either advance or inhibit a career for women (Cromie and O'Sullivan, 1999). The phe-nomenon of the women's invisibility sees their involvement relegated to operational and support roles, rather than top management. Despite slow improvements in European female board committee representa-tion over the past years, it has been shown that women on executive committees have been promoted more frequently to more influential roles, such as members of the Audit, Compensation, and Nominating Committees (Dalton and Dalton, 2009).

b.3. Better remuneration and security

Salganicoff (1990) reported better positions, higher incomes and more flexibility in work schedules for women who work in a family business in comparison with more conventional jobs. In a family business, a female family member is likely to be retained in employment for longer than a woman who is not a member of the family (Cromie and O'Sullivan, 1999). Young women see the family business as offering a life-long option without the need to climb a corporate ladder (Frishkoff and Brown, 1993). It is noteworthy that women's economical contributions to the family are broadly based, including a mix of paid employment and diverse types of unpaid family work (e.g. housework; and care of children, ill and disabled family members or elderly parents). This kind of work is difficult to measure, since it is not included in traditional eco-nomic production estimation (Voydanoff, 1990).

b.4. Mentoring

The most important factors that facilitate women's career development are communication and interpersonal skills, competency on the job and education. Clearly the most often mentioned facilitator for career devel-opment is mentoring. According to a study from Marlow) nearly two-thirds of the responding executives had mentors.

c. Organizational characteristics

c.1. Family and firm values

Women's success in business depends on their personality traits and on a system of values in which the family receives top priority. This sort of 'value arrangement' makes it possible to combine work more effectively with the sphere of family and household by taking advantage of the sup-port of one's nearest and dearest (Turetskaia, 2003).

c.2. The presence of women in ownership, top management and governance roles

The presence of women on the owner-management team of a family busi-ness is positively associated with the presence of other women in other top management roles as CEO, board member (greater balance in the board of directors) and successor CEO (Allen and Langowitz, 2003). Yet, woman-owned family firms are more than twice likely to employ female family members full-time and nearly three times as to employ more than one female family member full-time (Allen and Langowitz, 2003). Such presence in the board and top management roles seems to benefit performance (Smith et al., 2008). Smith and colleagues (2006) have observed the 2,500 largest Danish firms (1993–2001) and found a positive effect of women in top management positions and performance, if even this relation is mediated by the qualifications of female top managers. Similarly, management teams with an equal gender mix seem to perform better than male-dominated and female-dominated teams in terms of sales, profits and earnings per share (Hoogendoorn et al., 2013). If there are enough women who are equally qualified as men, it is in firms' best interest to increase the share of women in their boards. When becoming CEOs, women introduce a number of changes in the management style whereby they add their softer feminine approach as a new quality to the existing style. This assumption is very relativistic since the research indicated that female CEOs behave unlike other female family members involved in the business (Vadnjal and Zupan, 2009).

RUNNING THE COMPANY

Among women who have succeeded in reaching top management positions and running a business we can distinguish between women who are in leadership positions in the family business because they have inherited the firm, and women who are the founders of their own company. Literature shows some specific characteristics of firms run by women, as well of women's styles of leadership and management.

Women working in the family firm
Women involved in a family firm can be wives or daughters of the founder or the CEO who have been involved (formally or informally) in the company as a consequence of a succession process. Owning and running a family business requires a lifestyle that influences many aspects of women's lives: i.e. their role in society and in the family, their use of time, their recognition and standard of living, and perhaps most important, their role and responsibilities to their families (Ramadani, 2015; Ramadani, Hisrich et al., 2015). The hours needed by the business and less time available for children and the family may result in more stress on the entrepreneur herself and create new family problems that did not exist previously. This problem is particularly acute when the woman entrepreneur works in the home as much as she did before starting the venture, with little assistance in household chores from the spouse or children (Hisrich and Fülöp, 1997; Caputo et al., 2016).

Women entrepreneurs/founders of a firm

Literature on women entrepreneurs focuses on motivations to start a new venture. It distinguishes between motivations driven by the willingness to change a negative situation and motivations driven by self-fulfillment. As for the first type of motivations, barriers in the labor market have been proposed to have the side effect of propelling women into self-employment. According to Aldrich (1989) this has happened frequently in immigrant groups (Ramadani et al., 2013). Bane and Ellwood (1986) have proposed that women maintaining families are slightly more likely to rise out of poverty through earnings rather than through marriage. Thus, self-employment is not a means of taking advantage of the opportunities of the labor market and achieving a higher socio-economic standing; rather, it is a way of escaping unemployment lines and circumventing the conflict between family responsibilities and work obligations. According to Bane and Ellwood (1986), women in Germany are more likely to choose a business career as an employee rather than in self-employment when they are in their prime working age, educated, not married and have no children. While women clearly choose self-employment over a simple paid job when they have children, when the alternative choice is not to work at all, married women with children choose to stay at home rather than having their own business (Constant, 2006). Moreover, for some women entrepreneurs, being an owner-manager is an extension of her parent and spouse/partner roles, and it is instrumental to these dominant roles in her socialization (Terjesen and Ratten, 2007; Dana and Dana, 2008; Ramadani, Dana et al., 2015; Ramadani, Hisrich et al., 2015).

On the contrary, for other women entrepreneurs starting a business is a way to create their own employment, an instrument for personal development, and a flexible response to their economic and professional needs, while adapting to their family responsibilities (Lee-Gosselin and Grisé, 1990).

With regard to factors that favor the choice to become an entrepreneur and establish a company, the main conclusions to be drawn from the study conducted by Akehurst et al. (2012) are that, firstly, the type of financial support received affects the motivation and obstacles for women entrepreneurs. Secondly, in terms of demographic factors, not having a partner positively influences their ambition to start a business. The age at which women undertake a new business project also affects both the entrepreneurial nature of the women, the obstacles they come up against and their business success. Lastly, women entrepreneurs who start larger firms and those who start business using family loans tend to be more successful.

Peus et al. (2015) investigated how women in Asia and the U.S. become leaders and how they enact their leadership. Women leaders across continents stressed the importance of success factors at the individual level (achievement and learning orientation) and at the interpersonal level (role models) as well as barriers at the social systems level (gender stereotypes). Networks and access to them is another crucial point to aid female entrepreneurship (Scott, 2005; Caputo et al., 2016).

In line with this, a study conducted by Roomi (2009) based on interviews of 50 women entrepreneurs in the East of England region shows that the use of networks and interpersonal relationships by women business owners help them in accessing information, advice and ideas as well as financial and human resources. Women-only networks were mentioned in playing a crucial role in developing and building contacts with like-minded entrepreneurs and a critical source for ideas, information and advice in the earlier phases (existence and survival) of business development (Roomi, 2009). Women entrepreneurs can more successfully use their social capital in the survival, success and take-off stages of their businesses if they start building it in during start-up (existence) or even in the pre-start-up phase (Roomi, 2009). Linking individual women through one-on-one mentoring or in networks and organizations helps to shift their identities, thereby enabling women entrepreneurs individually and collectively to change the material and discursive aspects of the places where they live and work (Hanson, 2009).

Referring to women's leadership and management styles, there are no differences in leadership practices between women managers with dependent children and those without, providing empirical support for the fact that mothers are not less capable of leadership practices than nonmothers (Nuosce, 2007). Compared to men, however, women owners overall are less primarily focused on profit. This does not mean, however, that financial success is unimportant to women owners. They may stress financial success along with other goals, such as building positive relations with customers (Bird and Sapp, 2004). Female entrepreneurs are more oriented toward controlling their own time, often at the expense of greater profit, and they attempt to find a satisfying balance between work and home, even if this may imply limiting the expansion of the business (Chirikova and Krichevskaia, 2002). Woman-owned family firms place greater emphasis on philanthropy, especially those activities with educational focuses and community engagement (Allen and Langowitz, 2003). Female-owned family firms experience greater family loyalty to the business, agreement with its goals and pride in the business than male-owned family firms. This is also demonstrated by a 40 percent lower rate of family member attrition in the business (Allen and Langowitz, 2003).

As far as some personal characteristics of women entrepreneurs are concerned, some management consultants reported that women business owners listen better and act on what they hear, whereas men tend to think they do not need advice (Nelton, 1998). A study conducted by Danes et al. (2005) on language patterns of family business owners, showed that women have a higher emotional discourse style score for managing the business than men, and they balance their emotional language with the practicality of planning tasks and creating efficiencies. Women usually talk about the same decision in mainly emotional discourse terms. Danes and colleagues (2005, 127) write: "A unique insight into the role of women in the family businesses obtained from this study is their greater use of the emphasized ideas about the future and change compared with men". The higher use of phrases concerning future and change provides some evidence that women may be a key element (or at least a springboard) for innovation within family businesses (Danes et al., 2005). Indeed, more than two-thirds of woman-owned family businesses anticipate a positive future for their companies despite recessionary conditions (Allen and Langowitz, 2003).

With regard to strategy and decision making, woman-owned family firms rarely look outside the family for a chief executive, especially when compared to male-owned firms (Allen and Langowitz, 2003). Employees exhibit relatively high levels of satisfaction with female management. Women who build management and worker teams are able to handle family emergencies without disrupting business operations, while those who do not delegate may have to halt the conduct of business in order to tend to family matters, and consequently suffer reduced firm performance (Shelton, 2006).

Adame et al. (2015) have analyzed empirical data from 87 Spanish SMEs. The study's main finding, contrary to earlier literature, is that the presence of women does not determine the level of implementation of work–life balance policies. Conversely, the absence of women does seem to determine the absence of such policies.

Although women still believe that humane management and the "technique of attentiveness" are essential tools for today executives, they do not limit their own management strategies to these principles (Chirikova and Krichevskaia, 2002). With the current economic environment most women managers view the principle that power should be concentrated in a firm as the most important factor relative to other management skills. Moreover, because of the economic environment and the consequent decline in the availability of financial resources, the typical female management style is gradually losing its gender connotations as male and female management techniques begin to converge. Under present conditions management strategies are becoming increasingly complex. These techniques are aimed both at "macro-policy", the construction of general strategies for company development, and at "micro-policy", which takes into account the interests and motives of many people in the company (Chirikova and Krichevskaia, 2002).

4. Conclusions and future research directions

The analysis of previous literature on women in family business shows both light and shadow. On the one hand, it seems that nowadays women have to cope with fewer obstacles than in the past, as social values and economic and organization contexts are fast changing. The financial crisis that began in 2008, may have also had a positive impact, as it pushed companies to develop their social capital in terms of their networks and relationships with other companies. This implies a necessity to adopt selection and evaluation criteria for people to be involved in top leadership positions in companies more focused on skills, competences and capabilities, rather than on other less meritocratic 'rules' such as primogeniture. The fact that women are more educated than men and act according to a 'feminine' management and leadership style is more consistent with today's requirements and competitive environment. Thus, this should also help to increase women's participation in companies' life. However, some shadows remain, as data on the low number of women involved in boards and top management roles,

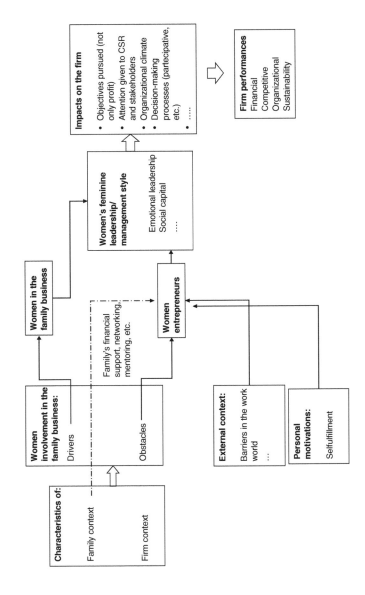

Figure 5.5 Proposed research framework

also in family firms, prove. As a matter of fact, women in family business still have to cope with the phenomena of the glass ceiling, invisibility and glass cliff. Also, women entrepreneurs who establish their own company experience more difficulties than men in financing the venture, entering networks and gaining a reputation among stakeholders (Ramadani, 2015; Ramadani, Dana et al., 2015; Caputo et al., 2016).

The framework proposed by Martinez-Jimenez (2009) allows us to articulate the discussion of previous studies by integrating it with some new relevant issues. However, the richness of the topic seems difficult captured with a categorical framework. So we propose a model that can summarize more in-depth relevant variables and relations when studying the role of women in family business (Figure 5.5).

Each rectangle (and the variables written inside) of our research framework represents a specific research stream that can be tackled using different theories and methods, consistent with the analyzed issues. Figure 5.5 can also be used to give a clearer picture of the issues to be managed and relations among them to family business' owners, managers, consultants and policymakers.

In conclusion, it is only fair to acknowledge that we have come a long way in the quest for gender diversity in business – but business cannot meet this challenge alone. That will require concerted, concrete, repeated action upstream of working life at all levels of society and in all institutions, by individuals and by groups. Slowly this will create the cultural and organizational basis for change (McKinsey, 2007).

References

Adame, C., Caplliure, E. M., and Miquel, M. J. (2016). Work – life balance and firms: A matter of women? *Journal of Business Research,* 69(4), 1379–1383.

Akehurst, G., Simarro, E., and Mas-Tur, A. (2012). Women entrepreneurship in small service firms: Motivations, barriers and performance. *The Service Industries Journal,* 32(15), 2489–2505.

Aldrich, H. (1989). Networking among women entrepreneurs. In O. Hagan, C. Rivchun and D. Sexton (eds.), *Women owned businesses* (pp. 103–132). New York: Praeger.

Allen, I. E., and Langowitz, N. S. (2003). *Women in family-owned businesses.* Boston, MA: MassMutual and Center for Women's Leadership, Babson College.

Almallah, S., and Schwartz, T. (2008). Women, wealth, leadership: Family firms advance. *Grand Rapids Business Journal,* 26(46), 20.

Anshu, M. (2012). Women in family business. *International Journal of Computer Science and Management Studies,* 12(2), 34–40.

Aronoff, C. (1998). Megatrends in family business. *Family Business Review,* 11(3), 181–186.

Bane, M., and Ellwood, D. (1986). Slipping into and out of poverty: The dynamics of spells. *Journal of Human Resources,* 21(1), 1–23.

Baum, J. R., Olian, J. D., Erez, M., Schnell, E. R., Smith, K. G., Sims, H. P., Scully, J. S., and Smith, K. A. (1993). Nationality and work role interactions: A cultural contrast of Israeli and U.S. Entrepreneurs versus managers needs. *Journal of Business Venturing*, 8(6), 499–512.

Bird, S., and Sapp, S. (2004). Understanding the gender gap in small business success: Urban and rural comparisons. *Gender & Society*, 18(1), 5–28.

Bork, D. (1993). *Family business, risky business* (2nd ed.). Aspen, CO: Bork Institute for Family Business.

Cadieux, L., Lorrain, J., and Hugron, P. (2002). Succession in women-owned family businesses: A case study. *Family Business Review*, 15(1), 17–30.

Caputo, A., Mehtap, S., Pellegrini, M. M., and Al Refai, R. (2016). Supporting opportunities for female entrepreneurs in Jordan. *International Journal of Entrepreneurship and Small Business*, 27(2/3), 384–409.

Carter, S., Mwaura, S., Ram, M., Trehan, K., and Jones, T. (2015). Barriers to ethnic minority and women's enterprise: Existing evidence, policy tensions and unsettled questions. *International Small Business Journal*, 33(1), 49–69.

Chirikova, A., and Krichevskaia, O. (2002). The woman manager: Business strategies and self-image. *Sociological Research*, 41(1), 38–54.

Cinamon, R., and Rich, G. (2002). Gender differences in the importance of work and family roles: Implications for work – family conflict. *Sex Roles*, 47(11), 531–541.

Cole, P. (1997). Women in family business. *Family Business Review*, 10(4), 353–371.

Constant, A. (2006). Female proclivity to the world of business. *Kyklos*, 59(4), 465–480.

Cromie, S., and O'Sullivan, S. (1999). Women as managers in family firms. *Women in Management Review*, 14(3), 76–88.

D'Arquer, J. (1992). PYME y empresa familiar. *Alta Dirección*, 28(166), 17–22.

Dalton, D., and Dalton, C. (2009). Women gain (hidden) ground in the boardroom. *Harvard Business Review*, 87(1), 23.

Dana, L. P., and Dana, T. E. (2008). Ethnicity and entrepreneurship in Morocco: A photo-ethnographic study. *International Journal of Business and Globalisation*, 2(3), 209–226.

Danes, S. M., Haberman, H. R., and McTavish, D. (2005). Gendered discourse about family business. *Family Relations*, 54(1), 116–130.

Danes, S. M., Stafford, K., and Loy, J. T.-C. (2007). Family business performance: The effects of gender and management. *Journal of Business Research*, 60(10), 1058–1069.

Dugan, A. M., Krone, S. P., Le Couvie, K., Pendergast, J. M., Kenyon-Rouvinez, D. H., and Schuman, A. M. (2011). *A Woman's Place: The Crucial Roles of Women in Family Business*. New York: Palgrave MacMillan.

Dumas, C. (1989a). Daughters in family-owned businesses: An applied systems perspective. Unpublished doctoral dissertation, the Fielding Institute, Santa Barbara, CA.

Dumas, C. (1989b). Understanding of father-daughter and father-son dyads in family-owned businesses. *Family Business Review*, 2(1), 31–46.

Dumas, C. (1992). Integrating the daughter into family business management. *Entrepreneurship Theory and Practice*, 16(4), 41–56.

Dumas, C. (1998). Women's pathways to participation and leadership in the family-owned firm. *Family Business Review*, 11(3), 219–228.

Eagly, A. H., Makhijani, M. G., and Klonsky, B. G. (1992). Gender and the evaluation of leaders: A meta-analysis. *Psychological Bulletin*, 111(1), 3–22.

Eddleston, K. A., and Powell, G. N. (2012). Nurturing entrepreneurs' work-family balance: A gendered perspective. *Entrepreneurship Theory and Practice,* 36(3), 513–541.

Fitzgerald, M., and Muske, G. (2002). Copreneurs: An exploration and comparison to other family businesses. *Family Business Review,* 15(1), 1–16.

Folker, C. (2008). Women in family firms: Characteristics, roles and contribution. *Small Business Institute Research Review,* 35, 157–168.

Frishkoff, P. A., and Brown, B. M. (1993). Women on the move in family business. *Business Horizons,* 36(2), 66–70.

Galiano, A. M., and Vinturella, J. B. (1995). Implications of gender bias in the family business. *Family Business Review,* 8(3), 177–188.

García-Élvarez, E., López-Sintas, J., and Gonzalvo, P. (2002). Socialization patterns of successors in first- to second-generation family businesses. *Family Business Review,* 15(3), 189–203.

Gilligan, C. (1987). *In a different voice: Psychological theory and women's development.* Cambridge, MA: Harvard University Press.

Gillis-Donovan, J., and Moynihan-Bradt, C. (1990). The power of invisible women in the family business. *Family Business Review,* 3(2), 153–167.

Goitein, S. D. (1967). A Jewish business woman of the eleventh century. *The Jewish Quarterly Review,* 57, 225–242.

Grant, J. and Tancred, P. 1992. 'A Feminist Perspective on State Bureaucracy', in A. J. Mills and P. Tancred (eds.) *Gendering Organisational Analysis.* London: Sage.

Haberman, H., and Danes, S. M. (2007). Father – daughter and father – son family business management transfer comparison: Family FIRO model application. *Family Business Review,* 20(2), 163–184.

Hamilton, E. (2006). Whose story is it anyway? Narrative accounts of the role of women in founding and establishing family businesses. *International Small Business Journal,* 24(3), 253–271.

Hanson, S. (2009). Changing places through women's entrepreneurship. *Economic Geography,* 85(3), 245–267.

Harveston, P. D., Davis, P. S., and Lyden, J. A. (1997). Succession planning in family business: The impact of owner gender. *Family Business Review,* 10(4), 373–396.

Hisrich, R., and Fülöp, G. (1997). Women entrepreneurs in family business: The Hungarian case. *Family Business Review,* 10(3), 281–302.

Hollander, B. S., and Bukowitz, W. R. (1990). Women, family culture and family business. *Family Business Review,* 3(2), 139–151.

Hoogendoorn, S., Oosterbeek, H., and Van Praag, M. (2013). The impact of gender diversity on the performance of business teams: Evidence from a field experiment. *Management Science,* 59(7), 1514–1528.

Howorth, C. A., Westhead, P, Rose, M. B., and Hamilton, E. E. (2010). Family firm diversity and development: An introduction. *International Small Business Journal,* 28(5), 437–451.

Humphreys, M. (2013). Daughter succession: A predominance of human issues. *Journal of Family Business Management,* 3(1), 24–44.

Jaffe, D. (1990). Working with the ones you love: Strategies for a successful family business. Emeryville, CA: Conari Press.

Jennings, J., Breitkreuz, R., and James, A. (2013). When family members are also business owners: Is entrepreneurship good for families? *Family Relations,* 62(3), 472–489.

Keating, N. C., and Little, H. M. (1997). Choosing the successor in New Zealand family farms. *Family Business Review,* 10(2), 157–171.

Khan, B. (2015). Invisible women: Entrepreneurship, innovation and family firms in France during early industrialization. Working Paper 20854 National Bureau of Economic Research. www.nber.org/papers/w20854

Koffi, V., Guihur, I., Morris, T., and Fillion, G. (2014). Family business succession: How men and women predecessors can bring credibility to their successors? *Entrepreneurial Executive,* 19, 67–85.

Lee-Gosselin, H., and Grisé, J. (1990). Are women owner-managers challenging our definitions of entrepreneurship? An in-depth survey. *Journal of Business Ethics,* 9(4), 423–433.

Lesser, E. L. (2000). Leveraging social capital in organizations. In E. L. Lesser (ed.), *Knowledge and social capital.* Boston, MA: Butterworth-Heinemann.

Lipman, J. (1984). *Gender roles and power.* Englewood Cliffs, NJ: Prentice Hall.

Livingstone, D., Pollock, K., and Raykov, M. (2014). Family binds and glass ceilings: Women managers' promotion limits in a 'Knowledge Economy'. *Critical Sociology,* 42(1), 145–166.

Llano, C., and Olguin, F. (1986). La sucesión en la empresa familiar. In V. F. Pascual (ed.), *La Empresa Familiar* 2 (pp. 36–66). Barcelona, Spain: Universidad de Navarra, IESE.

Lyman, A. R. (1988). Life in the family circle. *Family Business Review,* 1(4), 383–398.

Lyman, A., Salganicoff, M., and Hollander, B. (1985). Women in family business an untapped resource. *SAM Advanced Management Journal,* 50(1), 46–49.

Marlow, N. D., Marlow, E. K., and Arnold, V. A. (1995). Career development and women managers: Does 'one size fit all'? *Human Resource Planning,* 18(2), 38–49.

Martinez-Jimenez, R. (2009). Research on women in family firms: Current status and future directions. *Family Business Review,* 22(1), 53–64.

McKinsey &Company. (2007). Women matter: Gender diversity, a corporate performance driver. McKinsey & Company, available on McKinsey website: http://www.mckinsey.com/business-functions/organization/our-insights/gender-diversity-a-corporate-performance-driver

McManus. (1999). Inside the family firm. *NZ Business,* 13(10), 30–36.

Mehtap, S., Caputo, A., and Pellegrini, M. M. (2016). Encouraging female entrepreneurship in Jordan: Environmental factors, obstacles and challenges. In V. Ramadani, L. P. Dana, S. Gërguri-Rashiti and V. Ratten (eds.), *Entrepreneurship and management in an Islamic context* (pp. 207–225). Berlin: Springer.

Mehtap, S., Pellegrini, M. M., Caputo, A., and Welsh, D. (forthcoming). Entrepreneurial intentions of young women in the Arab world: Socio-cultural and educational barriers. *International Journal of Entrepreneurial Behavior & Research.*

Morrison, A., White, R. P., and Van Velsor, E. (1994). *Breaking the glass ceiling: Can women reach the top of America's largest corporations?* Reading, MA: Addison-Wesley.

Nekhili, M., and Gatfaoui, H. (2013). Are demographic attributes and firm characteristics drivers of gender diversity? Investigating women's positions on French boards of directors. *Journal of Business Ethics,* 118(2), 227–249.

Nelton, S. (1998). The rise of women in family firms: A call for research now. *Family Business Review,* 11(3), 215–218.

Nelton, S. (1999). Why women are chosen to lead: Women are leading more companies. *Nation's Business,* 87(4), 48–51.

Nuosce, M. (2007). The relationship between role salience, work-family conflict, and women's managerial leadership practices. Electronic Dissertation.

Overbeke, K. K., Bilimoria, D., and Perelli, S. (2013). The dearth of daughter successors in family businesses: Gendered norms, blindness to possibility, and invisibility. *Journal of Family Business Strategy,* 4(3), 201–212.

Pellegrini, M. M., Ciappei, C., and Cannoni, T. (2012, September–December). Communicational topics in governance processes of family business succession. *Sinergie: Italian Journal of Management,* 89, 131–146.

Peus, C., Braun, S., and Knipfer, K. (2015). On becoming a leader in Asia and America: Empirical evidence from women managers. *The Leadership Quarterly,* 26(1), 55–67.

Poza, E., and Messer, T. (2001). Spousal leadership and continuity in the family firm. *Family Business Review,* 14(1), 25–36.

Ramadani, V. (2015). The woman entrepreneur in Albania: An exploratory study on motivation, problems and success factors. *Journal of Balkan and Near Eastern Studies,* 17(2), 204–221.

Ramadani, V., Dana, L., Ratten, V., and Tahiri, S. (2015). The context of Islamic entrepreneurship and business: Concept, principles and perspectives. *International Journal of Business and Globalisation,* 15(3), 244–261.

Ramadani, V., Gërguri, S., Dana, L.-P., and Tašaminova, T. (2013). Women entrepreneurs in the Republic of Macedonia: Waiting for directions. *International Journal of Entrepreneurship and Small Business,* 19(1), 95–121.

Ramadani, V., Hisrich, R. D., and Gërguri-Rashiti, D. (2015). Female entrepreneurs in transition economies: Insights from Albania, Macedonia and Kosovo. *World Review of Entrepreneurship, Management and Sustainable Development,* 11(4), 391–413.

Roomi, M. A. (2009). Impact of social capital development and use in the growth process of women-owned firms. *Journal of Enterprising Culture,* 17(4), 473–495.

Rosenblatt, P. C., De Mik, L., Anderson, R. M., and Johnson, P. A. (1985). *The family in business.* San Francisco, CA: Jossey-Bass.

Rowe, B., and Hong, G. (2000). The role of wives in family businesses: The paid and unpaid work of women. *Family Business Review,* 13(1), 1–13.

Ryan, M., and Haslam, S. (2005). The glass cliff: Evidence that women are over-represented in precarious leadership positions. *British Journal of Management,* 16(2), 81–90.

Salganicoff, M. (1990). Women in family businesses: Challenges and opportunities. *Family Business Review,* 3(2), 125–137.

Sánchez-Sellero, C., and Sánchez-Sellero, P. (2013). El modelo de salarización en el mercado laboral gallego: Influencia del género. *Intangible Capital,* 9(3), 678–707.

Scott, A. (2005). Networking event to aid entrepreneurs. *Fairfield County Business Journal,* 44(18), 10.

Sharma, P. (2004). An overview of the field of family business studies: Current status and directions for the future. *Family Business Review,* 17(1), 1–36.

Sharma, P., Chrisman, J. and Chua, J., (2005). Trends and directions in the development of a strategic management theory of the family firm. *Entrepreneurship Theory and Practice,* 29(5), 555–576.

Shelton, L. (2006). Female entrepreneurs, work – family conflict, and venture performance: New insights into the work – family interface. *Journal of Small Business Management,* 44(2), 285–297.

Smith, N., Smith, V., and Verner, M. (2006). Do women in top management affect firm performance? A panel study of 2,500 Danish firms. *International Journal of Productivity and Performance Management,* 55(7), 569–593.

Smith, N., Smith, V., and Verner, M. (2008). *Women in top management and firm performance.* Aarhus School of Business, University of Aarhus.

Songini, L., and Dubini, P. (2003). *Glass ceiling in SMES: When women are in command.* Milan: SDA Bocconi.

Songini, L., Gnan L., (2004). Glass ceiling or women in command? The role of professionalization in women's family firms. In J. H. Astrachan, and S. Tomaselli, Family firms in the wind of change. IFERA-FBN Publications, 172–195.

Songini, L., and Gnan, L. (2014). The glass ceiling in SMEs and its impact on firm managerialisation: A comparison between family and non-family SMEs. *International Journal of Business Governance and Ethics,* 9(2), 170–196.

Stavrou, E. T. (1999). Succession in family businesses: Exploring the effects of demographic factors on offspring intentions to join and take over the business. *Journal of Small Business Management,* 37(3), 43–61.

Terjesen, V., and Ratten, V. (2007). La vita imprenditoriale. In M. Radović-Marković (ed.), *The perspective of women's entrepreneurship in the age of globalization* (pp. 41–53). Charlotte, NC: IAP.

Thébaud, S. (2015). Business as plan B: Institutional foundations of gender inequality in entrepreneurship across 24 industrialized countries. *Administrative Science Quarterly,* 60(4), 671–711.

Turetskaia, G. (2003). The family and women's business activities. *Sociological Research,* 42(3), 53–65.

Vadnjal, J., and Zupan, B. (2009). The role of women in family businesses. *Economic and Business Review,* 11(2), 159–177.

Vera, C., and Dean, M. (2005). An examination of the challenges daughters face in family business succession. Family Business Review, 18(4), 321–345.

Voydanoff, P. (1990). Economic distress and family relations: A review of the eighties. *Journal of Marriage and the Family,* 52(4), 1099–115.

Ward, J. L. (1987). *Keeping the family business healthy: How to plan for continuing growth, profitability, and family leadership.* San Francisco: Jossey-Bass.

Welsh, D., Memili, E., Kaciak, E., and Ochi, M. (2014). Japanese women entrepreneurs: Implications for family firms. *Journal of Small Business Management,* 52(2), 286–305.

6 Innocent sampling in research on gender and entrepreneurship

Annie Roos and Johan Gaddefors

In this chapter we challenge and problematize what we consider to be 'innocent sampling strategies' in research on gender and entrepreneurship. To accomplish this we introduce the topic by engaging in an author dialogue (Hosking and Hjorth, 2005; Welter et al., 2016). Next, we conduct a review of sampling strategies in method literature and develop our results into what one might call an analytical tool. Lastly, we use our tool on a sample of articles and discuss the implications of their chosen sampling strategies. The idea is to show how different sampling strategies open and close interpretative spaces for developing our understanding. Our aim in this work is to investigate how different sampling strategies contribute to theory building in gender and entrepreneurship theory.

Researching gender comes with many challenges. West and Zimmerman (1987) have pointed towards the challenge of how 'doing gender' in a research situation as unavoidable. They argue that the researcher always has gender prejudices and perceptions about the interviewees, affecting the research situation before it even begins. The situation is also the other way around: the interviewees have prejudices and perceptions about the researcher and the research project. Unavoidable biases are thus in play in the gendered research situation. Following this, Deutsch (2007) talks about how it is easier to observe and analyze conformity (doing gender) than the resistance of gender (undoing gender). Martin (2003) talks about the difficulties in researching the doing of gender practices because of the invisible, collective and routine nature of gender. As discussed by Henry et al. (2015), a challenge is that studies that are interpretative in their methods are not as easy to get published as more traditional studies with a well-known method for collecting data. With these challenges, researchers have a hard time grasping the complexity of gender, leaving gender and entrepreneurship research treading water when it comes to advancing gender equality.

Treating gender as an isolated variable (Alvesson and Billing, 1997) creates another challenge, for example, when separating the business sphere from the household sphere (Bruni et al., 2004; Martin, 2006). However, public and private spheres are intertwined and gender is not left at the door when moving from one of the loosely bound spheres to the other (Martin, 2006). Thus, a number of shortcomings can be identified in existing sampling strategies. We figure that an alternative approach may be better suited to solve some of these shortcomings. There seem to be arguments for a 'full-picture' view of gender and entrepreneurship in research, a picture where public and private spheres are connected, where both the conformity and resistance of gender are easier to observe, where the anomalies of research are embraced and not suppressed, and where the choice of epistemology is made on elaborated arguments.

In the next section we lay the groundwork for the chapter, arguing for our positions within the research fields. Then, we evaluate how others feel that sampling should be done. We begin with a literature review on sampling and move on to see how this has been carried out in peer-reviewed articles within our field. Lastly we return to our author-dialogue style and discuss how different ways of sampling in gender and entrepreneurship research could advance theory building. Let the conversation begin!

Positioning ourselves

A   So Johan, even though we come from different perspectives, I feel that we are bound together by what I would say is a critical view on entrepreneurship. To me, a critical view is not taking mainstream ideas for granted. Instead, it is taking a phenomenon like entrepreneurship and examining it from different perspectives and angles to see whether we could perceive the phenomena in new ways. What would you say is a critical view on entrepreneurship from your perspective?

J   The word *critical* has a lot of baggage with it, high expectations and a number of connotations. To some people, *critical* refers to whining and complaining; others think it has to do with being mutinously cautious in order to get everything right. I basically agree with those understandings, but when we talk about *critical* in this chapter, I think we have to consider theoretical takes. I prefer to start with critical theory understood as a tradition in social science based on thinkers like the Frankfurt school, poststructuralism and certain versions of feminism (Alvesson, 2003). To be *critical* is to take part in a movement aiming for emancipation, to reflect on established, dominant structures like ideas and institutions by critically examining for example, asymmetric power relations or male dominance. If we talk about a critical view on entrepreneurship I think Steyaert and Katz (2004) have a good point when they argue for "entrepreneuring" rather than entrepreneurship, emphasizing the discursive movement often lost and forgotten in entrepreneurship theory. Ogbor (2000) reminds us of the effects of ideological control in conventional entrepreneurship discourses such as gender bias, ethnocentricity and a prevailing focus on 'the entrepreneur'. I would also like to add the concept of context. To me a critical view of entrepreneurship needs to take into account the context. If we disregard the context of an entrepreneurial adventure we would probably not grasp the essentials of the entrepreneurial process (Welter, 2011).

A   But how would you define *context* when it comes to entrepreneurship? Welter's definition (2011) in her well-cited paper comes to my mind. Do you depart from that as well?

J   Well, there are a number of competing views on this that I find interesting, but to me it boils down to what Giddens (1984) refers to as "structuring", the interplay between agency and structure. When it comes to structure, I find Welters suggestion easy to work with. She identifies four different contexts: business, social, spatial and institutional. In other words, I find it useful to discuss the structuring of the rural (spatial).

A   That sounds a bit like a critical perspective on entrepreneurship. My impression is that this has gained momentum lately, within both gender research and policy. There is a need to further acknowledge that different epistemologies yield different results and realizing that researching gender does not mean to advance gender equality, per se (Ahl, 2006; Calás et al., 2007). Depending on epistemology, the underlying claims of the research and the research itself could continue to conform to stereotypical gender practices. Quantitatively oriented researchers started out by showing how women owned fewer and smaller businesses than men and how this was likely related to the lack of entrepreneurial characteristics that women possessed (see for example Fischer et al., 1993). These studies focused on the supposed differences between men entrepreneurs and women entrepreneurs (see for example Cliff, 1998). This was later critiqued by a number of scholars arguing that women do entrepreneurship differently than men and thus have different needs and opportunities (see for example Bird and Brush, 2002). To overcome gender inequality, it was argued that there should be a masculine way of doing entrepreneurship and a feminine way of doing entrepreneurship.

J   Are these still viable research foci?

A   I would say that a lot of research is still done within these two streams. However the ever-growing movement within gender and entrepreneurship research argues for a social constructionist perspective (Ahl, 2006). Social constructionism in entrepreneurship means that research and concepts are something that are constructed in interaction with other people (Lindgren and Packendorff, 2009). Research and concepts are not out there as tangible things for us as researchers to identify and collect. Rather than contrasting women and men, and using women and men as substitutes for analyzing gender, the focus is on researching the *process* in which gender evolves. Examples of questions to ask in a social constructionist perspective of gender are "How is gender related to other phenomena?" and "How is it constructed in different situations?" Is this view in line with your thoughts?

J   It is. I think of the reality we act within as socially constructed (Berger and Luckmann, 1967). What is interesting is how this construction is a joint effort between people, a negotiated understanding developed in a shared process (Fletcher, 2006). In fact, this view is very close to the structuring between agency and structure that we discussed when we talked about context. Thus, social construction theory gives us a dynamic view on how structure is being renegotiated, and, structuration theory gives us an understanding of how agency is involved. Finally, the theory of entrepreneuring gives us ideas of how structures change and take on new forms. To grasp this process requires

Table 6.1 Research on gender and entrepreneurship sorted according to levels of analyses and contexts

Level of analysis / Context	Individual	(Family) firm	Network	Communities
Business	Bock (2004)	Warren-Smith (2012)	Petridou and Glaveli (2008)	
Institutional	Baker et al. (1997)	Hamilton (2006)	Al-Dajani et al. (2015)	Lindberg et al. (2014)
Spatial	Cassel and Pettersson (2015)	Ekinsmyth (2013)	Hanson and Blake (2009)	Berg (1997)
Social	Mulholland (1996)	Harveston et al. (1997)	Lahiri-Dutt and Samanta (2006)	Hanson (2009)

a reflexive-interpretative, language-sensitive, local, open and nonauthoritative research method. That is (one of) our challenge(s)!

A   I ask myself how these contexts you talked about are linked to gender. Are the contexts gendered? Gender has been studied from different levels of analysis, such as individual, (family) firm, networks and communities as a whole. Using Welters' (2011) conceptual framework we can identify four contexts; social, institutional, spatial and business. This yields a four by four matrix with 16 possible ways for how gender and entrepreneurship have been researched, as shown in Table 6.1. To see whether this framework holds any credibility we identified an article published in a peer-review journal for nearly every box. Not going into all 15articles we identified, we would still argue that we see that research can be done within all contexts and all level of analysis. We argue in this chapter that to be able to grasp the complexity of entrepreneurship we as a research community need to attend to all of the level of analyses and different contexts.

J   Interesting framework! I wonder how the sampling process in gender and entrepreneurship research look on a larger scale. What factors are taken into account when choosing what to study? And in what order are things done?

A   Yes, I feel that to be able to take our argument of how to advance sampling in gender and entrepreneurship research we need to see how this framework fits in the literature.

A review of sampling strategies in entrepreneurship research

We started our journey as many before us, by reviewing literature. We asked what is emphasized when it comes to sampling. But who. did we ask? What sampling strategy did we use? We decided to search for insights about sampling in the methods literature on different levels: textbooks, handbooks, well-cited works and finally critical perspectives (see Table 6.2). To start our quest and get some *basic* views on sampling we began by looking into two undergraduate textbooks about method. One was Bryman and Bell (2015), which focuses on methods in business research, and the other was Robson (2011), which targets people interested in researching social sciences. The typical textbook approach is to identify differences between quantitative and qualitative sampling. Quantitative sampling involves trying to fit the sample as closely to the whole population as possible. Qualitative sampling strategies are more focused on digging deep and are based on the purpose of the research. It is sampling based on criteria and can be either theoretically or purposively driven. For these reasons, qualitative research is lacking in (population) generalization, but can contribute with a theoretical generalization.

Two themes kept coming back as we continued our literature review with four research handbooks on methodology: the sampling strategy starts with the research question and that the choice of unit of analysis is crucial. We chose Miles and Huberman (1994), Silverman (1993), Van de Ven (2007) and Titscher et al.(2000) since they are well-cited both by students and in research articles. All four handbooks argue for a sampling process based in a theoretical framework. For Titscher et al. a good way to minimize the sample is to have a theoretically based research question. Silverman emphasizes that cases should be chosen in order to test theory. Van de Ven argues for specific hypotheses guided by theory as research questions. He also emphasizes that the research question needs to be based in the real world. Miles and Huberman argue that research questions should set boundaries for the study, where the theoretical framework can either be permanent or change throughout the study. For Miles and Huberman, sampling can change during the study through the evolving theoretical framework.

Both Miles and Huberman and Titscher et al. touch upon how it is possible to go for a broader sample, like a context, instead of, for example, individuals. Miles and Huberman write about sampling a setting and then subsettings, such as first choosing a community, then a school and then classes. Titscher et al. have a similar way of first choosing a theme, such as a social phenomenon, and then aiming for actual texts to study. Miles and Huberman say the same thing in a different way when emphasizing that sampling can occur within and across cases and thus arguing that cases are more than merely individuals. Hence, there is a difference between the case studied and the informants we interview, observe and survey. Still, Miles and Huberman acknowledge that usually people are studied with context as a background factor, wherein context is not the unit of analysis itself. From here we can see that there are differences in unit of analysis and the proxy for the unit of analysis.

For the next step in our review we chose three well-known and cited works on qualitative method: Eisenhardt (1989), Glaser and Strauss (1967), and Yin (1994). The sampling strategies they lay out contain similarities but differ on some points. Overall, Yin, and Glaser and Strauss, see sampling as a process

Table 6.2 Literature used in search for what is important when sampling

Themes important when sampling as discussed in. . .

Textbooks		Research handbooks		Theoretical works		Critical perspectives		
Population sampling	Purposive sampling	Sampling guided by RQ	Unit of analysis	Evolving sampling	Fixed sampling	Context	Reflexivity	Process
Bryman and Bell (2015); Robson (2011)	Bryman and Bell (2015); Robson (2011)	Miles and Huberman (1994); Titscher et al.(2000); Silverman (1993); Van de Ven (2007)	Miles and Huberman (1994); Titscher et al.(2000)	Glaser and Strauss (1967); Yin (1994)	Eisenhardt (1989)	Alvesson and Sköldberg (2000); Flyvbjerg (2001); Czarniawska (1998)	Alvesson and Sköldberg (2000); Flyvbjerg (2001); Czarniawska (1998)	Czarniawska (1998)

throughout the course of the research, moving from sample to sample. Their theories differ in where the initial sample comes from. Whereas Yin focuses on the need of having a research question from an initial theoretical framework to choose from, Glaser and Strauss are more interested in a topic or a problem that can guide the first interaction. A theoretical framework will 'blind' the researcher with bias and thus not serve its purpose within grounded theory. Glaser and Strauss emphasize the importance of the researcher, arguing that the first sample will always be a search for interesting interactions between people. Whereas Yin starts with an existing theory, Glaser and Strauss start with a spark, hunch or interest from the researcher.

Yin, and Glaser and Strauss, use a rather linear way of choosing the next sample. Controlled by the emerging theory, following the strategy from Glaser and Strauss, the researcher collects data (thus moving from sample to sample) and analyses the material simultaneously until the purpose of the research is met. Yin is quite vague on where to look for the next sample, but argues for the replication of cases (with confirming results) until the purpose of the research is met. For Yin, the purpose is met when the question is answered and analytical generalization is fulfilled, while for Glaser and Strauss the purpose is met when a theory has emerged. In contrast to both Yin and Glaser and Strauss, Eisenhardt argues that sampling should be made at the beginning of the research process and not throughout. The strategy for sampling cases, preferably those that are extreme or polarized, is to limit the effect external factors have on the result. For example, one can choose cases from four different industries to be able to generalize, while taking into account a wide range of contextual factors. As the purpose is to confirm or modify an already existing theory, cases should be chosen where the theory at hand is evident. Two distinct views on sampling are understood here: sampling is seen as evolving and lasting throughout the course of the research (Yin, and Glaser and Strauss) or as a fixed decision made by the researcher at the beginning of the research process (Eisenhardt).

So far the literature supports understanding people or phenomena in context and not context with people. Depending on which unit of analysis is chosen, different phenomena become the foreground of the study. If people are chosen as the unit of analysis, context will be a background factor and is usually minimized to the effect that it has on people's individual actions. In adding a critical theoretically driven perspective we hope to nuance this picture. Three sources have guided us: Alvesson and Sköldberg (2000), Flyvbjerg (2001) and Czarniawska (1998). From these three sources emerged three themes we sought to highlight: a *context* theme, wherein the context is taken into account; a *process* theme, wherein phenomena are looked upon as a process; and *reflexivity*, wherein the researcher's role in the sampling process is problematized.

All of these authors acknowledge that phenomena exist within a context. Alvesson and Sköldberg point towards the un-transferability of phenomena due to context dependency. Phenomena are thus so embedded in their contexts that a generalization across other contexts is impossible. Instead of identifying phenomena for generalization, Alvesson and Sköldberg support finding units of analysis that contribute to the evolving theory through understanding a phenomenon in a different way. Flyvbjerg states simply that cases exist in context. Czarniawska takes context a bit further by arguing that context in itself could be studied. A problem she sees with studying complex settings, such as organizations, is that the researcher is situated in their own body in a specific place and time. Since modern organizing occurs in many places at once and through "multitudes of kaleidoscopic movements"(1998: 28) the researcher thus can grasp only a portion of what is actually going on in the organization. With the organizers moving around in the organization, one round of interviews does not reflect the 'organizing' itself. Czarniawska's solution is to therefore study a context (she uses the term *action*), not an individual, through a multiplicity of techniques. This context is full of different patterns; practices get confirmed or rejected, boundaries are pushed and identities are discussed. When studying a context, the researcher can potentially grasp more of the complexity of modern organizing.

Czarniawska's notion of studying 'organizing' instead of organizations leads us to the second theme, where phenomena are sampled as a process. As Czarniawska so thoughtfully did, focus is placed on the verb, not the noun, as in *entrepreneuring* versus *entrepreneurship*. Studying a process instead of individuals enables us to follow how organizations, individuals and structures are constantly evolving through constructions in the process.

Flyvbjerg places focus on the researcher finding suitable cases to study. His standpoint is that finding cases requires experience and that no rule-based technique exists that can assist the researcher in finding worthy cases. The sampling strategy is based on the researcher's intuition, which is based on previous knowledge and the results the researcher hopes to find. This intuitive choice must afterwards be argued for with conventional criteria when preparing research for publication. Czarniawska also acknowledges that the researcher needs to balance methodological practices that have been institutionalized with personal interests and self-reflection. Because every researcher takes something for granted when choosing cases to study, the researcher is in some ways at the center of a study. From the viewpoint of this epistemology, researching your own views about a phenomena is just as relevant as any other research. Alvesson and Sköldberg reject the notion of choosing cases for any type of generalization, arguing that cases do not reflect or mirror an objective reality. As no institutional practices are considered, it is up to the researcher to choose cases best suited to the purpose of the study. Czarniawska puts forward that cases can even choose you, before you get to choose them. As with Alvesson and Sköldberg, Czarniawska argues that the purpose becomes the starting point for sampling.

Going back to Table 6.2, we have used sources from different types of literature to see what is emphasized when it comes to sampling. We choose, among many other options, to identify nine different themes of what is emphasized on sampling strategies in literature on method.

Our sampling process when investigating 'sampling 'in gender and entrepreneurship research

To best be able to ground our discussion on sampling and scientific method, we felt we needed to see how our identified sampling strategy themes were applied in practice. For this we choose to sample research articles from the gender and entrepreneurship research field. The sample was collected by means of the following steps. First we entered a search term into Google Scholar, an easy-access database chosen for its user-friendly interface. Since our research question is related to sampling in the field of gender and entrepreneurship, we used the search term *gender entrepreneurship*. The search yielded approximately 300,000 results, which we sorted by relevance. (Google Scholar offers an option to sort by relevance or date). Because we are interested in sampling within gender and entrepreneurship, we focused on the most relevant texts regardless of the year they were published. The relevance parameter on Google Scholar is based on the number of citations by the author, word matching with the content of the full text, the place of publication and how often the article has been cited in scholarly literature (Google, 2017). We choose to work with the first 30 texts,[1] believing this to be a manageable size that would still enable us to group the material. Among these 30 texts we then selected articles published in peer-reviewed research journals; 22 articles met this criterion. This was done for two reasons: first, our main focus is on sampling in research contexts and thus texts such as Microsoft PowerPoint presentations are not considered relevant; second, an article published in a peer-reviewed journal (as opposed to a book chapter by a famous scholar) means that the research community – through the voice of editors and reviewers (and not editors and publishing houses) – has approved the chosen sampling strategy. (See Appendix 1 for an account of the 30 texts and how they were classified.) Next, we read the articles and eliminated those that did not have any empirical material; in practice, this means that they did not have a section on method and sampling. The four articles that were eliminated were primarily conceptual papers. Eighteen papers remained after this step (see Table 6.3). Finally, from the remaining 18

Table 6.3 Our sample of 18 articles sorted alphabetically

Article number	Articles	Number of citations in Google Scholar
I	Ahl, Helene, and Susan Marlow. 2012. "Exploring the Dynamics of Gender, Feminism and Entrepreneurship: Advancing Debate to Escape a Dead End? *"Organization* 19 (5): 543–562.	115
II	Anderson, Erin R. 2008. " 'Whose Name's on the awning?' 'Gender, Entrepreneurship and the American Diner. *"Gender, Place and Culture* 15 (4): 395–410.	10

(Continued)

Table 6.3 (Continued)

Article number	Articles	Number of citations in Google Scholar
III	Bruni, Attila, Silvia Gherardi, and Barbara Poggio. 2004. "Doing Gender, Doing Entrepreneurship: An Ethnographic Account of Intertwined Practices. "*Gender, Work & Organization* 11 (4): 406–429.	429
IV	Brush, Candida G., Anne De Bruin, and Friederike Welter. 2009. "A Gender-Aware Framework for Women's Entrepreneurship." *International Journal of Gender and Entrepreneurship* 1 (1): 8–24.	363
V	Carter, Sara, Eleanor Shaw, Wing Lam, and Fiona Wilson. 2007. "Gender, Entrepreneurship, and Bank Lending: The Criteria and Processes Used by Bank Loan Officers in Assessing Applications." *Entrepreneurship Theory and Practice* 31 (3): 427–444.	227
VI	De Bruin, Anne, Candida G. Brush, and Friederike Welter. 2007. "Advancing a Framework for Coherent Research on Women's Entrepreneurship." *Entrepreneurship Theory and Practice* 31 (3): 323–339.	397
VII	Fischer, Eileen M., A. Rebecca Reuber, and Lorraine S. Dyke. 1993. "A Theoretical Overview and Extension of Research on Sex, Gender, and Entrepreneurship." *Journal of Business Venturing* 8 (2): 151–168.	844
VIII	Gupta, Vishal K., Daniel B. Turban, S. Arzu Wasti, and Arijit Sikdar. 2009. "The Role of Gender Stereotypes in Perceptions of Entrepreneurs and Intentions to Become an Entrepreneur." Entrepreneurship Theory and Practice 33 (2): 397–417.	403
IX	Kalleberg, Arne L., and Kevin T. Leicht. 1991. "Gender and Organizational Performance: Determinants of Small Business Survival and Success. "*Academy of Management Journal* 34 (1): 136–161.	1080
X	Kobeissi, Nada. 2010. "Gender Factors and Female Entrepreneurship: International Evidence and Policy Implications." *Journal of International Entrepreneurship* 8 (1): 1–35.	66
XI	Kourilsky, Marilyn L., and William B. Walstad. 1998. "Entrepreneurship and Female Youth: Knowledge, Attitudes, Gender Differences, and Educational Practices." *Journal of Business Venturing* 13 (1): 77–88.	486
XII	Laure Humbert, Anne, and Eileen Drew. 2010. "Gender, Entrepreneurship and Motivational Factors in an Irish Context." *International Journal of Gender and Entrepreneurship* 2 (2): 173–196.	50
XIII	McGehee, Nancy G., Kyungmi Kim, and Gayle R. Jennings. 2007. "Gender and Motivation for Agri-Tourism Entrepreneurship." *Tourism Management* 28 (1): 280–289.	159

Article number	Articles	Number of citations in Google Scholar
XIV	Minniti, Maria, and Carlo Nardone. 2007. "Being in Someone Else's Shoes: The Role of Gender in Nascent Entrepreneurship." *Small Business Economics* 28 (2–3): 223–238.	313
XV	Mueller, Stephen L. 2004. "Gender Gaps in Potential for Entrepreneurship across Countries and Cultures." *Journal of Developmental Entrepreneurship* 9 (3): 199.	187
XVI	Orhan, Muriel, and Don Scott. 2001. "Why Women Enter into Entrepreneurship: An Explanatory Model." *Women in Management Review* 16 (5): 232–247.	510
XVII	Wilson, Fiona, Jill Kickul, and Deborah Marlino. 2007. "Gender, Entrepreneurial Self-Efficacy, and Entrepreneurial Career Intentions: Implications for Entrepreneurship Education." *Entrepreneurship Theory and Practice* 31 (3): 387–406.	876
XVIII	Zhang, Zhen, Michael J. Zyphur, Jayanth Narayanan, Richard D. Arvey, Sankalp Chaturvedi, Bruce J. Avolio, Paul Lichtenstein, and Gerry Larsson. 2009. "The Genetic Basis of Entrepreneurship: Effects of Gender and Personality." *Organizational Behavior and Human Decision Processes* 110 (2): 93–107.	122

articles we copied the paragraphs about sampling into one document, aligning them next to each other. We then highlighted the core sentences that described the sampling processes of each of those studies.

Writing about our sampling process in a chapter about how to sample is slightly intimidating. It is in no way a structured literature review and it follows few prewritten rules. Put simply, our sample is a snapshot of a research field from an influential databases consisting of research literature. The articles mentioned here simply provide a way for us to illustrate our discussion on sampling and scientific methods. The 18 articles will, together with the nine themes we identified in the literature on sampling, be the basis for discussing how sampling have been done and possibly could be done. Our main focus here is positioning existing sampling strategies within our framework. We will link back to the argument of advancing sampling strategies in gender and entrepreneurship research in the next section. First, however, we examine our snapshot of how sampling have been done in research on gender and entrepreneurship.

Our results: mainstream articles and fascinating outliers

Applying the nine themes, which we identified when reviewing literature on sampling, to our 18 articles rendered a (rather complex) table (see Table 6.4).

In the table, the articles are categorized depending on whether their sampling strategy met the criteria of the theme. We analyzed this by reading the sampling paragraphs of the articles and matching the content to the identified themes. Depending on how the articles relate to our themes, two distinct groupings in Table 6.4 can be constructed. The first group is the *mainstream articles*, which overall have the same categorization, differing when it comes to unit of analysis and whether they used purposive or population sampling. The other group are the *outliers*, where the articles do not share similarities and are unique.

The main group, the mainstream articles, contains 14 articles that follow the same pattern. Within these articles the methodology is guided by a research question and samples are decided at the start of data collection. Not only do these articles have negative answers to the critical theoretically driven themes, failing to take into account the context of the research, but they also fail to consider how the researcher affects the research. Additionally, they do not explore entrepreneurship and gender as a process. The mainstream articles differ on two points: when it comes to unit of analysis and whether they have used purposive or population sampling. Three of the articles are driven by a purposive sample and the rest are based on a population sample. The unit of analysis and their proxy, hence the representation for the unit analysis, differ between articles depending on their topic. It is fairly clear that the focus is on the relationship between gender and *entrepreneurship as starting a business* and the representation of the relationship is students or entrepreneurs.

The remaining four articles form the outlier group, wherein every article is unique and lacks the same set of categories when matched to the themes. These outliers and are thus interesting in that they managed to make it through editors' rejections and into print, without complying with the mainstream way of sampling. In this second group, we have Article II, III, VI and XVI. Within this group we can see how Article II and III differ only in unit of analysis and whether the sampling was fixed or evolving. According to our analysis, in the initial sampling in Article III the two firms were fixed until the researcher arrived, then the sampling process evolved. Both of these articles focus on investigating the interplay between entrepreneurship and other phenomena. In Article III, gender is the other phenomena, while in Article II, space is added to the equation to evaluate the interplay between all three phenomena. When interplay is the focus of research there is logically also a need to study entrepreneurship as a process. If we consider entrepreneurship as something that is shaped by and shapes other phenomena, then entrepreneurship is not static but a process. With this reasoning, considering the context of the research object also comes naturally – for how can we study how entrepreneurship interacts with other phenomena without emphasizing phenomena that are the context?

Article VI is similar to Articles II and III in that it is not driven by a clear research question. Article VI differs from the others due to the way in which empirics are used as illustrative examples. As a result the themes of context, reflexivity of the researcher and entrepreneurship as a process are not present. The same is evident with Article XVI, where context, reflexivity and entrepreneurship

Table 6.4 Our sample categorized with the themes

			Themes important when sampling as discussed in...									
			Textbooks		Research handbooks			Theoretical works		Critical perspectives		
Article number	Data collection		Population sampling	Purposive sampling	Sampling guided by RQ	Unit of analysis	Proxy for unit of analysis	Evolving sampling	Fixed sampling	Context	Reflexivity	Process
The mainstream articles												
I	Illustrative cases		No	Yes	Yes	Entrepreneurial representation	Articles	No	Yes	No	No	No
IV	Review of academic literature		No	Yes	Yes	Women entrepreneurship research field	Articles	No	Yes	No	No	No
V	Experiment and focus groups		No	Yes	Yes	Consequence of gender in bank lending decisions	Loan officers	No	Yes	No	No	No
VII	Survey		Yes	No	Yes	The relationship between business size and entrepreneur experience	Individual entrepreneurs	No	Yes	No	No	No
VIII	Survey		Yes	No	Yes	The relationship between gender stereotypes and entrepreneurship	Individual students	No	Yes	No	No	No
IX	Survey		Yes	No	Yes	The relationship between gender and business survival rate	Individual entrepreneurs	No	Yes	No	No	No

(Continued)

Table 6.4 (Continued)

| | | Themes important when sampling as discussed in. . . | | | | | | | | | |
| | | Textbooks | | Research handbooks | | | Theoretical works | | Critical perspectives | | |
Article number	Data collection	Population sampling	Purposive sampling	Sampling guided by RQ	Unit of analysis	Proxy for unit of analysis	Evolving sampling	Fixed sampling	Context	Reflexivity	Process
The mainstream articles											
X	Secondary data	Yes	No	Yes	Factors affecting female entrepreneurship start-ups	Individual entrepreneurs	No	Yes	No	No	No
XI	Survey	Yes	No	Yes	The relationship between gender and entrepreneurial motivation	Individual students	No	Yes	No	No	No
XII	Survey	Yes	No	Yes	The relationship between gender and entrepreneurial motivation	Individual entrepreneurs	No	Yes	No	No	No
XIII	Survey	Yes	No	Yes	The relationship between gender and entrepreneurial motivation	Individual farmers	No	Yes	No	No	No
XIV	Secondary data	Yes	No	Yes	Factors affecting female entrepreneurship start-upwwws	Individual entrepreneurs	No	Yes	No	No	No
XV	Survey	Yes	No	Yes	Entrepreneurial traits	Individual students	No	Yes	No	No	No
The mainstream articles											
XVII	Survey	Yes	No	Yes	The relationship between gender and entrepreneurial motivation	Individual students	No	Yes	No	No	No

XVIII	Secondary data	Yes	No	Yes	The relationship between gender genetics and entrepreneurship start-ups	Individual non-entrepreneurs and entrepreneurs	No	Yes	No	No	No
The fascinating outliers II	Personal interviews	No	Yes	No	Interplay between gender, entrepreneurship and space	Individual entrepreneurs	Yes	No	Yes	Yes	Yes
III	Ethnography	No	Yes	No	Interplay between gender and entrepreneurship	2 organization	Yes	Yes	Yes	Yes	Yes
VI	Review of academic literature	Yes	No	No	Women entrepreneurship research field	Articles	No	Yes	No	No	No
XVI	Personal interviews	Yes	No	Yes	The relationship between gender and entrepreneurial motivation	Individual entrepreneurs	Yes	Yes	No	No	No

Table 6.5 Our sample, categorized with levels of analysis and contexts from Table 6.1

Level of analysis Context	Individual	(Family) firm	Network	Communities
Business	V, VII, VIII, IX, X, XI, XII, XIII, XIV, XV, XVI, XVII, XVIII			
Institutional	II	III		I, IV, VI
Spatial	II			
Social				

as a process are absent. Here the methodology is guided by a research question and the sampling is done in two steps: a first step where a pool of women entrepreneurs were gathered through business directories and networking, and a second step in which a random sample was drawn from this pool and further researched. Both Article VI and XVI have population sampling in their strategy.

With four exceptions (Article I, III, IV and VI) the proxy of unit of analysis is the entrepreneur, the nonentrepreneur, the farmer, investor or student possibly engaging in entrepreneurship. There is a need when undertaking surveys, for example, to determine who to call or send the questionnaire to. The proxy for any given unit of analysis is here an individual person. Whether it is students, entrepreneurs or farming families that are targeted, someone – one person –needs to take the time to answer the questions. In the exception of Articles I, IV and VI, the representation of the unit of analysis are articles. In Article III an ethnographic study was conducted in two organizations, thus taking into account more than individual explanations of an entrepreneur.

Weaving the results in Table 6.4together with the results in Table 6.1 enables us to understand how sampling affects the level of analysis and the context that are studied. It is evident that within our sample there is an excess of articles that research the individual level of analysis in the business context. However, five of the articles take another perspective. These articles branch out from the conventional way of looking upon gender and entrepreneurship. Moving on to the next section of this chapter, we discuss how different ways of sampling render the excessive favoring of the individual level of analysis in a business context.

A different way to sample as a way to advance research on gender and entrepreneurship

J Revisiting the first paragraphs of this chapter, we aim to investigate how different sampling strategies contribute to theory building in gender and to entrepreneurship theory. We want to challenge and problematize what we consider to be 'innocent sampling strategies' in research on gender and entrepreneurship. In our discussion before in this chapter we laid out different sampling strategies. Now we will turn to discussing the effects that different types of sampling have on research on gender and entrepreneurship.

A Linking back to Table6.5, I find it problematic that so many of the boxes are not filled. A lot of levels of analyses and contexts of gender and entrepreneurship are not researched on in our sample.

J Still, when we actively searched for articles that had different levels of analysis and contexts we did find –even though it was after some digging –articles that met the criteria (see Table6.1). So, it is possible to research gender and entrepreneurship in more ways than just focusing on the individual in the business context, but this is rarely done.

A If we sample for business owners, we will get business owners. There will perhaps be glimpses of entrepreneurial processes amongst everything else that is happening, but who we talk to and what we talk about is of course essential for the theory we are trying to develop. When it comes to researching entrepreneurship it is fairly easy for us to find people who run businesses in a traditional and mainstream way. In Sweden we can look in the local business registers and find a list of all the businesses that are registered for taxes. If we want some type of selection, there are numerous business associations that organize business owners in various categories. Or we could decide to set up parameters such as size, growth or sector to select a sample that fits our needs. What we have to ask ourselves is, what will this sample do to our study? What stories of entrepreneurship will be told – and maybe more importantly, what stories will *not* be told?

J We know that entrepreneurship theory is based on male business owners (Ogbor, 2000). And we know what happens when theory is based on male experiences and accumulated within research and policy. Berglund and Johansson (2007) showed how entrepreneurship discourses included words such as *profit, exploit* and *strategic*. Ogbor (2000) added *courage, achievement,* and *domination,* and Ahl (2006) included *strong, visionary* and *conquer*. To me this is an illustration of the need for a more elaborated sampling strategy in gender and entrepreneurship research. One way would be to consider other representations of entrepreneurship. I wonder how best to branch out from looking at businesses as entrepreneurship? How do we capture the process of entrepreneurship and thus move from subject to process as the unit of analysis?

A I would say that if we were to advance our research on gender and entrepreneurship away from focusing solely on the individual business context, the researcher could grasp a more nuanced picture of the interplay between gender and entrepreneurship. Public and private spheres of entrepreneurship are, for example, more evident within the level of analysis in family as showed by Ekinsmyth (2013), who focused on how spatial factors surrounding the home as a workplace affect how the entrepreneurial process is unfolded. Conformity and resistance of gender could be observed better in social contexts where, for example, Mulholland (1996) showed how women's roles are, through marginalization and to some extent liberation, negotiated in wealthy entrepreneurial families. Anomalies of research can be embraced when researching the social context, as the researcher is clearly involved in the social process happening in the research situation.

A With this way of approaching research on gender and entrepreneurship, epistemology becomes the core of the research process.

J What we argue for is not to research all at once, but try to fill the void outside of the individual business context. Sampling has consequences; I think it's time to for us to stand up for more well-considered sampling strategies.

Concluding thoughts on sampling in research on gender and entrepreneurship

In this chapter we identify and discuss how 'innocent sampling strategies' affect theory building in gender and entrepreneurship theory. Through our sample of research on gender and entrepreneurship we see that the sampling strategy chosen renders elaborations on an individual perspective in relation to the business context. When research is concentrated on one aspect of gender and entrepreneurship, we see that many research situations are missing. These unresearched situations could help us better understand the interplay between gender and entrepreneurship. We have illustrated that it is possible to do research on other contexts and levels of analysis, yet still this is not done. We argue that researchers should further acknowledge contexts and different levels of analysis in future research.

Note

1 As the result on Google Scholar is updated and revised monthly (Falagas et al., 2007), the result we found may not appear the same at another time. We did our search on January 31, 2017.

References

Ahl, H. (2006). Why research on women entrepreneurs needs new directions. *Entrepreneurship Theory and Practice*, 30(5), 595–621.

Al-Dajani, H., Carter, S., Shaw, E., and Marlow, S. (2015). Entrepreneurship among the displaced and dispossessed: Exploring the limits of emancipatory entrepreneuring: Entrepreneurship among the displaced. *British Journal of Management*, 26(4), 713–730.

Alvesson, M. (2003). Critical organization theory. In B. Czarniawska-Joerges and G. Sevón (eds.), *The Northern lights: Organization theory in Scandinavia* (pp. 151–174). Malmö: Liber.

Alvesson, M., and Billing, Y. D. (1997). *Understanding gender and organizations*. London: Sage.

Alvesson, M., and Sköldberg, K. (2000). *Reflexive methodology: New vistas for qualitative research*. Los Angeles, CA: Sage.

Baker, T., Aldrich, H. E., and Nina, L. (1997). Invisible entrepreneurs: The neglect of women business owners by mass media and scholarly journals in the USA. *Entrepreneurship & Regional Development*, 9(3), 221–238.

Berg, N. G. (1997). Gender, place and entrepreneurship. *Entrepreneurship & Regional Development*, 9(3), 259–268.

Berger, P. L., and Luckmann, T. (1967). *The social construction of reality: A treatise in the sociology of knowledge*. London: Penguin Press.

Berglund, K., and Johansson, A. W. (2007). Constructions of entrepreneurship: A discourse analysis of academic publications. *Journal of Enterprising Communities: People and Places in the Global Economy*, 1(1), 77–102.

Bird, B., and Brush, C. G. (2002). A gendered perspective on organizational creation. *Entrepreneurship Theory and Practice*, 26(3), 41–65.

Bock, B. B. (2004). Fitting in and multi-tasking: Dutch farm women's strategies in rural entrepreneurship. *Sociologia Ruralis*, 44(3), 245–260.

Bruni, A., Gherardi, S., and Poggio, B. (2004). Doing gender, doing entrepreneurship: An ethnographic account of intertwined practices. *Gender, Work & Organization*, 11(4), 406–429.

Bryman, A., and Bell, E. (2015). *Business research methods* (4th ed.). Oxford: Oxford University Press.

Calás, M. B., Smircich, L., and Bourne, K. A. (2007). Knowing Lisa? Feminist analyses of 'gender and entrepreneurship'. In D. Bilimoria and S. K. Piderit (eds.), *Handbook on women in business and management* (pp. 78–105). Cheltenham: Edward Elgar Publishing.

Cassel, S. H., and Pettersson, K. (2015). Performing gender and rurality in Swedish farm tourism. *Scandinavian Journal of Hospitality and Tourism*, 15(1–2), 138–151.

Cliff, J. E. (1998). Does one size fit all? Exploring the relationship between attitudes towards growth, gender, and business size. *Journal of Business Venturing*, 13(6), 523–542.

Czarniawska, B. (1998). *A narrative approach to organization studies*. London: Sage Publications.

Deutsch, F. M. (2007). Undoing gender. *Gender & Society*, 21(1), 106–127.

Eisenhardt, K. M. (1989). Building theories from case study research. *The Academy of Management Review*, 14(4), 532–550.

Ekinsmyth, C. (2013). Managing the business of everyday life: The roles of space and place in 'mumpreneurship'. *International Journal of Entrepreneurial Behavior & Research*, 19(5), 525–546.

Falagas, M. E., Pitsouni, E. I., Malietzis, G. A., and Pappas, G. (2007). Comparison of PubMed, scopus, web of science, and google scholar: Strengths and weaknesses. *The FASEB Journal*, 22(2), 338–342.

Fischer, E. M., Reuber, A. R., and Dyke, L. S. (1993). A theoretical overview and extension of research on sex, gender, and entrepreneurship. *Journal of Business Venturing*, 8(2), 151–168.

Fletcher, D. E. (2006). Entrepreneurial processes and the social construction of opportunity. *Entrepreneurship and Regional Development*, 18(5), 421–440.

Flyvbjerg, B. (2001). *Making social science matter*. Cambridge: Cambridge University Press.

Giddens, A. (1984). *The constitution of society: Outline of the theory of structuration*. Cambridge: Polity Press.

Glaser, B., and Strauss, A. (1967). *The discovery of grounded theory: Strategies for qualitative research*. Chicago: Aldine.

Google. (2017). About Google scholar. *Google Scholar.* https://scholar.google.com/intl/en/scholar/about.html (accessed February 22, 2017).

Hamilton, E. (2006). Whose story is it anyway? Narrative accounts of the role of women in founding and establishing family businesses. *International Small Business Journal,* 24(3), 253–271.

Hanson, S. (2009). Changing places through women's entrepreneurship. *Economic Geography,* 85(3), 245–267.

Hanson, S., and Blake, M. (2009). Gender and entrepreneurial networks. *Regional Studies,* 43(1), 135–149.

Harveston, P. D., Davis, P. S., and Lyden, J. A. (1997). Succession planning in family business: The impact of owner gender. *Family Business Review,* 10(4), 373–396.

Henry, C., Foss, L., and Ahl, H. (2015). Gender and entrepreneurship research: A review of methodological approaches. *International Small Business Journal,* 25(1), 1–25.

Hosking, D. M., and Hjorth, D. (2005). Relational constructionism and entrepreneurship: Some key notes. In D. Hjorth and C. Steyaert (eds.), *Narrative and discursive approaches in entrepreneurship: A second movements in entrepreneurship book.* Cheltenham: Edward Elgar Publishing.

Lahiri-Dutt, K., and Samanta, G. (2006). Constructing social capital: Self-help groups and rural women's development in India. *Geographical Research,* 44(3), 285–295.

Lindberg, M., Lindgren, M., and Packendorff, J. (2014). Quadruple Helix as a way to bridge the gender gap in entrepreneurship: The case of an innovation system project in the Baltic Sea region. *Journal of the Knowledge Economy,* 5(1), 94–113.

Lindgren, M., and Packendorff, J. (2009). Social constructionism and entrepreneurship: Basic assumptions and consequences for theory and research. *International Journal of Entrepreneurial Behavior & Research,* 15(1), 25–47.

Martin, P. Y. (2003). 'Said and done' versus 'saying and doing' gendering practices, practicing gender at work. *Gender & Society,* 17(3), 342–366.

Martin, P. Y. (2006). Practising gender at work: Further thoughts on reflexivity. *Gender, Work & Organization,* 13(3), 254–276.

Miles, M. B., and Huberman, A. M. (1994). *Qualitative data analysis: An expanded sourcebook* (2nd ed.). Thousand Oaks, CA: Sage.

Mulholland, K. (1996). Gender power and property relations within entrepreneurial wealthy families. *Gender, Work & Organization,* 3(2), 78–102.

Ogbor, J. O. (2000). Mythicizing and reification in entrepreneurial discourse: Ideology-critique of entrepreneurial studies. *Journal of Management Studies,* 37(5), 605–635.

Petridou, E., and Glaveli, N. (2008). Rural women entrepreneurship within co-operatives: Training support. *Gender in Management: An International Journal,* 23(4), 262–277.

Robson, C. (2011). *Real world research* (3rd ed.). Chichester: Wiley.

Silverman, D. (1993). *Interpreting qualitative data: Methods for analysing talk, text and interaction.* London: Sage (accessed 19 March 2015).

Steyaert, C., and Katz, J. (2004). Reclaiming the space of entrepreneurship in society: Geographical, discursive and social dimensions. *Entrepreneurship & Regional Development,* 16(3), 179–196.

Titscher, S., Meyer, M., Wodak, R., and Vetter, E. (2000). *Methods of text and discourse analysis.* Thousand Oaks, CA: Sage.

Van de Ven, A. H. (2007). *Engaged scholarship: A guide for organizational and social research*. Oxford: Oxford University Press.

Warren-Smith, I. (2012). Rural female entrepreneurs: Rational choices and socio-economic development. *International Journal of Entrepreneurship and Small Business*, 17(3), 338–354.

Welter, F. (2011). Contextualizing entrepreneurship: Conceptual challenges and ways forward. *Entrepreneurship Theory and Practice*, 35(1), 165–184.

Welter, F., Gartner, W. B., and Wright, M. (2016). The context of contextualizing contexts. In F. Welter and W. B. Gartner (eds.), *A research agenda for entrepreneurship and context*. Cheltenham: Edward Elgar Publishing.

West, C., and Zimmerman, D. H. (1987). Doing gender. *Gender and Society*, 1(2), 125–151.

Yin, R. K. (1994). *Case study research: Design and methods* (2nd ed.). Thousand Oaks, CA: Sage.

Appendix 1 – Our 30 texts and how they were classified

Reference	Type	Empirics
Ahl, Helene J. 2003. "The scientific reproduction of gender inequality – A Discourse Analysis of Research Articles on Women's Entrepreneurship."	Dissertation	-
Ahl, Helene, and Susan Marlow. 2012. "Exploring the Dynamics of Gender, Feminism and Entrepreneurship: Advancing Debate to Escape a Dead End?" *Organization* 19 (5): 543–562.	Article	Yes
Ahwireng-Obeng, Fred. 1993. "Gender, Entrepreneurship and Socioeconomic Reparation in South Africa." *The Review of Black Political Economy* 22 (2): 151–165.	Article	No
Anderson, Erin R. 2008. "'Whose Name's on the awning?' Gender, Entrepreneurship and the American Diner." *Gender, Place and Culture* 15 (4): 395–410.	Article	Yes
Bardasi, Elena, C. M. Blackden, and J. C. Guzman. 2007. "Gender, Entrepreneurship, and Competitiveness." The Africa Competitiveness Report 2007.	Microsoft Power Point	-
Bruni, Attila, Silvia Gherardi, and Barbara Poggio. 2004. "Doing Gender, Doing Entrepreneurship: An Ethnographic Account of Intertwined Practices." *Gender, Work & Organization* 11 (4): 406–429.	Article	Yes
Bruni, Attila, Silvia Gherardi, and Barbara Poggio. 2014. *Gender and Entrepreneurship: An Ethnographic Approach.* Routledge.	Book	-
Brush, Candida G., Anne De Bruin, and Friederike Welter. 2009. "A Gender-Aware Framework for Women's Entrepreneurship." *International Journal of Gender and Entrepreneurship* 1 (1): 8–24.	Article	Yes
Carter, Sara, Eleanor Shaw, Wing Lam, and Fiona Wilson. 2007. "Gender, Entrepreneurship, and Bank Lending: The Criteria and Processes Used by Bank Loan Officers in Assessing Applications." *Entrepreneurship Theory and Practice* 31 (3): 427–444.	Article	Yes

Reference	Type	Empirics
Carter, Sara, Eleanor Shaw, Fiona Wilson, and Wing Lam. 2006. "Gender, Entrepreneurship and Business Finance: Investigating the Relationship between Banks and Entrepreneurs in the UK." *Growth-Oriented Women Entrepreneurs and Their businesses – A Global Research Perspective*, 373–392.	Book chapter	-
De Bruin, Anne, Candida G. Brush, and Friederike Welter. 2007. "Advancing a Framework for Coherent Research on Women's Entrepreneurship." *Entrepreneurship Theory and Practice* 31 (3): 323–339.	Article	Yes
Fischer, Eileen M., A. Rebecca Reuber, and Lorraine S. Dyke. 1993. "A Theoretical Overview and Extension of Research on Sex, Gender, and Entrepreneurship." *Journal of Business Venturing* 8 (2): 151–168.	Article	Yes
Gupta, Vishal K., Daniel B. Turban, S. Arzu Wasti, and Arijit Sikdar. 2009. "The Role of Gender Stereotypes in Perceptions of Entrepreneurs and Intentions to Become an Entrepreneur." *Entrepreneurship Theory and Practice* 33 (2): 397–417.	Article	Yes
Kalleberg, Arne L., and Kevin T. Leicht. 1991. "Gender and Organizational Performance: Determinants of Small Business Survival and Success." *Academy of Management Journal* 34 (1): 136–161.	Article	Yes
Kobeissi, Nada. 2010. "Gender Factors and Female Entrepreneurship: International Evidence and Policy Implications." *Journal of International Entrepreneurship* 8 (1): 1–35.	Article	Yes
Kourilsky, Marilyn L., and William B. Walstad. 1998. "Entrepreneurship and Female Youth: Knowledge, Attitudes, Gender Differences, and Educational Practices." *Journal of Business Venturing* 13 (1): 77–88.	Article	Yes
Laure Humbert, Anne, and Eileen Drew. 2010. "Gender, Entrepreneurship and Motivational Factors in an Irish Context." *International Journal of Gender and Entrepreneurship* 2 (2): 173–196.	Article	Yes
Markets, Gender Entrepreneurship. 2007. "International Finance Corporation." GEM Country Brief-Jordan.	Quote	-
Marlow, S., and M. McAdam. 2012. "Advancing Debate: An Epistemological Critique of the Relationship between Gender, Entrepreneurship and Firm Performance." *International Journal of Entrepreneurial Behaviour & Research* 19 (1): 6–6.	Article not found	-
Marlow, Susan, and Dean Patton. 2005. "All Credit to Men? Entrepreneurship, Finance, and Gender." *Entrepreneurship Theory and Practice* 29 (6): 717–735.	Article	No

(*Continued*)

(Continued)

Reference	Type	Empirics
McGehee, Nancy G., Kyungmi Kim, and Gayle R. Jennings. 2007. "Gender and Motivation for Agri-Tourism Entrepreneurship." *Tourism Management* 28 (1): 280–289.	Article	Yes
Minniti, Maria, and Carlo Nardone. 2007. "Being in Someone Else's Shoes: The Role of Gender in Nascent Entrepreneurship." *Small Business Economics* 28 (2–3): 223–238.	Article	Yes
Minniti, Maria, and others. 2009. "Gender Issues in Entrepreneurship." *Foundations and Trends® in Entrepreneurship* 5 (7–8): 497–621.	Book chapter	-
Mueller, Stephen L. 2004. "Gender Gaps in Potential for Entrepreneurship across Countries and Cultures." *Journal of Developmental Entrepreneurship* 9 (3): 199.	Article	Yes
Mushaben, Joyce Marie. 2006. "Thinking Globally, Integrating Locally: Gender, Entrepreneurship and Urban Citizenship in Germany." *Citizenship Studies* 10 (2): 203–227.	Article	No
Nina Gunnerud, Berg. 1997. "Gender, Place and Entrepreneurship." *Entrepreneurship & Regional Development* 9 (3): 259–268.	Article	No
Orhan, Muriel, and Don Scott. 2001. "Why Women Enter into Entrepreneurship: An Explanatory Model." *Women in Management Review* 16 (5): 232–247.	Article	Yes
Torri, Maria Costanza. 2010. "Community Gender Entrepreneurship and Self-Help Groups: A Way Forward to Foster Social Capital and Truly Effective Forms of Participation among Rural Poor Women?" *Community Development Journal.*	Article not found	-
Wilson, Fiona, Jill Kickul, and Deborah Marlino. 2007. "Gender, Entrepreneurial Self-Efficacy, and Entrepreneurial Career Intentions: Implications for Entrepreneurship Education." *Entrepreneurship Theory and Practice* 31 (3): 387–406.	Article	Yes
Zhang, Zhen, Michael J. Zyphur, Jayanth Narayanan, Richard D. Arvey, Sankalp Chaturvedi, Bruce J. Avolio, Paul Lichtenstein, and Gerry Larsson. 2009. "The Genetic Basis of Entrepreneurship: Effects of Gender and Personality." *Organizational Behavior and Human Decision Processes* 110 (2): 93–107.	Article	Yes

7 How does spouse involvement affect business growth?

A matter of gender

*Eli Gimmon, Zeevik Greenberg
and Yanay Farja*

Introduction

This study explores the effect of home location as well as the involvement of spouses and other family members on business growth while comparing women- and men-owned ventures. We surveyed 266 ventures in Israel, of which 202 were men-owned and 64 were women-owned. Findings show that growth of women-owned ventures is not influenced by home-base location, while men-owned ventures grow less if located at home, and that the growth of women-owned ventures is much more affected than men-owned ventures by the involvement of their life partners. Following previous research we provide explanations for these findings.

Like the labour market, entrepreneurship is gendered as well. The rate of women entrepreneurs is still extremely low compared to man entrepreneurs. A gender-based analysis reveals substantial gaps between the rates of men and women entrepreneurs. The Global Entrepreneurship Monitor (GEM) survey (Singer et al., 2015), conducted in 73 countries, finds a balanced rate of women and man entrepreneurs in only 10 of them. Yet, a review of the periodic reports reveals a steady rise in the rate of women entrepreneurs (Kelley et al., 2012). In Israel, the rate of women involved in entrepreneurship increased from 4.7 per cent in 2007 (Menipaz et al., 2009) to 5.1 per cent in 2012 (Menipaz et al., 2013). Evidence on the performance of women entrepreneurs is mixed: on one hand, early research, such as that summarized in Brush (1992), shows that women underperform in many firm level measures, such as profitability, employment and production. On the other hand, Du Rietz and Henrekson (2000) find that when the analysis is conducted at a more disaggregated level, there is only weak evidence of underperformance of women compared to men.

Family is an important dimension of the entrepreneurial landscape around the world, and the footprints of the family into the venture are quite diverse (Howorth et al., 2010; Fletcher et al., 2012). According to Zachary et al. (2011) and Howorth et al. (2010), a family and firm's external context can significantly affect family business development. The role of family in business creation and growth was highlighted by Alsos et al. (2014) in regard to the use of kinship relations as a business resource base and the mitigation of risk and uncertainty through family self-imposed growth controls. While studying the influence of family on business performance, Casillas and Moreno (2010) found that family involvement has an effect on firm growth since it interacts with innovativeness and with risk-taking. Wright et al. (2014) suggested studying differences in family business models to explore the role the family plays in the entrepreneurial activities under various socio-economic contexts.

Family business and entrepreneurship

Family factors entail additional aspects to the complexity of gendered entrepreneurship. On one hand, women tend to launch new ventures in order to bypass the obstacles they face in the gendered labour market. Female entrepreneurs spend more time on childcare and housework than do female employees (Craig et al., 2012). On the other hand, by doing so, women reproduce the heteronormative assumptions of the gender contract. Namely, women take upon themselves the role of secondary breadwinners, if substantially or not, and limit their employment options so that their work will not interfere with their role in the household (Sa'ar, 2010). For self-employed women, working from home reduces the conflict between the need to work and pursue a career, and family expectations of them (König and Cesinger, 2015). Women-owned businesses are often based on the work of the woman alone, apparently evidence of the low revenue expectations of women entrepreneurs (Jasper et al., 2000; Welter, 2010). These characteristics of women's businesses can explain the difficulties that women entrepreneurs face in gaining legitimation from family members, customers and sponsors, since their businesses are perceived as leisure activity, with a limited growth potential (Reichborn-Kjennerud and Svare, 2014).

Gender differences were also found in the ways men and women operate their business: Women are more prone to professionally consult with a wide array of external sources, while many men prefer a single mentor (DeTienne and Chandler, 2007); women, more than men, tend to avoid financial and professional risks (Akehursta et al., 2012;Rad et al., 2014); many women entrepreneurs admit they shy away from anything that has to do with raising external funds, from institutional or private organizations, and perceive it as a financial risk of sorts (Marlow and McAdam, 2013).

Home location

Locating the business at home saves bureaucratic and licensing efforts, reduces the tensions related to the collisions between business and familial activities, eases the financial burden and gives the entrepreneur a sense of higher security while developing a new business (Hennon and Loker, 2000). Women who operate home-based businesses experience a lower level of stress from the conflicts of time division and home and family duties (Nordqvist and Melin, 2010) and work fewer hours compared to men in the same situation (Breen, 2010).

Locating the business at home also creates greater involvement of the spouse in the business. The main partner in the business is usually the spouse, followed by the children. Sharing the business with a spouse contributes to the feeling of financial and employment security by the business owner and his/her family partners, facilitates the bureaucratic side of the business, and allows the owner to share the burden of operational and emotional stresses (Nordqvist and Melin, 2010; Brannon et al., 2013). Kirkwood (2012) suggests that women entrepreneurs, on one hand, perceive that locating their business at home is an opportunity to create collaboration and sharing with their family members. Men, on the other hand, emphasize the financial benefits of reducing their operational costs by locating their business at home. Businesses owned by women are noted to have low operating costs (Brannon et al., 2013; Hennon and Loker, 2000). Jimenez (2009) suggests that the engagement of family members in the business contributes to the individual welfare of the owner.

We propose the following research questions:

P1: Are women-owned ventures likely to grow in the same rate as men-owned ventures?
P2: Are spouses and other family members involved more in women-owned ventures than in men-owned ventures?
P3: Does the involvement of spouses and other family members have the same effect on venture growth in women-owned ventures and in men-owned ventures?
P4: How does the business home location interact with the effect of the involvement of spouse and other family member on growth of women-owned ventures and men-owned ventures?

Method

A survey designed for this study was conducted in Israel in 2013. We surveyed 266 ventures, of which 202 were owned by men and 64 were owned by women. These new businesses were aged from one to 10 years with a mean of 5.59 years. We followed Chrisman et al. (1998), who considered "new" a venture that has not yet reached maturity, which is commonly reached between eight to 12 years old. Items in the questionnaire included demographic and socio-economic information about the entrepreneur who launched the business and characteristics of the business itself. Growth was measured in this study by the natural logarithm of the change in number of employees in the business. The questionnaire was pre-tested in a telephone pilot survey, resulting in the removal or modification of several items that showed low validity or were not sufficiently clear to respondents. Then we applied a telephone interview and a web-based questionnaire administered with Qualtrics©.

Results

Table 7.1 presents the descriptive statistics of all variables. In regard to P1 it shows that there is no difference by gender in rate of growth. However in regard to P2, family involvement in the business from both life partners and other family, ventures owned by women were found to have significantly such involvement more than ventures owned by men, though the prominent difference in family involvement is due to the spouse. Also family financing is more common for ventures owned by women than by men. Another significant difference is related to the business location at home, which is more common for women.

Table 7.1 Summary of descriptive statistics and differences by gender

Variable	Full sample	Ventures owned by men	Ventures owned by women	t-test of difference between men and women
Rate of growth	.4328588 (.8034121)	.4343959 (.8278985)	.3333462 (.6783811)	0.90
Growing business	.5524476 (.4981132)	.538835 (.4997039)	.5757576 (.4980147)	−0.52
Business at home	.2972028 (.4578277)	.2864078 (.4531835)	.3787879 (.4888024)	−1.41*
Life partner in business	.1818182 (.3863707)	.1553398 (.3631107)	.3030303 (.4630899)	−2.68***
Age of business	5.590909 (2.900173)	5.728155 (2.915707)	4.969697 (2.784405)	1.85**
Dependent on nearby customers	.2482517 (.4327559)	.2378641 (.4268127)	.3333333 (.4750169)	−1.54*
Family members in business	.4125874 (.4931627)	.3883495 (.488562)	.5 (.5038315)	−1.60*
Bank loans	.2937063 (.4562574)	.3009709 (.4597974)	.2575758 (.4406501)	0.67
Family loans	.0909091 (.2879837)	.0679612 (.2522924)	.1363636 (.345804)	−1.74**
Age of owner	44.46468 (11.46294)	44.07317 (11.5151)	45.71875 (11.2919)	−1.00
Owner with academic education	.4755245 (.500276)	.461165 (.4997039)	.6212121 (.4888024)	−2.28**
Married	.8014706 (.3996281)	.8106796 (.3927173)	.7727273 (.4222815)	0.67
Employed elsewhere	.1433566 (.3510504)	.1213592 (.3273398)	.1818182 (.3886502)	−1.25
N	266	202	64	

Standard errors in parentheses ***$p < 0.01$, **$p < 0.05$, *$p < 0.1$

The significant effects on business growth are presented in Table 7.2. For women-owned ventures, the life partner's involvement in the business was found to have a positive effect on growth but it had no effect in regard to men-owned businesses. The involvement in business of other family members has a weak positive effect on growth of women-owned ventures and no effect on men-owned ventures. When the owner has an additional job apart from the owned business, it has a negative effect on men-owned businesses and no effect on women-owned businesses. Also, operating the business from home has a negative effect on business growth for men and no effect for women. Interestingly, this effect turns to be clearer when adding an interaction to the regression (columns 2, 4, 6 in Figure 7.2) of the two factors: for men-owned businesses life partner involvement and being based at home shows that when the business is located at home the negative effect of this factor on growth is moderated by the spouse's involvement, which by itself turns out to have a positive (though weak) effect on growth. For women-owned businesses, when the business is located at home the positive effect of the spouse's involvement is increased. It should be noted that we also included in the regression an interaction between involvement of family members who are not the spouse and a variable home-base, but this does not have a significant effect on business growth.

In summary our study shows the following findings:

P1: Women-owned ventures grow at a similar rate to that of men-owned ventures.

P2: Life partners (spouses) are significantly more involved in women-owned ventures (30 per cent) than in men-owned ventures (16 per cent). To a lesser extent, this difference is shown in regard to the involvement of family members other than spouses. Also it should be noted that women (14 per cent) take family loans for their business at twice the rate as men (7 per cent).

P3: The involvement of spouses has a significant and much stronger effect on venture growth of women-owned ventures than men-owned ventures. The involvement of other family members has no significant effect in both cases.

P4: Home location is significantly more common for women-owned ventures (38 per cent) than men-owned ventures (29 per cent). Home location has no significant effect in regard to women-owned ventures but a significant negative effect on growth of men-owned ventures. The latter effect is moderated when the spouse is involved in the men-owned ventures. The interaction of home location with spouse involvement in women-owned ventures has no significant effect on growth. Also the interaction between home location and the involvement of other family members has no significant effect in regard to both genders.

Table 7.2 Regression: factors affecting growth

Variables	Full sample		Ventures owned by men		Ventures owned by women	
	(1)	(2) w/ interaction	(3)	(4) w/ interaction	(5)	(6) w/ interaction
	ln(growth)	ln(growth)	ln(growth)	ln(growth)	ln(growth)	ln(growth)
Business at home	-0.218**	-0.0879	-0.273**	-0.141	-0.145	0.147
	(0.105)	(0.157)	(0.129)	(0.180)	(0.183)	(0.344)
Life partner in business	0.239*	0.398**	0.200	0.392**	0.442**	0.684**
	(0.126)	(0.156)	(0.165)	(0.192)	(0.201)	(0.279)
Interaction home*life partner in business		-0.478*		-0.716*		-0.617
		(0.264)		(0.365)		(0.427)
Age of business	0.0258	0.0238	0.0423**	0.0406**	-0.0354	-0.0358
	(0.0169)	(0.0169)	(0.0204)	(0.0203)	(0.0326)	(0.0327)
Dependent on nearby customers	-0.218*	-0.207*	-0.290**	-0.300**	-0.0673	-0.00761
	(0.111)	(0.111)	(0.138)	(0.139)	(0.184)	(0.189)
Family members in business	-0.0823	-0.0915	-0.0387	-0.0396	-0.214	-0.286
	(0.0975)	(0.120)	(0.118)	(0.142)	(0.172)	(0.238)
Interaction home*family member in business		-0.0564		-0.0505		-0.116
		(0.214)		(0.257)		(0.415)
Bank loans	-0.0729	-0.0646	-0.105	-0.0818	-0.0158	-0.0308
	(0.105)	(0.105)	(0.126)	(0.126)	(0.196)	(0.198)
Family loans	-0.186	-0.191	-0.0999	-0.111	-0.317	-0.373
	(0.172)	(0.173)	(0.231)	(0.230)	(0.258)	(0.273)
Age of owner	0.00330	0.00368	0.00111	0.00196	0.0122	0.0123
	(0.00436)	(0.00437)	(0.00530)	(0.00530)	(0.00783)	(0.00792)
Owner with academic education	0.215**	0.208**	0.200*	0.180	0.287	0.293
	(0.0960)	(0.0958)	(0.117)	(0.116)	(0.184)	(0.187)

	(1)	(2)	(3)	(4)	(5)	(6)
Married	-0.0808	-0.0825	-0.0883	-0.0931	-0.217	-0.193
	(0.124)	(0.125)	(0.150)	(0.151)	(0.228)	(0.229)
Employed elsewhere	-0.386***	-0.431***	-0.499***	-0.560***	-0.117	-0.192
	(0.139)	(0.141)	(0.175)	(0.177)	(0.218)	(0.224)
Constant	0.286	0.260	0.356	0.314	0.0763	0.0199
	(0.246)	(0.247)	(0.284)	(0.285)	(0.535)	(0.538)
Observations	266	266	202	202	64	64
R-squared	0.108	0.120	0.127	0.145	0.207	0.239

Standard errors in parentheses *** $p < 0.01$, ** $p < 0.05$, * $p < 0.1$

Conclusions

We found significant differences between the genders in their business growth in the effect of two major factors: (a) the growth of women-owned ventures is not influenced by home-based location while men-owned ventures grow less if located at home, and (b) the growth of women-owned ventures is much higher with the involvement of their life partners. These differences can be explained by the advantage that women, unlike men, get when working from home in terms of their own time management (Nordqvist and Melin, 2010; Craig et al., 2012) and in terms of the help they may get from their life partner (Kirkwood, 2012). For the other gender, men-owned ventures grow less when located at home but at the home location the involvement of their spouse can better facilitate business growth. An explanation following DeTienne and Chandler (2007) is that women are more prone to professionally consult with a wide array of external sources.

An interesting finding with regard to family businesses is that having the involvement (not in financial terms) of family members other than the spouse does not help to grow the business, whether or not it is located at home. This finding is not in line with Discua-Cruz et al. (2013), who explored family businesses in Latin America and found that the involvement of family members contributes to the business by providing a higher level of networking. This finding can be explained in reference to family members like children who are not old enough to be capable of networking and are thus not effective in growing businesses.

This study has implications for women entrepreneurs, to whom it is recommended for the sake of business growth to launch their venture at home and recruit the involvement of their life partner. As for the other gender, men entrepreneurs should not locate their business at home. However, in the case that they do locate their business at home, they will do better if their spouse is involved in the business.

References

Akehursta, G., Simarrob, E., and Mas-Turb, A. (2012). Women entrepreneurship in small service firms: Motivations, barriers and performance. *The Service Industries Journal*, 32(15), 2489–2505.

Alsos, G. A., Carter, S., and Ljunggren, E. (2014). Kinship and business: How entrepreneurial households facilitate business growth. *Entrepreneurship & Regional Development*, 26(1–2), 97–122.

Brannon, D. L., Wiklund, J., and Haynie, J. M. (2013). The varying effects of family relationships in entrepreneurial teams. *Entrepreneurship: Theory and Practice*, 37(1), 107–132.

Breen, J. (2010). Gender differences in home-based business ownership. *Small Enterprise Research*, 17(2), 124–136.

Brush, C. G. (1992). Research on women business owners: Past trends, a new perspective and future directions. *Entrepreneurship: Theory and Practice*,16(4), 5–31.

Casillas, J. C., and Moreno, A. M. (2010). The relationship between entrepreneurial orientation and growth: The moderating role of family involvement. *Entrepreneurship and Regional Development*, 22(3–4), 265–291.

Chrisman, J., Bauerschmidt, A., and Hofer, C. W. (1998, Fall). The determinants of new venture performance – an extended model. *Entrepreneurship: Theory & Practice*, 23(1), 5–29.

Craig, L., Powell, A., and Cortis, N. (2012). Self-employment, work-family time and the gender division of labour. *Work, Employment and Society*, 26(5), 716–734.

DeTienne, D. R., and Chandler, G. N. (2007). The role of gender in opportunity identification. *Entrepreneurship: Theory and Practice*, 31(3), 365–386.

Discua-Cruz, A., Howorth, C., and Hamilton, E. (2013). Intra-family entrepreneurship: The formation and membership of family entrepreneurial teams. *Entrepreneurship Theory and Practice*, 37(1), 17–46.

Du Rietz, A., and Henrekson, M. (2000). Testing the female underperformance hypothesis. *Small Business Economics*, 14(1), 1–10.

Fletcher, D., Melin, L., and Gimeno, A. (2012). Culture and values in family business – a review and suggestions for future research. *Journal of Family Business Strategy*, 3(3), 127–131.

Hennon, C. B., and Loker, S. (2000). Gender and home-based employment in a global economy. In C. B. Hennon, S. Loker and R. Walker (eds.), *Gender and home-based employment*. Westport, CT: Auborn House.

Howorth, C., Rose, M., Hamilton, E., and Westhead, P. (2010). Family firm diversity and development: An introduction. *International Small Business Journal*, 28(5), 437–451.

Jasper, C. R., Goebel, K. P., Stafford, K., and Heck, R. K. Z. (2000). A gender comparison of business management practices of home-based business owners. In C. B. Hennon, S. Loker and R. Walker (eds.), *Gender and home-based employment*. Westport, CT: Auborn House.

Jimenez, R. M. (2009). Research on women in family firms: Current status and future directions. *Family Business Review*, 22(1), 53–64.

Kelley, D. J., Singer, S., and Herrington, M. (2012). *The global entrepreneurship monitor*. 2012 Global Report.

Kirkwood, J. (2012). Family matters: Exploring the role of family in the new venture creation decision. *Journal of Small Business and Entrepreneurship*, 25(2), 141–154.

König, S., and Cesinger, B. (2015). Gendered work – family conflict in Germany: Do self-employment and flexibility matter? *Work, Employment and Society*, 29(4), 531–549.

Marlow, S., and McAdam, M. (2013). Gender and entrepreneurship: Advancing debate and challenging myths; exploring the mystery of the under-performing female entrepreneur. *International Journal of Entrepreneurial Behavior & Research*, 19(1), 114–124.

Menipaz, E., Avrahami, Y., and Lerner, M. (2009). *Global entrepreneurship monitor: Israel national entrepreneurship report*. www.gemconsortium.org/docs/532/gem-israel-2007-report (Accessed April 29, 2015).

Menipaz, E., Avrahami, Y., and Lerner, M. (2013). *Global entrepreneurship monitor Israel 2012 national summary*. www.gemconsortium.org/docs/2802/gem-israel-2012-national-summary (accessed April 29, 2015).

Nordqvist, M., and Melin, L. (2010). Entrepreneurial families and family firms. *Entrepreneurship and Regional Development*, 22(3–4), 211–239.

Rad, A., Yazdanfar, D., and Öhman, P. (2014). Female and male risk aversion: An empirical study of loan officers' assessment of SME loan applications. *International Journal of Gender and Entrepreneurship*, 6(2), 121–141.

Reichborn-Kjennerud, K., and Svare, H. (2014). Entrepreneurial growth strategies: The female touch. *International Journal of Gender and Entrepreneurship*, 6(2), 181–199.

Sa'ar, A. (2010). Women's micro-entrepreneurship as a track for social mobility, some paradoxical aspects. *Israeli Sociology*, 11(1): 441–462 (in Hebrew).

Singer, S., Amorós, J. E., and Moska, D. (2015). *Global entrepreneurship monitor 2014*. London: Global Entrepreneurship Research Consortium.

Welter, F. (2010). Contextualizing entrepreneurship – conceptual challenges and ways forward. *Entrepreneurship Theory and Practice*, 35(1), 165–184.

Wright, M., Chrisman, J. J., Chua, J. H., and Steier, L. P. (2014). Family enterprise and context. *Entrepreneurship Theory and Practice*, 38(6), 1247–1260.

Zachary, R. K., Rogoff, E. G., and Phinisee, I. (2011). *Defining and identifying family entrepreneurship: A new view of entrepreneurs*. The Dynamics of Entrepreneurship: Evidence from Global Entrepreneurship Monitor Data, 57, Oxford Scholarship Online database.

8 Firm performance, corporate governance and gender diversity in top Italian family firms

Michela C. Mason and Josanco Floreani

Introduction

Family firms have received growing attention over the last 40 years, spurring a rich body of academic literature on the topic (e.g., Adams et al., 2005; Barontini and Caprio, 2006; Astrachan and Shanker, 2003; Corbetta, 1995; Zahra and Sharma, 2004). Family firms are a very heterogeneous group with respect to size, branch, age and structure (Birley, 2001; Handler, 1989). It is well recognized in the literature that family firms are heterogeneous in their governance structures (e.g., Corbetta and Salvato, 2004). For example, levels of ownership and management may vary (Chrisman et al., 2012) to produce different types of firm (Miller et al., 2013) that, in turn, may act differently with respect to their performance (e.g., Anderson and Reeb, 2003). However, the relationship between family involvement and firm performance is far from clear (Gedajlovic et al., 2012; Mazzi, 2011). From the theoretical point of view, scholars continue to be divided between those emphasizing the benefits of family involvement and those pointing to its drawbacks (e.g. Schulze et al., 2002). In addition, empirical research continues to provide a variety of findings (Gedajlovic et al., 2012; O'Boyle et al., 2011), which reflect a number of caveats in existing research. The level and characteristics of the family's involvement and influence on the business is a complicating factor (Habbershon et al., 2003; Habbershon and Williams, 1999; Klein et al., 2005). In addition, scholars have outlined the absence of a framework regarding the family firm (Chrisman et al., 2005; Craig and Moores, 2010), which makes it very complicated to interpret research results adequately.

Following this field of research, the present chapter contributes to the literature on family firm governance and performance, with a specific focus on the gender literature. In this chapter, we argue that a consideration of the effects of family governance can better explain the financial performance of family firms.

We focus on Italian family firms, which represent the backbone of the Italian economic system (Belcredi and Enriques, 2014). In 2014, the Italian Association of Family Firms estimated roughly 784,000 family firms in Italy, accounting for 85 percent of total Italian firms and employing 70 percent of the total labour force. Moreover, individuals or private non-financial companies hold more than 50 percent of the share capital of Italian listed companies, whereas in Europe the figure is nearly 30 percent on average (Bianco et al., 2015). Italian family firms are characterized by a high ownership concentration, with an important involvement of the controlling family in management and a limited participation of women (Barontini and Bozzi, 2010; Bianco et al., 2015). Previous studies on the Italian market account for the superior performance of family firms (Bianchi and Bianco, 2008). Given this, we test if any relationship between specific aspects of governance and a set of performance indicators for Italian family firms exist that would allow us to draw implications for entrepreneurs.

We chose a qualitative-quantitative methodology to investigate how the Italian context influences the relationship between family governance and performance.

At a first stage, we performed a meta-analysis (Ramos et al., 2016) aimed to investigate how the context influences the effects of family governance on Italian family firms' performance.

In the second stage, we investigated the impact of governance on firm performance (dependent variable), while taking into account the composition of the firms' ownership structure (Giovannini, 2010). Our governance measures captured both the ownership structure and the board composition, investigating in particular the role of female management in driving performance. Specifically, we wanted to shed light on female participation on Italian corporate boards as well as on the relevance of family connection to the controlling shareholder. Accordingly, the next section discusses the methodological framework while the following section presents our results. Then the main findings are discussed followed by the conclusions of the study.

Literature review

Research on family firms exists at the crossroads of a plethora of theories on the firm, ranging from agency theory to the behavioural agency paradigm and ending with the resource-based view (see Le Breton-Miller et al., 2015; Mason and Floreani, 2016). According to Klein (2010) the basis for the firm governance discussion in science was until recent times almost exclusively constituted by the principal-agent theory. Recently, researchers using the strategic management approach have begun to increasingly rely on other theoretical perspectives, such as the resource-based view and the stewardship theory.

Indeed, it is well recognized in the literature that family firms are heterogeneous in their governance structures (Corbetta and Salvato, 2004). Although one may be tempted to think that family firms can be regarded as entities sharing common features while being substantially different in behaviour from non-family firms, actually they comprise an heterogeneous world. Heterogeneity among family firms can arise due to a variety of factors such as: governance arrangements (Carney,2005), critical resources (Habbershon and Williams, 1999), goals (Berrone et al., 2012) and capital structure (Anderson and Reeb, 2003). Very often family firms pursue non-economic goals, which is a source of different behaviours among them. Access to resources and capabilities is particularly interesting, and this is why the resource-based view is particularly challenging for family firms.

Access to financial resources is one of the major concerns for family businesses, distinguishing them from non-family firms as recognized by the financing (and equity) gap literature. Specifically, family ownership is probably the most pervasive ownership structure found in many national contexts such as Italy (Barontini and Caprio, 2006; La Porta et al.,1998). Moreover, there is a growing interest in academic literature in this field, specifically regarding the effects of ownership concentration (particularly in families), on their financial performance, although following different methodological approaches.

The evidence regarding the performance implications of family ownership is mixed. Some studies find family ownership positively impacts firm performance (Anderson and Reeb, 2003; Barontini and Caprio, 2006; Hamadi, 2010; Maury, 2006; Singal and Singal, 2011; Wagner et al., 2015). Other studies conclude that family ownership coincides with poorer firm performance (Bennedsen and Nielsen, 2010). Still more studies detect no significant relationship between family ownership and firm performance (Aguilera and Crespi-Cladera, 2012; O'Boyle et al., 2011). An important distinction that sheds light on ownership-performance research is between listed and non-listed family firms. Many studies find a positive relationship between family ownership and firm performance in listed family firms (Anderson and Reeb, 2003; Lee,2006; Maury, 2006). However, studies in private family firms find no relation between family ownership and firm performance in general (Che and Langli, 2015). All these contributions try to investigate the effectiveness of ownership structure on performances. Board composition (proportion of executive directors, CEO duality, diversity of family directors, outside boards) might have an influence on firm performance (Cabrera-Suárez and Martin-Santana, 2015). In the ownership-related literature, an interesting and still promising field of research (among others see Adams and Ferreira, 2009; Dezsö and Ross, 2012; Amore et al., 2014) is dedicated to gender interactions in the top layers of the firms with corporate performances. Despite significant interest from practitioners, policymakers and academics, research has failed to explore board independence structure in a gender diversity framework. Scholars have called for further investigation of board gender diversity–firm outcome relationships (Adams et al., 2015; Bilimoria, 2008; Terjesen et al., 2009)

We attempted to get some insights into these issues by conducting a systematic literature review to deepen our understanding of the issue. The review focused specifically on the experiences of Italian family firms and their performance.

The systematic literature review follows. It was aimed at exploring the current state of research regarding performance of Italian family firms, and, specifically, the relationships between family ownership concentration, presence of CEO duality (i.e., the practice of a single individual serving simultaneously as CEO and board), presence of family directors, presence of women on the board and overall performance of the firm. Regarding the choice of review methodology, in the field of family business systematic literature review appears a useful and reliable methodology, allowing researchers to develop an accurate picture of extant contributions, and identify avenues and gaps to be addressed by future research. The systematic literature review developed in this chapter builds upon the procedures developed in previous research (e.g., Denyer and Tranfield, 2009; Wang and Chugh, 2014). Regarding the construction of the initial database, the following criteria have been applied:

- Only articles in peer-reviewed journals published in English and in Italian were considered; hence, book chapters, conference proceedings, non-English and non-Italian articles were not included.
- Following Ramos et al. (2016), a time span beginning in1986 (the year in which the first journal devoted to family business, *Family Business*, was first published) to present was considered.

The selection of papers involved some of the most popular scientific databases available: Elsevier Scopus, EBSCO Business Source Complete, Google Scholar and ISI Web of Knowledge. In each of these databases, the following keywords were entered: *family business, family business performance, family business involvement, Italian family firms, Italian firm performance.*

After having obtained the initial database, the following restriction criteria were applied:

- papers not extensively discussing about the relationship family firm-performance;
- papers considering Italian family firms, but not specifically considering performance;
- papers considering only non-Italian family firms; and
- papers published in journals not listed in the following categories of the Association of Business Schools (ABS) Academic Journal Quality Guide 2015: "Entrepreneurship and Small Business", "International Business", and "Strategic Management", "Organisation studies", "General Management" and "Finance and Accounting". Note that, journals not included in these categories, but listed in the Journal Quality Guide (GEV-13) of the Italian National Agency for the Evaluation of Universities and Research Institutes (ANVUR) were not excluded.

Finally, to identify possible avenues of future research, thematic codes suggested by extant research (e.g., Wagner et al., 2015) were considered: 1) year of publication, 2) number of firms in the sample, 3) countries included in the sample, 4) publication of the article (i.e., availability on-line. Articles available only in Italian were labelled as "not published") and 5) major findings.

Due to the small number of articles identified, coding was carried out manually, after a careful reading and identification of relevant information. To ensure reliability, each researcher independently read and coded each paper. Differences in terms of coding were discussed among the researchers, and articles were then revised again until an agreement was reached. Table presents the results of our systematic literary review.

Table 8.1 Results of the systematic literary review

Authors	Year	Sample (N. family firms)	Countries	Published	Main findings
Barontini, R.; Caprio, L.	2006	675	Belgium, Denmark, Finland, France, Germany, Italy, The Netherlands, Norway, Spain, Sweden, Switzerland	Yes	Family control does not hamper firm performance. Valuation and operating performance significantly higher in founder-controlled corporations, and in corporations where descendants are board members, but not executive directors.
Binacci, M.; Peruffo, E.; Oriani, R.; Minichilli, A.	2016	584	Italy	Yes	Non-family management teams (NFT) dominant functional diversity improves firm performance. NFT tenure diversity and family firm performance exhibit a U-shaped relationship. NFT size and family firm performance exhibit a U-shaped relationship.
Danes, S. M.; Stafford, K.; Teik-Cheok Loy, J.	2007	301	United States	Yes	For family business with female owners, personnel management has a much greater effect on gross revenue than in the case of male owners. Gender works as a moderator in the case of family businesses' responses to disruption.
De Massis, A.; Kotlar, J.; Campopiano, G.; Cassia, L.	2013	494	Italy	Yes	There is a significant, direct relationship between the degree of family ownership and performance of private family SMEs. The relationship is not linear. Firm performance benefits from a concentrated degree of ownership in the hands of a single member. Family involvement in Top Management moderates the relationship between family ownership dispersion and performance.

(*Continued*)

Table 8.1 (Continued)

Authors	Year	Sample (N. family firms)	Countries	Published	Main findings
De Massis, A.; Kotlar, J.; Campopiano, G.; Cassia, L.	2015	787	Italy	Yes	The relationship family ownership-performance is inverted U-shaped. Ownership dispersion among family members negatively affects performance. Firm performance benefits from a balance between family and non-family members in the top management team.
Erbetta, F.; Menozzi, A.; Corbetta, G.; Fraquelli, G.	2013	320	Italy	Yes	Family firms are more profitable than non-family firms. Family firms tend to be systematically less efficient.
Gallucci, C.; D'Amato, A.	2013	114	Italy	Yes	Family power and revenue are linked by a U-shaped relationship. Family power and profitability are linked by an inverted U-shaped relationship.
Gallucci, C.; Santulli, R.	2014	ND	ND	No	Overall, no significance can be suggested regarding the family involvement-firm performance relationship. The studies considered are strongly heterogeneous.
Gallucci, C.; Santulli, R.; Calabrò, A.	2015	114	Italy	Yes	Family firms involving the family in firm management and using the family as a strategic asset in terms of corporate branding achieve higher sales growth.
Giovannini, R.	2010	56	Italy	Yes	Family independence of the governance board increases with family divestment at IPO, presence of venture capitalists establishment of large and active boards, appointment and compensation committees. Firm performance is positively influenced by the presence of independent directors.
Kumar, P.; Zattoni, A.	2016	ND	ND	Yes	
Lee, Y. G.; Jasper, C.R.	2010	553	United States	Yes	Average levels of Perceived Business Success higher in female managers than in male.

Authors	Year	Sample	Country		Findings
Mari, M.; Poggesi, S.; De Vita, L.	2016	307 managers	Italy	Yes	Female managers more keen to develop innovative management practices. Profit growth higher in the case of female managers. Different responses between male and female managers. There were different responses between male and female managers regarding changes in business-related issues and personal issues (e.g., health).
Maury, B.	2006	1672	Austria, Belgium, Finland, France, Germany, Ireland, Italy, Norway, Portugal, Spain, Sweden, Switzerland, UK	Yes	Family firm performance benefits from being guided by female business owners. Female family business owners are pushed in performing well by their family ties. Active family control is associated with higher profitability with respect to non-family firms. This holds in different legal regimes. Active and passive family control are both associated with higher firm valuations.
Mazzi, C.	2011	ND	ND	Yes	The findings stated the need to further extend knowledge on the relationship between family business and corporate performance and the need to include additional moderating and mediating variables.
Minichilli, A.; Brogi, M.; Calabrò, A.	2016	219	Italy	Yes	During the financial–economic crisis family firms performed better than non-family owned firms. Mixed configurations in family firms (family CEOs but lower family ownership concentration) lead to better performance in difficult conditions.
Mustilli, M.; Campanella, F.; Graziano, D.	2013	992	Italy	No	Replacement of the management team after family succession causes deterioration of performance only in the case of second-generation family businesses.

(*Continued*)

Table 8.1 (Continued)

Authors	Year	Sample (N. family firms)	Countries	Published	Main findings
Perrini, F.; Rossi, G.; Rovetta, B.	2008	297	Italy	Yes	Ownership concentration in the five largest shareholders is beneficial to firm valuation. Managerial ownership is beneficial in non-concentrated firms only (the controlling owner might pursue personal interest through the appointment of management members).
Rubino, F.; Tenuta, P.; Cambrea, D. R.	2016	1613	Italy	Yes	CEO duality and busy directors positively impact a family firms' value. Gender diversity negatively impacts on a firm's value if a family member leads the firm.
Sciascia, S.; Mazzola, P.	2008	620	Italy	Yes	There is a negative quadratic relationship between family involvement in management and performance. There is no relationship between family involvement in ownership and performance.
Sciascia, S.; Mazzola, P.; Kellermanns, F. W.	2014	233	Italy	Yes	Founder-run family firms outperform true family firms. At later generational stages, a positive, significant relationship between family management and performance exists.
Songini, L.; Gnan, L.	2013	146	Italy	Yes	Family involvement in governance is negatively related to agency cost control mechanisms. The importance of agency cost control mechanisms is positively related to financial performance.
Venanzi, D.; Morresi, O.	2010	119	Italy	Yes	From the point of view of both the agency perspective and the stewardship perspective, no evidence is found that family firms perform better than non-family firms.

Wagner, D.; Block, J. H.; Miller, D.; Schwens, C.; Xi, G.	2015	ND	ND	Yes	Family firms exhibit superior performance with respect to non-family firms. If firms are public, or large, the positive effect of family firms on financial performance is higher. Moderating variables hugely impact the relationship between family firms and performance.
Wennberg, K.; Wiklund, J.; Hellerstedt, K.; Nordqvist, M.	2011	3280	Sweden	Yes	Family firms transferred to external owners outperform family businesses transferred within the family. Survival is higher for family businesses transferred within the family.

Methodology

Sample selection

Sample selection was based on the HSG-Global Family Business Index provided by the Center for Family Business at the University of San Gallen, in cooperation with EYs Global Family Business Center of Excellence. Being constructed on the top 500 family firms around the world by revenues, the index provides a representation of the upper echelon of family business globally. In a nutshell, the index constituents combine a $6.5 trillion in annual sales and nearly 21 million employees (see also the Global Family Business Index on http://familybusinessindex.com).

The Italian constituents represented our sample, comprising 28 Italian family firms, which we grouped in four sectors (manufacturing, construction, trade and services). Our sample makes an aggregate € 79.2 million in total revenues with 75,187 employees combined. We are aware that the universe of family businesses is substantially heterogeneous, including a great number of firms ranging from micro-businesses to large corporations. However, by investigating the upper echelon of Italian family firms, we intended to represent a substantial part of family business in Italy.

We surveyed the firms in our sample over a 10-year period, ranging from 2006–2015. The survey provides summary information for each firm such as date of establishment, the controlling family together with the equity stake and selected financial data. We collected annual financial and governance data from the AIDA database provided by the Bureau Van Dijk, which is specifically targeted to disseminate information on Italian firms, while the HSG was useful for deriving the age of each firm. All other information (e.g., generation of the family members running the firm, family and women presence on board) was collected manually from the firms' web pages and from online databases. Figure 8.1 provides a geographical representation of our sample.

Measures

Our hypotheses were tested using regression analysis through the use of the variables grouped into three categories. The first category comprises our *dependent variables*, which measured firm accounting performance; the second encompasses the *independent variables* describing the measures of composition of firm's board and ownership; the third is composed of the *control variables* to minimize potential confounds.

In order to assess performance (i.e., the *dependent variable*), two measures were adopted: return on assets (ROA) and return on equity (ROE). ROA is defined as the net operating income before extraordinary items, divided by total assets; ROE is the ratio of net income on own founds. The measurement of the performance of firms using ROA and ROE is widely supported in the family business literature (e.g., Sciascia and Mazzola, 2008 and Minichilli et al., 2010).

Figure 8.1 Sample representation

Regarding independent variables, we followed prior research in including the composition of a firm's board as an important determinant of performance with respect to female (e.g., Terjesen et al., 2009), family directors (e.g., Chu, 2011) and duality (e.g., Duru et al., 2016). The inclusion of female involvement in the board as an independent variable is due to women's relational skills, monitoring capacity, business involvement and personal charisma (Dezső and Ross, 2008; Adams and Ferriera, 2009; Dobbin and Jung, 2011). Like previous studies (e.g., Carter et al., 2003; Erhardt et al., 2003; Campbell and Minguez-Vera, 2008; Adams and Ferreira, 2009) we measured female involvement (FEM_BOARD)

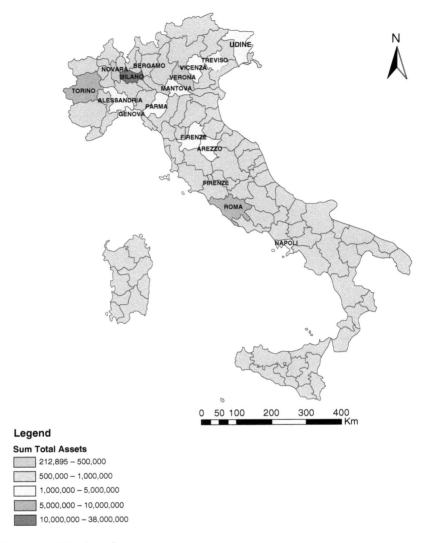

Legend

Sum Total Assets

	212,895 – 500,000
	500,000 – 1,000,000
	1,000,000 – 5,000,000
	5,000,000 – 10,000,000
	10,000,000 – 38,000,000

Figure 8.1 (Continued)

by the proportion of women sitting in the board. Our second set of independent variables are family ownership. Following D'Angelo et al. (2016) we measured the percentage of family ownership in its continuous form, taking values between 0 and 100 (FOWN).

Furthermore, we considered CEO duality (i.e., separation of the board chairman and CEO roles) in line with former research (Deman et al., 2016). This independent variable (CEO_D) is coded by a dummy variable (duality = 1).

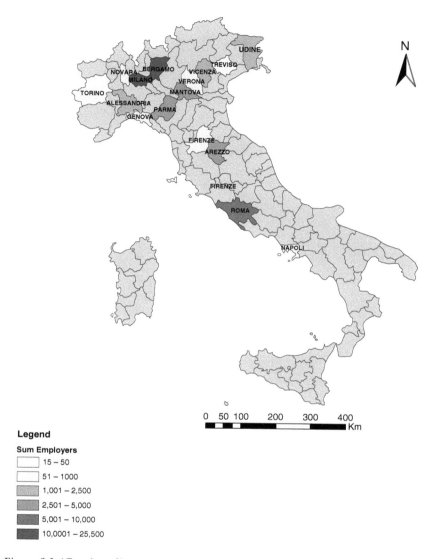

Figure 8.1 (Continued)

We also included FAM_CEO (i.e., presence of family members who serve as the firm's CEO or fill other top management positions) that, in line with research on family involvement in management, (e.g., Anderson and Reeb, 2003), is coded by a dummy variable (presence = 1).

Finally, we included eight *control variables.*

In line with previous studies (e.g., Ruigrok et al., 2014; Anderson and Reeb, 2003) two control variables were adopted to measure firm size: the number of full-time employees (LOG_EMPL) and the number of total assets (LOG_TA).

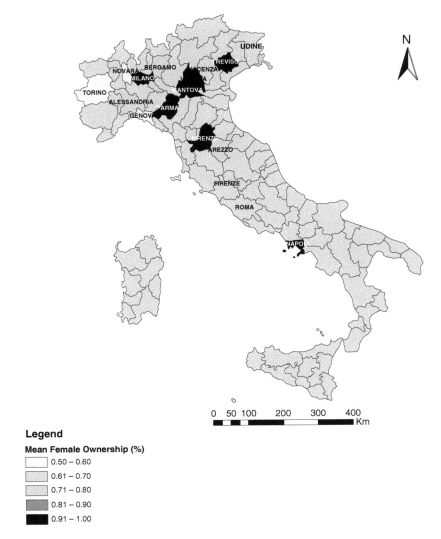

Figure 8.1 (Continued)

Given the distribution of firm sizes and the resultant kurtosis impact, the empirical norm of transforming the two size variables via natural log was followed (e.g., Zellweger et al., 2012).

The third control variable is industry (IND), introduced to control for possible confounding influences arising from the different sectors (Raes et al., 2013). The measures of industry referred to Standard Industry Classification Code one–digit code. Sector dummies (manufacturing, trade, construction and service) were included in the model with manufacturing as the base group.

Another control variable is the generational variable (GEN) for the generation that is managing the firm. We measured generational influence (generational variable GEN) by the individual generation of family members who actually control the company in terms of ownership (i.e., firm's development along the ownership dimension). We applied this control to account for possible generational influences (e.g., Bammens et al., 2008; Lubatkin et al., 2005; Sonfield and Lussier, 2004; Kellermanns et al., 2008).

In line with other research (McConnell and Servaes, 1990; Morck et al., 1988; Short and Keasey, 1999) we include a control variable as a proxy for the level of indebtedness (LEV). Leverage was measured by the ratio of total debt divided by total equity to proxy for financial leverage.

The CASH_H variable was included to control the effect of cash holdings for firm performance. It is measured as the logarithm of year-end cash balances (Isshaq et al., 2009).

The control variable adopted to control earnings quality is EBITDA on sales (EBITDA_S), since EBITDA can be considered as a proxy variable of operating cash flow (Tutino and Regoliosi, 2013).

We also included sales turnover ratio as additional control variable (Liu and Natarajan, 2012), which was calculated as dividing sales on total assets (TURN). Table 8.2 summarizes all the variables used in this chapter and their description.

Estimation method

Panel data with random effects methodology, for data from the 28 sampled Italian family firms for the period 2006 to 2015, provide a framework for estimating the performance–family involvement relation.

The general specification of the equation to be estimated is:

$$\Upsilon_{i,t} = \alpha_i + \beta X_{i,t} + \gamma Z_{i,t} + \delta FOWN_{i,t} + u_{i,t}$$

Table 8.2 Description of variables

Dependent variables	
ROE	Net income/own founds
ROA	Net operating income before extraordinary items/total assets
Independent Variables	
FEM_BOARD	Presence of at least one female in board positions coded by a dummy variable (presence = 1)
FAM_CEO	Presence of family members in CEO positions coded by a dummy variable (presence = 1)
CEO_D	Separation of the board chairman and CEO roles coded by a dummy variable (duality = 1)
FOWN	Proportion of total equity owned by the family (the ownership is either direct or indirect through other entities)

(*Continued*)

Table 8.2 (Continued)

Control Variables	
LOG_EMPL	Logarithmic (number of full-time employees)
MAN, TRADE, CONST, SERVICE	Four industry dummy variables defining manufacturing, trade, construction and service firms, with manufacturing as the base group
GEN	The generation of family members that actually controls the company in terms of ownership
LEV	Leverage ratio (total debt/total equity)
CASH_H	Logarithmic (year-end cash balances)
LOG_TA	Logarithmic (total assets)
EBITDA_S	EBITDA/sales
TURN	Sales on total assets

where i denotes the family firm and t the time periods. α_{it} is a parameter that represents the specific effects of each cross-section; namely, each firm. This parameter is constant over time. u_{it} gathers the effects of any absent variables that are specific to the cross-section and Y represents the dependent variable (ROE and ROA). X is the vector of control variables (i.e., logarithm of firms' employees, logarithm of total assets, firms' generational stage, leverage, logarithm of cash holdings, EBITDA on sales ratio, turnover and economic activity). Z is the vector of the governance variables – i.e., female presence on the board, FIM (Family Involvement in Management, and CEO duality) – while FOWN represents family ownership concentration. Economic activity is captured by four variables grouping manufacturing, trade, construction and service firms. We measured the relation between economic activity and performance through a difference-in-difference approach with manufacturing firms as the base group.

We estimated three models. The first tested for the impact of control variables. The second introduced our governance variables, while the third included family ownership. We tested our model assuming both ROE and ROA as performance measure.

We employed GLS panel data. The panel data methodology combines cross-sections (information from several individuals at a given moment) for several points in time. Panel data has several advantages for econometric estimation: as Baltagi (2008: 7) asserts, panel data give "informative more data, more variability, less collinearity among the variables, more degrees of freedom and more efficiency." Our model specification included dummy variables which prevent any estimation in a fixed effects regression given the collinearity with the intercept. We, therefore, ran a random effects regression.

Empirical analysis

Table 8.3 presents summary statistics (at the firm-year level) for our measures of firm accounting performance, the control variables and family involvement in ownership.

Table 8.3 Summary statistics

	Mean	Median	Lower quartile	Upper quartile	Standard dev.
ROE	0.079	0.057	0.007	0.146	0.187
ROA	0.024	0.000	−0.005	0.051	0.058
LOG_EMPL	2.673	2.949	1.914	3.486	1.051
LOG_TA	6.033	6.277	5.777	6.454	0.658
GEN	2.357	2.000	2.000	3.000	0.856
LEV	1.431	0.315	0.070	0.820	5.685
CASH_H	9.612	10.199	8.593	11.677	2.834
EBITDA_S	−3.948	0.065	−0.196	0.188	41.503
TURN	0.530	0.214	0.002	0.742	0.754
FOWN	0.708	0.670	0.510	1.000	0.218

The results in Table 8.2 show that firms in our sample experienced quite low accounting performances on average and in median terms. In particular, firms in our sample suffered of lower operational performances.

At a first glance, leverage and the EBITDA-to-sales ratio complete a picture of financial fragility of the family firms in our sample. On average, the debt ratio is substantially high (1.4), while the ROS figures show negative returns. However, we observed great variability as well. Both LEV and EBITDA_S volatility are high. Aside firms operating with high levels of financial leverage we found firms whose debt-to-equity ratio do not prompt substantial concerns (the median value equals 0.31 with a lower quartile of 0.07). In turn, the EBITDA_S ratio shows even greater volatility with a 6.5 percent median value coupled with a −19.6 percent lower quartile and a 18.8 percent upper quartile.

Ownership statistics confirm that firms under investigation are closely held, with an average 70.8 percent equity holding in the hands of the controlling family. Much of the family firms in our sample are run by the second generation of the family. Table 8.4 summarizes the correlations.

Our governance measures included three dummy variables measuring the family involvement in management and, in particular, female representation in the board. Table 8.5 presents summary statistics for these variables.

We, then, turn to the estimations of our econometric model. We measured accounting performances as the ROE and ROA respectively (dependent variables). We tested three models. The first model regresses accounting performance against the control variables. The second model includes our governance variables while the third model included ownership. Table 8.5 summarizes the results.

Beginning with the ROE and testing for the impact of control variables (Model 1), our results account for a negative (−0.082) and statistically significant impact of turnover. We found that service firms experience a lower ROE (−0.098) than the base group (manufacturing firms) with a 5 percent significance level. Introducing governance variables (Model 2) improved the goodness of fit. As Table 8.4 shows, our model helps explaining in particular the variance between

Table 8.4 Correlation matrix

	ROE	ROA	LOG_EMPL	LOG_TA	GEN	LEV	CASH_H	EBITDA_S	TURN	FOWN
ROE	1									
ROA	0.3548*	1								
LOG_EMPL	0.0589	0.5104*	1							
LOG_TA	-0.0218	-0.0771	-0.0334	1						
GEN	-0.0506	0.1515	0.4588*	0.2316*	1					
LEV	0.1619	0.4200*	0.2785*	-0.4392*	0.1408	1				
CASH_H	0.058	0.1916	0.3870*	0.7110*	0.4277*	-0.0088	1			
EBITDA_S	-0.0833	0.0693	0.141	0.0009	0.0503	0.0156	-0.0176	1		
TURN	-0.1381	0.177	0.4507*	0.1962	0.3615*	0.0442	0.3109*	0.0847	1	
FOWN	-0.0161	0.1928	0.2540*	-0.1973*	-0.2374*	-0.1077	-0.3041*	0.1709	-0.0497	1

Table 8.5 Regression results

	Dependent variable: ROE			Dependent variable: ROA		
	Model 1	Model 2	Model 3	Model 1	Model 2	Model 3
LOG_EMPL	0.01723	0.03364	0.09686***	0.03130***	0.03284**	0.03567***
LOG_TA	0.02582	-0.05668	-0.15068**	-0.03092*	-0.03851**	-0.04417**
GEN	-0.02735	-0.04770*	-0.09353***	-0.00844	-0.01033	-0.01227
LEV	-0.00057	0.00050	-0.02306	-0.01423***	-0.01367***	-0.01373***
CASH_H	-0.00083	-0.00090	-0.00435	-0.00157	-0.00140	-0.00133
EBITDA_S	-0.00035	-0.00028	0.00002	0.00000	0.00001	0.00001
TURN	-0.08212***	-0.09968***	-0.12261***	-0.00756	-0.00947	-0.00956
TRADE	0.00472	-0.02016	-0.04118	0.04418***	0.03932**	0.03857**
CONST	-0.02754	-0.14852*	-0.23873**	0.02567	0.01338	0.00917
SERV	-0.09897**	-0.03212	-0.01752	-0.01166	-0.00751	-0.00505
FEM_BOARD		0.13115***	0.11165**		0.01844	0.01867
FAM_CEO		-0.04168	-0.07502*		0.00655	0.00479
CEO_D		-0.14374***	-0.19483***		-0.01871	-0.02018
FOWN			-0.32749**			-0.01096
Cons	0.038647	0.56532	1.45246	0.18043	0.22072	0.26138
N. Groups (Obs)	24(205)	24(205)	24(205)	24(205)	24(205)	24(205)
Wald χ^2	18.58	31.93	36.73	58.39	58.45	54.03
(p value)	(0.0459)	(0.0025)	(0.0008)	(0.000)	(0.000)	(0.000)
Rsq within	0.0269	0.0495	0.0959	0.0732	0.0821	0.0901
Rsq between	0.2864	0.3910	0.4010	0.6511	0.6619	0.6416
Rsq overall	0.1137	0.1793	0.1974	0.4074	0.4226	0.4135

***1% significance level, **5% significance level; *1% significance level.

groups, which rises from 0.28 to 0.39. Turnover is still significant, and with the same sign, as in Model 1. Service firms still experience lower returns than the base sample. What is interesting to point out is the impact of governance variables. Our results show that female representation on the board is positively (0.131) and significantly associated with the ROE. By contrast, duality is negatively related (−0.143) with the return on equity.

Model 3 includes FOWN. Interestingly, ownership concentration is negatively (−0.327) and significantly associated with ROE. Moreover, FAM_CEO becomes statistically significant and negatively related with performance (−0.075) showing how family involvement in management tends to undermine performances. Duality and FEM_BOARD enter the relation with the same sign as in Model 2 and remain statistically significant. As in Model 2, generation remains negatively and statistically related with the ROE. Contrary to the previous model, firm's dimension becomes significantly related with the ROE, although with ambiguous effects of total assets (negatively related with performance) and employees (positive relation with the ROE). However, FOWN do not significantly add to the goodness of fit.

When turning to testing the determinants of the ROA, things substantially change. The goodness of fit is much higher, as shown by the between group and overall r-square. The three models present the same patterns and relations. All of them point to a significant, negative association of LEV and total assets with operational performance, while the number of employees positively and significantly enters the relation. The magnitude of coefficients do not substantially change. As for industry, in all three models those firms operating in the trade sector experience higher operational performances than the base sample, with the coefficients being statistically significant. On balance, only financial and dimensional variables play a significant role in driving ROA. By contrast, governance variables and FOWN do not significantly enter the relation with the return on assets. Moreover, such variables do not substantially add to the goodness of fit.

Discussion

Our analysis is grounded in a wide field of research addressing family firm performance under various perspectives covering ownership structure, family involvement, gender diversity, family generation and succession. A bourgeoning field of theory predicts potential, different and contrasting impacts of ownership and family involvement in management. In a nutshell, our results track those of prevailing literature although with a few distinguishing features. Going through the results, we elicit a few considerations with implications for family firm management.

Generation, ownership structure and governance variables become significant in driving returns on equity. Combining such attributes of family involvement we might derive an interesting tale. All of them lead to an unambiguous relation with ROE, where family involvement both in ownership and management is detrimental to performance.

Linking our results to the prevailing theoretical paradigms on family firms allows us to ruling out the hypothesis that a strong family commitment to the firm contributes to performance improvement. Evidence against the stewardship argument elicit to reconsider our results in the light of alternative theoretical paradigms. In our view, the agency theory reveals itself to be a convincing argument for bringing together different attributes of family firms in our sample and their effects on performance within a unifying framework. The basics of agency theory would point to a positive association between family involvement and performance by lowering agency costs.

However, family involvement might give rise to other agency costs should family members be driven by self-interest. Lower agency costs due to higher family involvement might be offset by conflicts between family managers or contrasting values and priorities. Moreover, a strong family involvement might favour the affirmation of non-monetary goals or constrain the effectiveness of management. Eventually, the link between family and the firm might shape an incentive to underinvest.

Within this framework, the negative relation of duality with ROE suggests that introducing a wedge between family and outside directors could actually exacerbate conflicts leading to poorer performances.

The effect of generation completes the story. The negative association we accounted for is not new in family firm studies. Indeed, it suggests that while the founder brings to the firm unique, high-level value-creating skills and capabilities, succession leads to a reduction in those skills.

Gender diversification is another significant attribute in our sample of family firms. More than half of the firms under investigation have a female presence in the board. On average, roughly 20 percent of board members are female. Not only listed family firms, for which a minimum 20 percent of female board members is mandated, but also non-listed family firms as well entrust women with managerial responsibilities. It is worth noting that not women in the board do not necessarily belong to the founding family. On balance, gender diversification appears as a phenomenon going beyond normative prescriptions, and is supportive to performance according to our study and prevailing literature.

Apart from allowing us to envision a policy tool for promoting equal opportunities across genders, gender diversification bears implications for board composition. Our results are in line with those of prevailing literature on gender diversification and make the case for entrepreneurs considering the inclusion of on women in the board, although such a conclusion requires further investigation considering, for example, different attributes of female board members (e.g. skills, education, previous experience and so on).

At a first glance, it is straightforward to observe that neither governance variables nor the generation of family members running the firm affects operational performance.

These results contrast previous research (e.g. Anderson and Reeb, 2003) accounting for a positive association of family involvement in management with firm's operational performance. In the same vein, the irrelevance of generation might appear straightforward. Indeed, a lot of research found an association between operational performance and the firm's age, which is strictly correlated with generation, meaning that the founder contributes shaping the firm's values and culture, and endowing the firm with unique skills affecting operations and strategies.

Finally, assessing a firm's accounting performances requires considering financing policies as well. In our sample, financial leverage significantly and negatively affects operational performances, suggesting that the capital structure is a concern for family firms in our sample. Indeed, especially for family firms, capital structure policies (i.e. choosing the right mix of debt and equity) might lead to biased performance results. It is often recognized that family firms are undercapitalized. The book value of equity, which is the basis for ROE calculations, often does not reflect the true capitalization of firms. Factors such as confusion between an entrepreneur's personal wealth and the family firm's own funds or fiscal considerations may prevent entrepreneurs from investing in a firm's equity capital. Rather, very often they prefer other forms of investment that are pledged against bank financing. Moreover, many firms in our sample are indirectly controlled through a chain of companies, which refer to the controlling family. Such an ownership structure arguably affects a firm's equity capital and, ultimately, to its leverage ratios.

Conclusions

This chapter investigated the drivers of family firm performance, following qualitative and quantitative approaches. The systematic literature review did not lead to conclusive results on the association of financial and governance variables with performance.

Firstly, the overall results of our qualitative analysis (i.e. systematic literary review) suggest a positive relationship between the family business status and its overall performance. Such a general consideration alone should encourage additional future research efforts in this field. Another interesting suggestion is the potential role of family ownership and structure for protecting performance as a key strategic asset to overcome sharp moments of crisis (e.g., Minichilli et al., 2015). However, family managerial control might, in some cases, lead to potential management problems, hampering the firm's growth. In this sense, the level of concentration of family power among members appears determinant on the overall success of family management in terms of performance (e.g., De Massis et al., 2015). Moreover, it should be noted that family firms generally benefit from the presence of a – relatively limited –presence of independent management members (e.g. Giovannini, 2010).

Regarding the role of female members in family firms' management boards, the research underlines a highly positive impact: female members tend to be associated with superior performance, innovative management practices and an overall better organizational climate.

Secondly, our quantitative analysis (i.e. regression models) partially confirms the agency theory perspective. Specifically, the negative impact of family management is in line with agency theory, in contrast with the stewardship perspective, which asserts that family managers ensure firm continuity and the establishment of strong relations with customers to sustain family firms. Additionally, the negative impact of CEO duality on performance supports the agency predictions that duality compromises the monitoring and control of the CEO.

As regards family ownership, the negative association with performance suggests that when families have a great control of the firm, the potential for entrenchment and poor performance is greater.

We, then, investigated the effect of gender diversity on performance. In line with the agency theory, a more heterogeneous board turns to better performance by reducing agency conflicts.

References

Adams, R., Almeida, H., and Ferreira, D. (2005). *Understanding the relationship between founder-CEOs and firm performance*. SSRN. http://ssrn.com/abstract=470145.

Adams, R. B., and Ferreira, D. (2009). Women in the boardroom and their impact on governance and performance. *Journal of Financial Economics*, 94(2), 291–309.

Aguilera, R. V., and Crespi-Cladera, R. (2012). Firm family firms: Current debates of corporate governance in family firms. *Journal of Family Business Strategy*, 3(2), 66–69.

Amore, M. D., Garofalo, O., and Minichilli, A. (2014). Gender interactions within the family firm. *Management Science*, 60(5), 1083–1097.

Anderson, R. C., and Reeb, D. M. (2003). Founding-family ownership and firm performance: Evidence from the S&P 500. *The Journal of Finance*, 58(3), 1301–1328.

Astrachan, J. H., and Shanker, M. C. (2003). Family businesses' contribution to the US economy: A closer look. *Family Business Review*, 16(3), 211–219.

Baltagi, B. (2008). *Econometric analysis of panel data*. Chichester: John Wiley & Sons.

Bammens, Y., Voordeckers, W., and Van Gils, A. (2008). Boards of directors in family firms: A generational perspective. *Small Business Economics*, 31(2), 163–180.

Barontini, R., and Bozzi, S. (2010). *CEO compensation and performance in family firms*. SSRN. https://papers.ssrn.com/sol3/papers.cfm?abstract_id=1557321

Barontini, R., and Caprio, L. (2006). The effect of family control on firm value and performance: Evidence from continental Europe. *European Financial Management*,12(5), 689–723.

Belcredi, M., and Enriques, L. (2014). Institutional investor activism in a context of concentrated ownership and high private benefits of control: The case of Italy. European Corporate Governance Institute (ECGI), Law Working Paper No. 22.

Bennedsen, M., and Nielsen, K. M. (2010). The economic consequences of succession in Danish firms. In M. Neville and K. Engsig Sørensen (eds.), *Company law and SMEs*. København: Thomson Reuter.

Berrone, P., Cruz, C., and Gomez-Mejia, L. R. (2012). Socioemotional wealth in family firms: Theoretical dimensions, assessment approaches, and agenda for future research. *Family Business Review*, 25(3), 258–279.

Bianchi, M., and Bianco, M. (2008). *Italian corporate governance in the last 15 years: From pyramids to coalitions?* SSRN. https://papers.ssrn.com/sol3/papers2.cfm?abstract_id=952147

Bianco, M., Ciavarella, A., and Signoretti, R. (2015). Women on corporate boards in Italy: The role of family connections. *Corporate Governance: An International Review*, 23(2), 129–144.

Bilimoria, D. (2008). Directions for future research on women on corporate boards of directors. In *Women on corporate boards of directors: International research and practice* (pp. 233–240). Cheltenham: Edward Elgar.

Binacci, M., Peruffo, E., Oriani, R., and Minichilli, A. (2015). Are all Non-Family Managers (NFMs) equal? The impact of NFM characteristics and diversity on family firm performance. *Corporate Governance: An International Review*, 24(6), 569–583.

Birley, S. (2001). Owner-manager attitudes to family and business issues: A 16 country study. *Entrepreneurship Theory and Practice*, 25, 63–76.

Cabrera-Suárez, M. K., and Martín-Santana, J. D. (2015). Board composition and performance in Spanish non-listed family firms: The influence of type of directors and CEO duality. *BRQ Business Research Quarterly*,18(4), 213–229.

Campbell, K., and Mínguez-Vera, A. (2008). Gender diversity in the boardroom and firm financial performance. *Journal of Business Ethics*,83(3), 435–451.

Carney, M. (2005). Corporate governance and competitive advantage in family-controlled firms. *Entrepreneurship Theory and Practice*, 29(3), 249–265.

Carter, D. A., Simkins, B. J., and Simpson, W. G. (2003). Corporate governance, board diversity, and firm value. *Financial Review*, 38(1), 33–53.

Che, L., and Langli, J. C. (2015). Governance structure and firm performance in private family firms. *Journal of Business Finance & Accounting*, 42(9–10), 1216–1250.

Chrisman, J. J., Chua, J. H., Pearson, A. W., and Barnett, T. (2012). Family involvement, family influence, and family-centered non-economic goals in small firms. *Entrepreneurship Theory and Practice*, 36(2), 267–293.

Chrisman, J. J., Chua, J. H., and Sharma, P. (2005). Trends and directions in the development of a strategic management theory of the family firm. *Entrepreneurship Theory and Practice*, 29(5), 555–576.

Chu, W. (2011). Family ownership and firm performance: Influence of family management, family control, and firm size. *Asia Pacific Journal of Management*, 28(4), 833–851.

Corbetta, G. (1995). Patterns of development of family businesses in Italy. *Family Business Review*, 8(4), 255–265.

Corbetta, G., and Salvato, C. (2004). Self-serving or self-actualizing? Models of man and agency costs in different types of family firms: A commentary on "comparing the agency costs of family and non-family firms: Conceptual issues and exploratory evidence". *Entrepreneurship Theory and Practice*, 28(4), 355–362.

Craig, J., and Moores, K. (2010). Strategically aligning family and business systems using the balanced scorecard. *Journal of Family Business Strategy*, 1(2), 78–87.

D'Angelo, A., Majocchi, A., and Buck, T. (2016). External managers, family ownership and the scope of SME internationalization. *Journal of World Business*, 51(4), 534–547.

Danes, S. M., Stafford, K., and Loy, J. T. C. (2007). Family business performance: The effects of gender and management. *Journal of Business Research*, 60(10), 1058–1069.

De Massis, A., Kotlar, J., Campopiano, G., and Cassia, L. (2013). Dispersion of family ownership and the performance of small-to-medium size private family firms. *Journal of Family Business Strategy*, 4(3), 166–175.

De Massis, A., Kotlar, J., Campopiano, G., and Cassia, L. (2015). The impact of family involvement on SMEs' performance: Theory and evidence. *Journal of Small Business Management*, 53(4), 924–948.

Deman, R., Jorissen, A., and Laveren, E. (2016). Board monitoring in a privately held firm: When does CEO duality matter? The moderating effect of ownership. *Journal of Small Business Management*. Online first, http://onlinelibrary.wiley.com/doi/10.1111/jsbm.12251/full

Denyer, D., and Tranfield, D. (2009). Producing a systematic review. In D. A. Buchanan and A. Bryman (eds.), *The Sage handbook of organizational research methods* (pp. 671–689). Thousand Oaks, CA: Sage Publications Ltd.

Dezsö, C. L., and Ross, D. G. (2008). *'Girl Power': Female participation in top management and firm performance*. University of Maryland Robert H Smith School of Business.

Dezsö, C. L., and Ross, D. G. (2012). Does female representation in top management improve firm performance? A panel data investigation. *Strategic Management Journal*, 33(9), 1072–1089.

Dobbin, F., and Jung, J. (2011). Board diversity and corporate performance: Filling in the gaps: Corporate board gender diversity and stock performance: The competence gap or institutional investor bias? *NCL Review*, 89, 809–2228.

Duru, A., Iyengar, R. J., and Zampelli, E. M. (2016). The dynamic relationship between CEO duality and firm performance: The moderating role of board independence. *Journal of Business Research*, 69(10), 4269–4277.

Erbetta, F., Menozzi, A., Corbetta, G., and Fraquelli, G. (2013). Assessing family firm performance using frontier analysis techniques: Evidence from Italian manufacturing industries. *Journal of Family Business Strategy*, 4(2), 106–117.

Erhardt, N. L., Werbel, J. D., and Shrader, C. B. (2003). Board of director diversity and firm financial performance. *Corporate Governance: An International Review*, 11(2), 102–111.

Gallucci, C., and D'Amato, A. (2013). Exploring nonlinear effects of family power on the performance of Italian wine businesses. *International Journal of Wine Business Research*, 25(3), 185–202.

Gallucci, C., Santulli, R., and Calabrò, A. (2015). Does family involvement foster or hinder firm performance? The missing role of family-based branding strategies. *Journal of Family Business Strategy*, 6(3), 155–165.

Gedajlovic, E., Carney, M., Chrisman, J. J., and Kellermanns, F. W. (2012). The adolescence of family firm research taking stock and planning for the future. *Journal of Management*, 38(4), 1010–1037.

Giovannini, R. (2010). Corporate governance, family ownership and performance. *Journal of Management & Governance*, 14(2), 145–166.

Habbershon, T. G., and Williams, M. L. (1999). A resource-based framework for assessing the strategic advantages of family firms. *Family Business Review*, 12(1), 1–25.

Habbershon, T. G., Williams, M., and MacMillan, I. C. (2003). A unified systems perspective of family firm performance. *Journal of Business Venturing*, 18(4), 451–465.

Hamadi, M. (2010). Ownership concentration, family control and performance of firms. *European Management Review*, 7(2), 116–131.

Handler, W. C. (1989). Methodological issues and considerations in studying family businesses. *Family Business Review*, 2(3), 257–276.

Isshaq, Z., Bokpin, G. A., and Mensah Onumah, J. (2009). Corporate governance, ownership structure, cash holdings, and firm value on the Ghana stock exchange. *The Journal of Risk Finance*, 10(5), 488–499.

Kellermanns, F. W., Eddleston, K. A., Barnett, T., and Pearson, A. (2008). An exploratory study of family member characteristics and involvement: Effects on entrepreneurial behavior in the family firm. *Family Business Review*, 21(1), 1–14.

Klein, P., Shapiro, D., and Young, J. (2005). Corporate governance, family ownership and firm value: The Canadian evidence. *Corporate Governance: An International Review*, 13(6), 769–784.

Klein, S. B. (2010, March). Corporate Governance, family business complexity and succession. In *"Transfer of Ownership in Private Businesses – European Experiences" International Conference*, Stockholm, Sweden.

Kumar, P., and Zattoni, A. (2016). Family business, corporate governance, and firm performance. *Corporate Governance: An International Review*, 24(6), 550–551.

Le Breton-Miller, I., Miller, D., and Bares, F. (2015). Governance and entrepreneurship in family firms: Agency, behavioral agency and resource-based comparisons. *Journal of Family Business Strategy*, 6(1), 58–62.

Lee, J. (2006). Family firm performance: Further evidence. *Family Business Review*, 19(2), 103–114.

Lee, Y. G., Jasper, C. R., and Fitzgerald, M. A. (2010). Gender differences in perceived business success and profit growth among family business managers. *Journal of Family and Economic Issues*, 31(4), 458–474.

Liu, X. G., and Natarajan, R. (2012). The effect of financial analysts' strategic behavior on analysts' forecast dispersion. *The Accounting Review*, 87(6), 2123–2149.

Lubatkin, M. H., Schulze, W. S., Ling, Y., and Dino, R. N. (2005). The effects of parental altruism on the governance of family-managed firms. *Journal of Organizational Behavior*, 26(3), 313–330.

Mari, M., Poggesi, S., and De Vita, L. (2016). Family embeddedness and business performance: Evidences from women-owned firms. *Management Decision*, 54(2), 476–500.

Maury, B. (2006). Family ownership and firm performance: Empirical evidence from Western European corporations. *Journal of Corporate Finance*,12(2), 321–341.

Mazzi, C. (2011). Family business and financial performance: Current state of knowledge and future research challenges. *Journal of Family Business Strategy*,2(3), 166–181.

McConnell, J. J., and Servaes, H. (1990). Additional evidence on equity ownership and corporate value. *Journal of Financial Economics*, 27, 595–612.

Miller, D., Minichilli, A., and Corbetta, G. (2013). Is family leadership always beneficial? *Strategic Management Journal*, 34(5), 553–571.

Minichilli, A., Brogi, M., and Calabrò, A. (2015). Weathering the storm: Family ownership, governance, and performance through the financial and economic crisis. *Corporate Governance: An International Review*, 24(6), 552–568.

Minichilli, A., Corbetta, G., and MacMillan, I. C. (2010). Top management teams in family-controlled companies: 'Familiness', 'faultlines', and their impact on financial performance. *Journal of Management Studies*,47(2), 205–222.

Morck, R., Shleifer, A., and Vishny, R. W. (1988). Management ownership and market valuation: An empirical analysis. *Journal of Financial Economics*, 20(1–2), 293–315.

Mustilli, M., Campanella, F., and Graziano, D. (2014). Management team replacement and family business performance: An empirical test in Southern Italy. *Sinergie Italian Journal of Management*, 1, 215–231.

O'Boyle, E. H., Rutherford, M. H., and Pollack, J. M. (2011). Examining the relation between ethical focus and financial performance in family firms: An exploratory study. *Family Business Review*, 23(4), 310–326.

Perrini, F., Rossi, G., and Rovetta, B. (2008). Does ownership structure affect performance? Evidence from the Italian market. *Corporate Governance: An International Review*, 16(4), 312–325.

Porta, R. L., Lopez-de-Silanes, F., Shleifer, A., and Vishny, R. W. (1998). Law and finance. *Journal of Political Economy*, 106(6), 1113–1155.

Raes, A. M., Bruch, H., and De Jong, S. B. (2013). How top management team behavioural integration can impact employee work outcomes: Theory development and first empirical tests. *Human Relations*, 66(2), 167–192.

Ramos, H. M., Buck, W. P., and Ong, S. L. (2016). The influence of family ownership and involvement on Chinese family firm performance: A systematic literature review. *International Journal of Management Practice*, 9(4), 365–393.

Rubino, F. E., Tenuta, P., and Cambrea, D. R. (2013). Board characteristics effects on performance in family and non-family business: A multi-theoretical approach. *Journal of Management & Governance*, 1, 1–36.

Ruigrok, W., Georgakakis, D., and Greve, P. (2014). Transparency differences at the top of the organization: Market-pull versus strategic hoarding forces. In J. Forssbaeck and L. Oxelheim (eds.), *The Oxford handbook of economic and institutional transparency* (p. 371). Oxford:

Santulli, C. G. R. (2016). Imprese familiari e performance: Una meta-analisi degli studi empirici. *Sinergie Italian Journal of Management*, 34(99), 365–383.

Schulze, W. S., Lubatkin, M. H., and Dino, R. N. (2002). Altruism, agency, and the competitiveness of family firms. *Managerial and Decision Economics*, 23(4–5), 247–259.

Sciascia, S., and Mazzola, P. (2008). Family involvement in ownership and management: Exploring nonlinear effects on performance. *Family Business Review*, 21(4), 331–345.

Sciascia, S., Mazzola, P., and Kellermanns, F. W. (2014). Family management and profitability in private family-owned firms: Introducing generational stage and the socioemotional wealth perspective. *Journal of Family Business Strategy*, 5(2), 131–137.

Short, H., and Keasey, K. (1999). Managerial ownership and the performance of firms: Evidence from the UK. *Journal of Corporate Finance*, 5, 79–101.

Singal, M., and Singal, V. (2011). Concentrated ownership and firm performance: Does family control matter? *Strategic Entrepreneurship Journal*, 5(4), 373–396.

Sonfield, M. C., and Lussier, R. N. (2004). First-, second-, and third-generation family firms: A comparison. *Family Business Review*, 17(3), 189–202.

Songini, L., and Gnan, L. (2013). Family involvement and agency cost control mechanisms in family small and medium-sized enterprises. *Journal of Small Business Management*, 53(3), 748–779.

Terjesen, S., Sealy, R., and Singh, V. (2009). Women directors on corporate boards: A review and research agenda. *Corporate Governance: An International Review*, 17(3), 320–337.

Tutino, M., and Regoliosi, C. (2013). Corporate governance and profitability: Value relevance of compliance to corporate governance best practice in Italian listed SMEs. *International Journal of Auditing Technology*, 1(3–4), 241–260.

Venanzi, D., and Morresi, O. (2010). Is family business beautiful? Evidence from Italian stock market. https://www.researchgate.net/publication/228239588_Is_Family_Business_Beautiful_Evidence_from_Italian_Stock_Market

Wagner, D., Block, J. H., Miller, D., Schwens, C., and Xi, G. (2015). A meta-analysis of the financial performance of family firms: Another attempt. *Journal of Family Business Strategy*, 6(1), 3–13.

Wang, C. L., and Chugh, H. (2014). Entrepreneurial learning: Past research and future challenges. *International Journal of Management Reviews*,16(1), 24–61.

Wennberg, K., Wiklund, J., Hellerstedt, K., and Nordqvist, M. (2011). Implications of intra-family and external ownership transfer of family firms: Short-term and long-term performance differences. *Strategic Entrepreneurship Journal*, 5(4), 352–372.

Zahra, S. A., and Sharma, P. (2004). Family business research: A strategic reflection. *Family Business Review*, 17(4), 331–346.

Zellweger, T. M., Kellermanns, F. W., Chrisman, J. J., and Chua, J. H. (2012). Family control and family firm valuation by family CEOs: The importance of intentions for transgenerational control. *Organization Science*,23 (3), 851–868.

9 When do women make a difference in the family firm?

Understanding the Latin American context

Luz Elena Orozco Collazos, Isabel C. Botero, and Maria Piedad López Vergara

Introduction

Family firm performance has been a topic that has captured the interest of family business scholars for a long time (Sharma, 2004). Researchers have been primarily interested in three aspects of performance: (1) how does the performance of family firms differ from non-family firms? (2) what are the different factors that influence the performance of family firms? And, (3) what are the components of performance in a family firm? Several studies addressing the first question have found that family controlled businesses in public markets outperform non-family controlled businesses (Anderson and Reeb, 2003; Villalonga and Amit, 2006). When exploring the second question, researchers indicate that family ownership gives the family the power to influence the goals of businesses, their behaviors, and their performance outcomes (Chrisman et al., 2005; Dyer and Whetten, 2006). Finally, researchers argue that performance in a family firm includes some aspects that are financial in nature and others that are non-economic (i.e., socio-emotional wealth) and this is one of the primary differentiators between family and non-family firms (Chrisman et al., 2005; Gomez-Mejía et al., 2007).

Even though firm performance has been an important area of research, one aspect that we still do not understand is the role that women have in the performance of family firms. Research outside of the family business discipline suggests that females are likely to enhance the financial performance of a firm because of what they add while they enact their different roles within the business (Carter et al., 2003; Cox and Blake, 1991; Smith et al., 2006). For example, empirical studies have found that the presence of women in the boards of directors of a firm increases the diversity of points of view during decision-making, which is likely to enhance the financial performance of a firm (Adams and Ferreira, 2009; Campbell and Mínguez-Vera, 2008; Carter et al., 2003; Liu et al., 2014). Similarly, the presence of women in top management roles is likely to increase the financial performance of a firm through its effects on employee motivation and behavior (Dezsö and Ross, 2012; Smith et al., 2006; Vieito, 2012). However, we are unaware of research in the family business context that has explored whether the presence of females in family firms can affect their financial performance and, if so, why.

Women have traditionally played important roles within family firms. These roles range from those that are directly related to the business and its performance (i.e., specific position within the family business or within the board of directors) to "invisible roles" (i.e., those that are not directly recognized as part of the organization; Martinez Jimenez, 2009). Additionally, women are believed to possess unique psychological characteristics that can help family members navigate the complexities of working together, help the family and the business communicate their values, and help provide support during the succession process (Dumas, 1989; Salganicoff, 1990; Ward, 1987). Thus, we believe it is important to explore the role that female family members that work in the family business can have in the financial performance of the firm.

Building on previous research findings that suggest that women can influence performance when they are part of the board (Carter et al., 2003; Smith et al., 2006), and when they belong to the top management team (Krishnan and Park, 2005; Shrader et al., 1997), we argue that women can influence the financial performance of firm when they have a higher ownership percentage in the firm. Given that gender stereotypes affect the types of roles and activities that women engage in when they are part of a business (Jaffe, 1990; Salganicoff, 1990), the benefits of the female presence in a firm are more likely to occur when they have higher ownership in the firm. Higher ownership provides women with greater power to influence the strategic decisions of the firm and to enact roles that can benefit the financial performance of the firm. We also suggest that family ownership creates a context that facilitates the opportunity of female ownership when female family members are knowledgeable about the business and highly involved in its operations. In particular, small family businesses provide an environment in which family females can become owners through inheritance or through their involvement in the operations of the business. However, we believe that these relationships are affected by the cultural norms of a region. Some cultural norms promote gender stereotypes that can affect the types of roles and activities that women are expected to or can engage in when they are part of a business (Jaffe, 1990; Salganicoff, 1990). Therefore, on one hand, cultural norms that promote the active and professional participation of women in the firm could enhance the relationships between family ownership, the percentage of female owners, and financial performance of the firm. On the other hand, cultural norms that hinder the participation of females in the workforce are likely to diminish the relationships among these variables.

With this in mind, this chapter presents an empirical study of the relationship between family ownership and the percentage of women ownership in a firm, the relationship between the percentage of women ownership and the financial performance of the firm, and the moderating effects of cultural norms about participation of women in the workforce (See Figure 9.1). To test our ideas we collected data from 13,704 privately owned firms in Colombia. In the following pages we describe the rationale for our ideas, present the methodology and results from our study, and discuss the contributions and implications of our results.

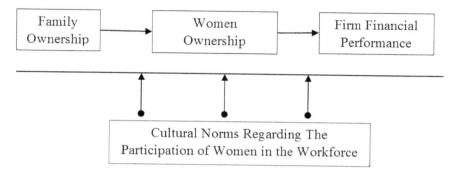

Figure 9.1 Visual model of relationships proposed

Women in family firms

The study of the influence of women in family businesses has captured the attention of scholars since the early 1990s. Women play important roles within the family firm both in the family system and in the business system (Gupta and Levenburg, 2013). Women can influence family firms through their roles as wives, mothers, and/or daughters (i.e., invisible roles; Gillis-Donovan and Moynihan-Bradt, 1990), or through roles in the business (i.e., accountant, manager, CEO, or board member). Independent of the type of role they enact, women are believed to have an important positive influence on the family firm through their actions. Because of this, the research about women that has been conducted in the context of family firms has tried to understand why and how women contribute to the family firm, how can they gain leadership positions within the firm, how to increase the involvement their involvement inside the firm, and the opportunities/advantages that family firms can offer women (Cole, 1997; Cromie and O'Sullivan, 1999; Dumas, 1998; Rowe and Hong, 2000; Salganicoff, 1990). Most of this research has been grouped in three focus areas: (1) factors contributing to the invisibility of women in the family firm, (2) positive aspects of the visibility of women in family firms, and (3) conditions for the successful engagement of women in the family firm (Gupta and Levenburg, 2013; Martinez Jimenez, 2009).

Studies in the first area suggest that the involvement of women in the family firm can be characterized as unpaid and focused on the enactment of informal roles without any position of authority, or any influence. Researchers suggest that, given the traditional roles played in the family, women are more likely to be involved in the family aspects rather than the business aspects of the firm (Ward and Sorenson, 1989). The argument made suggests that societies around the world are more likely to be governed by patriarchal norms where men are the head of the family and women are responsible for caring for the family (Gupta and Levenburg, 2013; Martinez Jimenez, 2009). These norms are then carried over to the business, which facilitates the entry of male children, and can diminish the likelihood for women to join the family firm (Llano and Olguin, 1986). However, researchers also indicate that women have a very important role in the preservation and transmission of the family culture, legacy, and tradition. Because of this, women are expected to be involved in a business and keep their loyalties around the care of the family (Poza and Messer, 2001).

Studies in the second area have found that emotional leadership is what characterizes the important role of women in family firms (Martinez Jimenez, 2009; Salganicoff, 1990). Given the way women are socialized, they are likely to develop psychological and behavioral characteristics that enable the adoption of a holistic perspective towards the firm (Salganicoff, 1990). This approach helps women focus on goals and values that encompass both the family and the business, and help in their survival and development. Women are also better equipped to understand risk and engage in different efforts to protect the family business.

The third area of studies has focused on the conditions necessary for the successful engagement of women in the firm. This area has focused on understanding the importance of work–life balance and how family firms can facilitate the way women manage their roles inside the family and the business (Gupta and Levenburg, 2013). These researchers suggest that family firms need to proactively engage in actions and behaviors that will enable women to be actively involved in the business. Therefore, they need to develop interventions that will help women manage their role in the family and the business.

As it is evident from this short review, the research about women in family firms has been very descriptive so far, and has focused less on explaining how, when, or why women's role can have an effect in the family firm. This is interesting, because outside of the family business field there has been a move to understand the role that women play in the performance of the firm in contexts that are traditionally dominated by men. In the next section we summarize this research and apply it to the context of family firms.

Effects of women on the performance of a firm

The introduction of the "glass ceiling" metaphor (i.e., the barrier preventing women from rising above a certain organizational level; Morrison et al., 1992), created an increased focus on trying to understand and explain the value that women can bring into an organization (Burgess and Tharenou, 2002; Burke, 1997). Since the early 1990s researchers have been interested in exploring how women can contribute to the performance of a firm. Given the disproportionate presence of women in top management when compared to men, scholars first began to explore the influence of women on the performance of a firm by studying board composition and its effects on performance (Carter et al., 2003). Authors argue that the role of the board is to protect all of the stakeholders of the firm, and that women represented 60 percent of all of the purchases in a country like the US. Thus, boards needed to include females to be able to mirror the outside market (Daily et al., 1999).

Cox and Blake (1991) and Robinson and Dechant (1997) argue that bringing diversity to a board is important because: (1) it promotes a better understanding of the marketplace, (2) it increases creativity and innovation, (3) it produces more effective problem solving, (4) it enhances effective corporate leadership, (5) it promotes more effective global relationships, and (6) it can help with integrating a diverse workforce. Thus, the presence of women in boards can increase diversity of opinions, bring a different strategic input to the board, influence the leadership and decision-making style of the organization, provide female role models and mentors, improve the image of the firm with stakeholder groups, and ensure better board room behavior (Burgess and Tharenou, 2002). Based on these arguments, studies began to explore how diversity in boards influenced the performance of the firm, and found that having a diverse board increased the financial performance in firms (Carter et al., 2003), and the presence of females in a board affected the quality of the monitoring role in the board and thus financial performance (Adams and Ferreira, 2009; Liu et al., 2014; Lückerath-Rovers, 2013).

A second line of research explores the effects of women in the top management of a firm (Dezsö and Ross, 2012; Smith et al., 2006; Vieito, 2012). These researchers argue that the presence of women in top management facilitates the inclusion of diverse alternatives when compared with a more homogeneous top management team. The presence of females in top management teams can also have a positive effect on performance due to the effects that diversity can have in perceptions and intentions of important stakeholders. Furthermore, the presence of women in top management can also have a positive effect on the career aspirations of other women in the firm given their symbolic role and disposition to mentor others (Dezsö and Ross, 2012). Likewise, women managers positively influence top management and middle management task performance given their capacity to consider the opinions of others and cooperate with others (Dezsö and Ross, 2012).

Building on this line of research and on resource dependence theory (Pfeffer and Salancik, 1978), we believe that the presence of females in top management of family firms can affect the performance of the organization. Women possess particular characteristics that make them important resources for organizations. In particular, women have unique attributes and behaviors that can help the firm (i.e., benevolence, concern, lower power orientation, focus on community, and participative communication; Adams and Funk, 2012; Bear et al., 2010; Nielsen and Huse, 2010). These behaviors can help family firms by enriching discussions and decision-making processes (Dezsö and Ross, 2012), and this can lead to better performance (Vieito, 2012; Wiersema and Bantel, 1992). However, the presence of females in the family firm will have an effect on performance only under conditions in which females can exercise their power in the decision-making process. In particular, given that previous research in family firms has highlighted the importance of female roles in the family firm, and the difficulties that females face in the family business culture (Curimbaba, 2002; Hollander and Bukowitz, 1990), we believe that the unique characteristics that females bring into the organization will help the business when females have power to implement their ideas in the strategy and its execution. Thus, we argue that it is not the presence of females that influences the performance of the firm; rather it is their ability to implement these ideas through ownership in the firm. In the following section we develop this rationale and explain why the percentage of women ownership can affect the financial performance a firm.

Effects of percentage of female owners on performance of a firm

Ownership is an important characteristic that describes the legal rights that individuals have over an object (Etzioni, 1991). Ownership is important because it carries with it the legal right to influence decisions (Pierce et al., 1991). Formal ownership is often defined in relation to three basic and fundamental rights: (1) the right to possess some share of the physical or financial value of the object, (2) the right to exercise influence/control over the object, and (3) the right for information about the status of what is owned (Pierce et al., 1991). Thus, when an individual has some legal ownership over a firm, they have influence over its strategic decisions. Translating this idea into the effects that women can have in the performance of the firm, we argue that even though the presence of women can have an important influence in the behavior and decision of what a firm does, their ideas and suggestions are not always implemented. Because of this, it is not the mere presence of women that matters, it is their ability to influence decision-making inside the firm. One way in which females can influence decision-making in a firm is through having a percentage of ownership.

Research on family firms has paid special attention to financial performance (Rutherford et al., 2008). However, one aspect that has not been directly explored is the effect of women ownership in the financial performance of the firm. We do know that percentage of ownership can have an effect on performance. In particular, research has found that lone-founder family firms (i.e., those with a high concentration of ownership in one person) tend to outperform other family firms (Miller et al., 2007). Building on this idea, we argue that the percentage of female ownership can also have a positive effect on performance. According to agency theory (Jensen and Meckling, 1976), an owner's ultimate goal is to improve the performance of the firm. Therefore, one of the ways in which the presence of females can affect the performance of the firm is through their percentage of ownership. Ownership enables female members to have greater influence in the strategic direction of the firm. Thus, the diverse perspectives that women bring to the firm are more likely to be heard and incorporated when they are part owners of a business. Building on this rationale, we hypothesize the following.

H1: The percentage of women ownership in a firm will be positively related to the firms' financial performance.

Family ownership as an enabler of women ownership

In recent years, researchers have been interested in understanding the different factors that promote women entrepreneurship and ownership in firms (Mari et al.,

2016). Although initially the focus was on the individual characteristics of women and how they facilitate or promote ownership, there has been a shift to explore how other factors such as social norms, institutional factors, cultural issues, and family context affect women's interest in and legitimacy to act as entrepreneurs and owners of a firm (Mari et al., 2016). Using the family-embeddedness approach, Aldrich and Cliff (2003) suggest that the family system is likely to influence the venture process through the resources, norms, attitudes, and values that it provides to family members. In turn, this unique cultural context provides an opportunity for family members to learn about ownership and management of a firm. We build on this idea to suggest that family ownership creates unique environments that are likely to promote women ownership within a firm. From our point of view, family ownership can promote female ownership in a firm in at least two ways. First, family ownership creates a context in which females can learn about what ownership entails. Matthews and Moser (1996) argue that family members can serve as role models that are likely to enhance the desire of family members to have ownership of a firm. Thus, similar to what is suggested by social learning theory (Bandura, 1977), family ownership creates the opportunity of females to learn by observing other family members, imitating and modeling their behavior to understand how to become active owners of a firm. Second, family ownership can promote female ownership in a firm because of the legal characteristics of the entity. Based on this approach, we could argue that given that inheritance laws require non-gender discrimination in many parts of the world, it could facilitate the likelihood of having a higher percentage of women ownership in a family-firm in contrast to non-family firms.

Family firms create a unique context for the active participation of female family members within the firm (Cromie and O'Sullivan, 1999). Females who are active members of a family firm have a strong commitment to the family and the business (Cappuyns, 2007; Poza and Messer, 2001). These females are likely to increase family unity and the continuity of the business (Poza and Messer, 2001). Additionally, we know that given the central role that active female family members play in the family firm, they are likely to focus on issues and goals that transcend the family and the business to help with the survival of the firm (Lyman, 1989). Building on this idea, we suggest that family ownership also provides a unique context that can result in higher female ownership in a firm because it provides spaces for females to learn about ownership and become interested in being an active owner in a firm. Building on this rationale, we hypothesize the following.

H2:   *Family ownership will be associated with a higher percentage of women ownership in a firm.*

Family ownership and performance

Family businesses represent an important type of organization around the world. Previous research has found that family ownership has positive effects on the performance of a firm (Anderson and Reeb, 2003). Research to date argues that one of the reasons for this increased performance is that family businesses have different sets of goals that focus on financial and non-financial aspects of performance (Gomez-Mejía et al., 2007). In this project we continue to build on previous work to suggest that these non-financial goals create a context that allows for unique processes to occur within the family firm. In turn, these unique processes drive the better performance of family firms. In this study we suggest that one of the reasons why family firms can have a better performance than non-family firms is because they create an environment that promotes women ownership in the firm. When women have higher ownership they are able to influence the strategic choices and direction of the firm. Thus, they are able to add diversity into the decision-making process, and are able to enhance the capability of a firm to understand multiple stakeholders. This, in turn, influences the financial performance of the firm. Thus, we hypothesize the following.

H3: The percentage of women ownership will mediate the relationship between family ownership and the financial performance of the firm.

The role of cultural norms in understanding the influence of females in a firm

The cultural context is an important consideration for research about family firms. Researchers have argued that characteristics of a culture can influence the relationship between variables in family firms (Sharma and Chua, 2013) and the way in which family business are defined (Astrachan et al., 2002). Thus, this chapter also considers the role of cultural norms to better understand the relationships proposed.

In its most general sense, culture can be defined as "the collective programming of the human mind that distinguishes the members of one human group from those of another" (Hofstede, 1984: 21). Culture is learned through the values, norms, rituals, and symbols that each society creates to reinforce its beliefs. In this chapter we focus on the importance of cultural norms as a contextual moderator of the relationships proposed. Norms represent an informal guideline of what is considered correct and incorrect behavior within a particular social unit (Eagly and Chaiken, 1993). Norms are important because they affect the intentions and behaviors that individuals are willing and unwilling to engage in (Fishbein and Ajzen, 1975). Building on this idea, we describe cultural norms as the expectations that a culture has regarding behaviors that are acceptable. Many societies tend to define what women can do based on their cultural norms regarding the roles that females should have within the family and their domestic obligations. Thus, women may experience an added complexity in their roles and behaviors based on the expectations that come from cultural norms.

Previous research has suggested that cultural norms at a societal level can play a role in the extent to which women can have an influence in a firm. For instance, Baughn and colleagues (2006) studied 41 countries and found that cultural norms that promote female participation in entrepreneurial activities are more likely to facilitate female entrepreneurship. When studying family firms, Amore and colleagues (2014) found that female directors improve a firm's performance based on the cultural norms of the location of the firm. Lerner and Malach-Pines (2011) also found that gender norms within a culture influenced the characteristics of family firms. Thus, we believe that the relationships between family ownership, percentage of female ownership, and financial performance are likely to be influenced by the cultural norms based on the location of the firm. The cultural norms that we are particularly interested are those that describe the participation of women in the workforce.

For the purpose of this project we explored the cultural context of Colombia, is a country located in the northern tip of South America. It is the third largest country in Latin America, with a population surpassing 48 million. Seventy percent of this population lives in urban areas. There are close to 1 million companies in the country (30 percent are formal organizations listed within chambers of commerce, and 70 percent are informal in nature). The country has five different cultural regions, each with unique characteristics (Gutiérrez de Pineda, 2000). Regional differences are rooted in the socio-economic dynamics of each region. These dynamics indicate that family is the institution that governs different aspects of life, including the norms that guide gender roles and the participation of women in the workforce. Gutiérrez de Pineda (2000) indicates that in the Bogotá and Central Region, cultural norms suggest that women should be responsible for managing the accounting and buying within the home. Engaging in these activities gives women authority within the home and their community. In other regions (i.e., West, Pacific, and Caribbean), the patriarchal figure has a dominant role at home, while women are expected to focus on childbearing

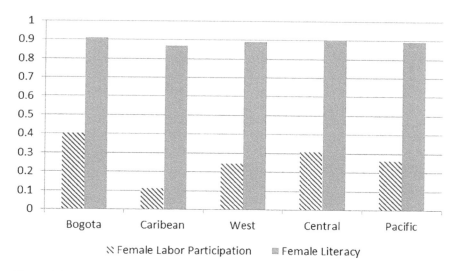

Figure 9.2 Female literacy and participation in the labor force for Colombian regions. Based on the Colombian General Census from 2005.

and childcare (Gutiérrez de Pineda, 2000). These differences between regions are also manifested in the participation of women in the workforce. Data from the Colombian Census of 2005 indicate that, independent of the level of female literacy, regions differ based on the participation of women in the workforce (See Figure 9.2). Thus, we argue that even though female literacy does not differ greatly within regions in Colombia, there is a big difference in cultural norms regarding the participation of women in the workforce. Because of this, we expect that in regions where the participation of women in the workforce is more accepted, family ownership will influence the percentage of female ownership in a firm, and the percentage of female ownership in the firm will influence financial performance. However, in regions where the cultural norms do not promote the participation of women in the workforce these relationships will not occur. Building on this idea, we hypothesize the following.

H4:   *Cultural norms regarding the participation of women in the workforce will moderate the relationship between family ownership, percentage of women ownership, and financial performance such that norms that facilitate the participation of women in the workforce will enhance the relationship between these variables, and norms that hinder the participation of females in the workforce will diminish this relationship.*

Method

Sample and procedure

Our sample is based on 13,704 firms obtained from the Colombian Superintendent of Societies in 2008. Given that Colombian firms are required to report their financial and other information annually to this organization, we used the list provided as the base of our study and complemented it with data from other sources. Seventy-seven percent of the sample was family controlled firms (i.e., 51 percent or higher family ownership). Firms ranged in age between 0.5 and 104 years with an average age of 18.6 years (SD = 12.8 years). Regarding industry, 31 percent were commerce-based firms;28 percent were manufacturing; 32 percent were service; and the rest were agriculture, mining, transportation, or public service firms. Finally when considering firm size, their average sales were COP $20.5 million (around USD $10.25 million) with a maximum of COP $4,000 million (around USD $1,335 million).

Measures

Financial Performance. The financial performance of each firm was assessed using return on assets (ROA). This information was calculated based on information from the Colombian Superintendent of Societies 2008 data. Given that these data were not normally distributed, we used a log-transform to normalize the distribution in our analysis.

Percentage of Women Ownership. We calculated the proportion of women owners from the ownership total count (i.e., number of owners identified by our information). The sex of the owners was established following an exhaustive review of the owner names and their Colombian ID numbers. When the sex was not possible to determine, it was recoded as a missing value. The identification of sex was aided by the fact that in Colombia, at least until 2005, ID numbers (parallel to Social Security numbers in the US) were assigned using ranges according to gender, with the range of 20 million to 70 million limited to women.

Family Ownership. This was a dummy variable with 0 being "no family ownership" and 1 being "family ownership" (0= no, 1 = yes). Firm ownership information was gathered from the Benchmark[1]database. Ownership in family firms tends to be consistent over time (Gersick et al., 1997). Thus, we used the information from 2012. One of the authors cross-referenced the identification number for each firm obtained from the initial list with the information from the Benchmark database. This enabled us to identify the names of all owners and their amount of ownership. This information was used to determine which organizations had 51 percent of ownership in the hands of family. Family relationships were determined by crossing first and second last names from the ownership dataset.[2]

Cultural Norms Regarding Participation of Women in Workforce. This was measured by dividing the sample into the five cultural regions identified by Gutiérrez de Pineda (2000). Each region represents a section of Colombia that has different expectations regarding the role of women and their participation in the workforce.

Control Variables. Four control variables were used in our analysis: firm size, firm age, industry, and ownership concentration. Size was measured based on total assets of the firm. The company's age was calculated based on the year the company was registered in the Colombian Chamber of Commerce. We used 2008 as the year to calculate age. The industry for each company was determined using the International Standard Industrial Classification of All Economic Activities (ISIC). Six dummy variables were created to represent the following categories: agriculture or extraction (i.e., mining), manufacturing, commerce, services, transportation, and public services. Ownership concentration was calculated using the Herfindall index for the distribution of ownership among the firm's owners.

Results

Table 9.1 presents the descriptive statistics and the bivariate correlation for all of the variables in the study.

H1, H2, and H3 were tested using hierarchical regression and the mediation principles from Baron and Kenny (1986) and James and Brett (1984). These authors suggest that to test for mediation using regression analysis three steps need to be followed. First, independent variables (i.e., family ownership) should be related significantly to the dependent variable (i.e., financial performance) (Step 2). Second, independent variables (i.e., family ownership) should

Table 9.1 Descriptive statistics and correlation

	1	2	3	4	5	6	7	9	9	10	11	12	13
Mean	0.02	0.76	0.26	0.19	0.42	15.07	2.67	0.07	0.28	0.31	0.32	0.01	0.00
Std. deviation	0.20	0.42	0.28	0.39	0.24	1.75	0.76	0.26	0.45	0.46	0.47	0.10	0.07
1 ROA													
2 Family Firm	.035**												
3 W % ownership	.013	.395**											
4 Fem Leg Repr.	.007	.038**	.303**										
5 Herfind. Index	.001	-.158**	-.207**	.000									
6 Firm Size	.868	-.157**	-.233**	-.100**	-.047**								
7 Firm Age	.020*	.087**	.040**	-.034**	-.085**	.194**							
9 Mining/Agric	-.041**	.011	.008	.006	-.064**	.045**	.037**						
9 Manufacturing	.003	.003	-.054**	-.058**	-.022**	.134**	.090**	-.175**					
10 Commerce	-.001	.065**	.061**	-.010	.041**	-.091**	-.080**	-.191**	-.417**				
11 Services	.024**	-.068**	-.009	.065**	.015	-.056**	-.020*	-.195**	-.426**	-.465**			
12 Transportation	-.006	.005	.002	-.010	-.006	-.032**	-.028**	-.029**	-.064**	-.069**	-.071**		
13 Public services	-.011	-.044**	-.030**	-.007	.019*	.000	-.011	-.019*	-.041**	-.045**	-.046**	-.007	

** . Correlation is significant at the 0.01 level (2-tailed).

* . Correlation is significant at the 0.05 level (2-tailed).

be significantly related to the mediator (i.e., percentage of women ownership). Third, the mediator (i.e., percentage of women ownership) should be significantly related to the dependent variable (i.e., financial performance). And, fourth, a hierarchical regression should be conducted to evaluate the effects of mediators (Step 2) and independent variables (Step 3) on the dependent variable. If the effect of both mediator and independent variables is still significant in Step 3 there is evidence for partial mediation. If the effect of mediators is significant but not the effects of independent variables there is evidence of full mediation. We used hierarchical regression and entered controls (i.e., Herfindall index, firm size, firm age, and industry) in Step 1. We evaluated the significance of each step with change in F(ΔF) and interpreted betas with t-values. Table 9.2 shows the results of all of these analyses.

As can be seen in Table 9.2, for Model 2, the addition of family ownership in Step 2 increased the variance explained in financial performance (ΔF = 101.19, p

Table 9.2 Hierarchical regression results for the complete sample

Dependent variable	Financial firm performance			Percentage of women ownership
	Model 1	Model 2	Model 3	Model 4
Step 1: Controls				
Herfindall Index	0.01	0.01	0.01	−0.21**
Firm Size	0.18**	0.18**	0.18**	−0.25**
Firm Age	−0.01	−0.01	−0.01	0.08**
Mining/Agric	−0.05**	−0.05**	−0.05**	−0.02*
Manufacturing	−0.02*	−0.02*	−0.02*	−0.06**
Services	0.01	0.01	0.01	−0.05**
Transportation	0.00	0.00	0.00	−0.01
Public services	−0.01	−0.01	−0.01	−0.03**
ΔR^2	0.03	0.03	0.03	0.11
ΔF	57.13**	57.13**	57.13**	212.41**
Step 2				
W % ownership	0.06**		0.06**	
Family Firm		0.07**		0.34**
ΔR^2	0.00	0.01	0.00	0.10
ΔF	47.92**	101.19**	47.92**	1833.15**
Step 3				
Family Ownership			0.06**	
ΔR^2			0.00	
ΔF			37.97**	
F	56.28**	62.40**	54.59**	417.70**
R^2	0.04	0.04	0.04	0.22
Adjusted R^2	0.03	0.04	0.04	0.21

Note: Model statistics are standardized betas.

* Significance at $p < .05$, ** Significance at $p < .01$

< .01). Analyses show a significant increase in firm performance based on family ownership (β = .07, p < .01). Second (see Table 9.2, Model 4), results also show that the addition of family ownership in Step 2 significantly increased the variance explained in the percentage of women ownership in a firm (ΔF = 1,833.15, p < .01), and family ownership was positively related to the percentage of women ownership in the firm (β = .34, p < .01), supporting H2. Third, (see Table 9.2, Model 1), results indicate that the addition of percentage of female ownership in Step 2 significantly increased the percentage of variance explained in financial performance (ΔF = 47.92, p < .01). The percentage of female ownership was positively related to financial performance (β = .06, p < .01), supporting H1. Finally, as seen in Table 9.2, for Model 3, both the addition of percentage of women ownership in Step 2 (ΔF = 47.92, p < .01), and family ownership in Step 3(ΔF = 37.97, p < .01) significantly increased the variance explained in financial performance. Results indicate that in Step 3 both percentage of women ownership (β = .04, p < .01), and family ownership (β = .06, p < .01) were positively related to firm performance. This suggests partial and not full mediation providing some support to H3.

To test H4 we conducted mediation analysis based on region. As can be seen in Table 9.3, our analyses show that the results vary per region. In particular, the results for the Central and Bogota Regions are similar to the complete data sample. However, the results for the other regions support either a full mediation or no mediation. These results provide some support for H4.

Discussion

The primary purpose of this study was to explore the effect of female ownership on the financial performance of a firm. In particular, we wanted to know whether family ownership affected the percentage of female owners in the firm, and whether the percentage of female ownership in a firm would affect the financial performance of the firm. By exploring these issues we wanted to answer the question: when do females make a difference in the performance of the firm? We explored this idea in the context of Colombia, a Latin American country where patriarchal norms are an important part of societal culture. We argued that in countries with such engrained patriarchal norms, the best way to test the influence of females on performance is by exploring conditions under which women can exercise power and control in the firm. We found that the percentage of female ownership in a firm positively influences the financial performance of the firm; family ownership enhanced the likelihood of women having ownership in a firm; and these results vary based on the cultural norms of the region.

Our results have important implications for research. To our knowledge this is the first quantitative study to explore the effects of family ownership and percentage of women ownership on the performance of a firm. Thus, a contribution is that our study builds on previous qualitative explorations of the role of females in family firms and provides some initial evidence of the effects of female ownership on performance. This is important because first, it helps us better understand

Table 9.3 Results of mediation analysis per region

B	Bogota		Caribbean		East		Central		Pacific	
		ΔF	β	ΔF	B	ΔF	β	ΔF	β	ΔF
Steps for mediation										
FO -> FP	.07**	26.08**	.09**	10.53**	.09**	61.17**	.07**	14.93**	.06**	7.90**
FO -> % of WO	.35**	926.65**	.33**	155.31**	.32**	101.61**	.30**	325.56**	.33**	290.09**
% of WO -> FP	.07**	25.57**	.07**	6.05*	N.S.	N.S.	.07**	13.91**	.05**	5.30*
Full Model Step 3		12.59		6.58**				8.13**		4.59*
% of WO	.04**		.04				.05**		.04	
FO	.06**		.08*				.06**		.05**	
Type of mediation	Partial mediation		Full mediation		No mediation		Partial mediation		Full Mediation	

Note. FO = Family Ownership; WO = Women Ownership; FP = Financial Performance

N.S. – Non-Significant, * $p < .05$, ** $p < .01$

when women can make the greatest difference for a family firm. In our case, the greater percentage of female ownership seems to bestow women with greater power to implement their ideas. Several studies show that women can develop important ideas (Gupta and Levenburg, 2013). However, they are likely to enact roles that are traditionally invisible and make it more difficult for their ideas to be heard and implemented (Gillis-Donovan and Moynihan-Bradt, 1990). Thus, it may be that they are not able to be heard and their ideas implemented unless they have control and power in the decision-making process and the implementation of strategy. It is important to acknowledge that in our study we assume that lower percentage of ownership in female hands indicates that the influence of women on firm decisions is lower than when they have higher ownership in the firm. In contrast, a high percentage of female ownership allows women a higher capacity to act and greater influence on the firm. Given these findings, we suggest that future research should continue to explore the role that women have in a firm and how this differs based on the percentage of women ownership in the firm.

A second contribution of our study comes from understanding the role that family ownership plays in the facilitation of women ownership in the firm. Previous studies in the context of entrepreneurship (see Mari et al., 2016) suggest that most of the research trying to understand female ownership and start-up of firms has focused on the individual characteristics of female entrepreneurs and how they affect their willingness to start and own a business. Our results suggest that family ownership creates an environment that promotes a higher percentage of female ownership in a firm. It seems that family ownership creates a context in which females can learn about ownership based on the observation of others, and their involvement in the firm. Thus, our results complement the work of Aldrich and Cliff (2003) who argue that the family embeddedness in a firm influences the behaviors of female members through the resources it provides to learn about ownership, the values that it presents to family members, and the norms and attitudes it helps develop.

Another contribution is tied to the differentiation within family firms. This study shows that family firms differ in their resources and that some of these resources (i.e., percentage of women ownership) are important in explaining family firm performance. Whether or not some resources are valuable to the firm depends on the opportunity that the family firm gives themselves to use and leverage them. In the case of women, a high percentage of ownership reflects one aspect of the openness of family firm to diversity, and may be a relevant factor that can help in functions of control and decision-making regarding the firm. Our results show that, at least in the Colombian context, when family firms are open to women participation in the workforce and in ownership of the firm, this participation increases financial returns.

This study also contributes to understand how the normative environment within a culture influences how women can contribute to the performance of the family firm. Our results suggest that the cultural norms that exist within each country can influence how and when women contribute to the performance of the firm. In this sense, our results duplicate those of Amore and colleagues

(2014). In particular, our results indicate that cultural norms that promote the participation and development of women in the workforce can provide positive context that can benefit from the unique characteristics that women bring to the work context. Instead of being conclusive, these results motivate more research that deepens our understanding of the influence of culture in family firms. A final contribution of our work comes from the context of our data. To our knowledge this is one of the first studies that focus on the effects of females on performance in a Latin American country. This is important because it provides a baseline to understand the effects that culture can have to understand how the presence of women can impact the firm.

Even though our study has important contributions, it also has its limitations. First, our data are based on information from 2008. It may be that during this time the economic conditions also played an important role in performance that we are not able to capture in our variables. Because of this, future research should try to replicate our results. A second limitation comes from the use of databases. Even though our data are very rich, it does not enable us to assess information in different ways. This should be a consideration for future research. Finally, we only consider a few factors that can affect performance of a firm this could limit our interpretation of the results. Given this, future research should consider additional factors that could also play a role when understanding the performance of a firm.

Notes

1 Information system for analyzing the financial statements of Colombian firms. This product originated in 1999 from the alliance between BPR and Casa Editorial El Tiempo.
2 In Colombia, individuals have two last names, and usually women do not change them when they get married. When a woman takes her husband's last name, it becomes her first or her second last name.

References

Adams, R. B., and Ferreira, D. (2009). Women in the boardroom and their impact on governance and performance. *Journal of Financial Economics*, 94(2), 291–309.
Adams, R. B., and Funk, P. (2012). Beyond the glass ceiling: Does gender matter? *Management Science*, 58(2), 219–235.
Aldrich, H. E., and Cliff, J. E. (2003). The pervasive effects of family on entrepreneurship: Toward a family embeddedness perspective. *Journal of Business Venturing*, 18(5), 573–596.
Amore, M. D., Garofalo, O., and Minichilli, A. (2014). Gender interactions within the family firm. *Management Science*, 60(5), 1083–1097.
Anderson, R. C., and Reeb, D. M. (2003). Founding-family ownership and firm performance: Evidence from the S&P 500. *The Journal of Finance*, 58(3), 1301–1328.
Astrachan, J. S., Klein, S. B., and Smyrnios, K. X. (2002). The F-PEC scale of family influence: A proposal for solving the family business definition problem. *Family Business Review*, 15(1), 45–58.

Bandura, A. (1977). *Social learning theory.* Oxford: Prentice-Hall

Baron, R. M., and Kenny, D. A. (1986). The moderator-mediator distinction in social psychological research: Conceptual, strategic, and statistical considerations. *Journal of Personality and Social Psychology*, 51(6), 1173–1182.

Baughn, C. C., Chua, B. L., and Neupert, K. E. (2006). The normative context for women's participation in entrepreneruship: A multicountry study. *Entrepreneurship Theory and Practice*, 30(5), 687–708.

Bear, S., Rahman, N., and Post, C. (2010). The impact of board diversity and gender composition on corporate social responsibility and firm reputation. *Journal of Business Ethics*, 97(2), 207–221.

Burgess, Z., and Tharenou, P. (2002). Women board directors: Characteristics of the few. *Journal of Business Ethics*, 37(1), 39–49.

Burke, R. J. (1997). Women on corporate boards of directors: A needed resource. *Journal of Business Ethics*, 16(9), 909–915.

Campbell, K., and Mínguez-Vera, A. (2008). Gender diversity in the boardroom and firm financial performance. *Journal of Business Ethics*, 83(3), 435–451. doi:10.1007/s10551-007-9630-y

Cappuyns, K. (2007). Women behind the scenes in family businesses. *Electronic Journal of Family Business Studies*, 1(1), 38–61.

Carter, D. A., Simkins, B. J., and Simpson, W. G. (2003). Corporate governance, board diversity, and firm value. *Financial Review*, 38(1), 33–53.

Chrisman, J. J., Chua, J. H., and Sharma, P. (2005). Trends and directions in the development of a strategic management theory of the family firm. *Entrepreneurship Theory and Practice*, 29(5), 555–576.

Cole, P. M. (1997). Women in family business. *Family Business Review*, 10(4), 353–371.

Cox, T. H., and Blake, S. (1991). Managing cultural diversity: Implications for organizational competitiveness. *The Executive*, 1, 45–56.

Cromie, S., and O'Sullivan, S. (1999). Women as managers in family firms. *Women in Management Review*, 14(3), 76–88.

Curimbaba, F. (2002). The dynamics of women's roles as family business managers. *Family Business Review*, 15(3), 239–252. doi:10.1111/j.1741-6248.2002.00239.x

Daily, C. M., Certo, S. T., and Dalton, D. R. (1999). A decade of corporate women: Some progress in the boardroom, none in the executive suite. *Strategic Management Journal*, 1, 93–99.

Dezsö, C. L., and Ross, D. G. (2012). Does female representation in top management improve firm performance? A panel data investigation. *Strategic Management Journal*, 33(9), 1072–1089. doi:10.1002/smj.1955

Dumas, C. (1989). Understanding of father – daughter and father – son dyads in family-owned businesses. *Family Business Review*, 2(1), 31–46.

Dumas, C. (1998). Women's pathways to participation and leadership in the family-owned firm. *Family Business Review*, 11(3), 219–228.

Dyer, W. G., and Whetten, D. A. (2006). Family firms and social responsibility: Preliminary evidence from the S&P 500. *Entrepreneurship Theory and Practice*, 30(6), 785–802.

Eagly, A. H., and Chaiken, S. (1993). *The psychology of attitudes.* Fort Worth, TX: Harcourt Brace Jovanovich College Publishers.

Etzioni, A. (1991). The socio-economics of property. *Journal of Social Behavior and Personality*,6(6), 465–468.

Fishbein, M., and Ajzen, I. (1975). *Belief, attitude, intention, and behaviour: An introduction to theory and research.* Reading, MA: Addison-Wesley.

Gersick, K. E., David, J. A., McCollom Hampton, M., and Lansberg, I. (1997). *Generation to generation: Life cycles of the family business.* Cambridge, MA: Harvard Business School Publishing India Pvt. Limited.

Gillis-Donovan, J., and Moynihan-Bradt, C. (1990). The power of invisible women in the family business. *Family Business Review,* 3(2), 153–167.

Gómez-Mejía, L. R., Haynes, K. T., Núñez-Nickel, M., Jacobson, K. J., and Moyano-Fuentes, J. (2007). Socioemotional wealth and business risks in family-controlled firms: Evidence from Spanish olive oil mills. *Administrative Science Quarterly,* 52(1), 106–137.

Gupta, V., and Levenburg, N. M. (2013). Women in family business: Three generations of research. In K. X. Smyrnios, P. Z. Poutziouris and S. Goel (eds.), *Handbook of research on family business* (2nd ed., pp. 346–367). Cheltenham: Edward Elgar Publishing.

Gutiérrez de Pineda, V. (2000). *Familia y cultura en Colombia: Tipologías, funciones y dinámica de la familia: manifestaciones múltiples a través del mosaico cultural y sus estructuras sociales* (Quinta ed.). Medellín: Editorial Universidad de Antioquia.

Hofstede, G. (1984). *Culture's consequences: International differences in work-related values* (vol. 5). London: Sage Publications.

Hollander, B. S., and Bukowitz, W. R. (1990). Women, family culture, and family business. *Family Business Review,* 3(2), 139–151. doi:10.1111/j.1741-6248.1990.00139.x

Jaffe, D. (1990). *Working with the ones you love: Strategies for a successful family business.* Emeryville, CA: Conari Press.

James, L. R., and Brett, J. N. (1984). Mediators, moderators, and test of mediation. *Journal of Applied Psychology,* 69(2), 307–321.

Jensen, M. C., and Meckling, W. H. (1976). Theory of the firm: Managerial behavior, agency costs and ownership structure. *Journal of Financial Economics,* 3(4), 305–360.

Krishnan, H. A., and Park, D. (2005). A few good women – on top management teams. *Journal of Business Research,* 58(12), 1712–1720.

Lerner, M., and Malach-Pines, A. (2011). Gender and culture in family business: A ten-nation study. *International Journal of Cross Cultural Management,* 11(2), 113–131.

Liu, Y., Wei, Z., and Xie, F. (2014). Do women directors improve firm performance in China? *Journal of Corporate Finance,* 28, 169–184.

Llano, C., and Olguin, F. (1986). La sucesión en la empresa familiar. *La Empresa Familiar,* 2, 1.

Lückerath-Rovers, M. (2013). Women on boards and firm performance. *Journal of Management & Governance,* 17(2), 491–509.

Lyman, A. R. (1989). Life in the family circle. *Women in Management Review,* 4(3), 383–398.

Mari, M., Poggesi, S., and De Vita, L. (2016). Family embeddedness and business performance: Evidences from women-owned firms. *Management Decision,* 54(2), 476–500.

Martinez Jimenez, R. (2009). Research on women in family firms: Current status and future directions. *Family Business Review,* 22(1), 53–64. doi:10.1177/089448 6508328813

Matthews, C. H., and Moser, S. B. (1996). A longitudinal investigation of the impact of family background and gender on interest in small firm ownership. *Journal of Small Business Management*, 34(2), 29–43.

Miller, D., Le Breton-Miller, I., Lester, R. H., and Cannella Jr., A. A. (2007). Are family firms really superior performers? *Journal of Corporate Finance*, 13(5), 829–858.

Morrison, A. M., White, R. P., and Van Velsor, E. (1992). *Breaking the glass ceiling: Can women reach the top of America's largest corporations?* New York: Basic Books.

Nielsen, S., and Huse, M. (2010). Women directors' contribution to board decision-making and strategic involvement: The role of equality perception. *European Management Review*, 7(1), 16–16–29.

Pfeffer, J., and Salancik, G. R. (1978). *The external control of organizations: A resource dependence perspective.* New York: Harper and Row.

Pierce, J. L., Rubenfeld, S. A., and Morgan, S. (1991). Employee ownership: A conceptual model of process and effects. *Academy of Management Review*, 16(1), 121–144.

Poza, E. J., and Messer, T. (2001). Spousal leadership and continuity in the family firm. *Family Business Review*, 14(1), 25–36.

Robinson, G., and Dechant, K. (1997). Building a business case for diversity. *The Academy of Management Executive*, 11(3), 21–31.

Rowe, B. R., and Hong, G. S. (2000). The role of wives in family businesses: The paid and unpaid work of women. *Family Business Review*, 13, 1–13.

Rutherford, M. W., Kuratko, D. F., and Holt, D. T. (2008). Examining the link between "familiness" and performance: Can the F-PEC untangle the family business theory jungle? *Entrepreneurship: Theory & Practice*, 32(6), 1089–1109.

Salganicoff, M. (1990). Women in family businesses: Challenges and opportunities. *Family Business Review*, 3(2), 125–137.

Sharma, P. (2004). An overview of the field of family business studies: Current status and directions for the future. *Family Business Review*, 17(1), 1–36.

Sharma, P., and Chua, J. H. (2013). Asian family enterprises and family business research. *Asian Pacific Journal of Management*, 30(3), 641–656.

Shrader, C. B., Blackburn, V. B., and Iles, P. (1997). Women in management and firm financial performance: An exploratory study. *Journal of Managerial Issues*, 9(3), 355–372.

Smith, N., Smith, V., and Verner, M. (2006). Do women in top management affect firm performance? A panel study of 2,500 Danish firms. *International Journal of Productivity and Performance Management*, 55(7), 569–593.

Vieito, J. P. T. (2012). Gender, top management compensation gap, and company performance: Tournament versus behavioral theory. *Corporate Governance: An International Review*, 20(1), 46–63. doi:10.1111/j.1467-8683.2011.00878.x

Villalonga, B., and Amit, R. (2006). How do family ownership, control and management affect firm value? *Journal of Financial Economics*, 80(2), 385–417.

Ward, J. L. (1987). *Keeping the family business healthy: How to plan for continuing growth, profitability, and family leadership.* San Francisco, CA: Jossey-Bass.

Ward, J. L., and Sorenson, L. S. (1989). The role of mom. *Nation's Business*, 11(77), 40–41.

Wiersema, M. F., and Bantel, K. A. (1992). Top management team demography and corporate strategic change. *Academy of Management Journal*, 35(1), 91–121.

10 Female entrepreneurship in developing contexts

Characteristics, challenges, and dynamics

*Andrea Caputo, Luisa De Vita,
Michela Mari and Sara Poggesi*

Introduction

The economic impact of female entrepreneurship is increasing on a daily basis (e.g., Ramadani et al., 2015; Ramadani et al., 2015) and its contribution is noticeable worldwide (Dana, 1992). In 2010, research suggested that 187 million women were involved in entrepreneurial enterprises, which is almost 42 percent overall (GEM, 2010).

It is important to note that, surprisingly, this happens mostly in less-developed countries. For example, female entrepreneurs exist at a rate of 41 percent in Nigeria and Zambia, whereas they have a much lower number of only 2 percent in Japan (GEM, 2014). Not only that, but 61 out of the 83 economies included in the Global Entrepreneurship Monitor (GEM) report (2014) shows an increase in the gender gap between men and women entrepreneurs equal to 6 percent. The reason for this increase is often down to the difficulties women face working in employment that lead them to consider entrepreneurship as a way to make a living for themselves and their families (Poggesi, Mari, and De Vita, 2015).

Despite the studies that have already been done, there is a need for more research into the role female entrepreneurship plays, from a social perspective as well as an economic point of view (Caputo et al., 2016; De Vita et al., 2014). Economically, these women are a fundamental driver for growth; socially they are challenging gender stereotypes, or in other words "the behaviors, attitudes, values, beliefs and so on that a particular cultural group considers appropriate for males and females on the basis of their biological sex" (Bland, 2005).

This chapter to shed light on the main characteristics, challenges, and dynamics that female entrepreneurs have in developing countries. In particular, this is the result of bringing together results from ongoing research projects carried out by the authors in the last few years (e.g., Caputo, Lombardi et al., 2016; Caputo et al., 2016; De Vita et al., 2014).

To address the goal of this chapter, a critical review on research papers published on this topic is performed. The results of this review are categorized into six clusters – i.e., East Asia and the Pacific, Eastern Europe and Central Asia, Latin America and Caribbean, South Asia, Sub-Saharan Africa, and the Middle

East and North Africa – according to the World Bank's classification. Such a categorization allows cultural, political, and religious impacts to be included in this analysis, as well as considerations on legal and socio-cultural context.

Each region is the subject of one section in the chapter. Each section offers an overview of entrepreneurship in the region, and then presents the main trends in female entrepreneurship, identifying gaps and future research directions. After focusing the six regions identified, the chapter will then focus on Jordan, to provide insights into the different facets of female entrepreneurship in that country. Jordan is a country of particular interest because, as reported by GEM (2010), it shows one of the lowest rate of women in the labor force in the world. Although women generally have a high level of literacy, they still struggle to find employment (Itani et al., 2011). As a recent consequence, women are turning to entrepreneurship (Itani et al., 2011), leading Jordan to be one of the most active entrepreneurial economies in the Middle East, which, despite its small dimension, produces 75 percent of the region's online Arabic content (U.S. Department of Commerce, 2014).

East Asia and the Pacific

This is a massive region that incorporates some very different countries, such as China, Indonesia, Malaysia and Korea, varying in economic situation, history, culture, and values. In this region coexist low-income countries, such as Lao PDR, and high-income areas, such as Hong Kong, which is in the country with the highest number of citizens. Moreover, certain economies in this region are based on Confucian principles, according to which it is mandatory to coexist and work together to help one another out (for example, China and Thailand), and others are restricted by socialist-oriented regulations which make things very challenging.

The integration between these countries can be very difficult because of the above depicted differences. However, two elements seem to pool these countries: 1. The economic growth and 2. the low level of female inclusion in the economy.

Specifically focusing on the second point, female entrepreneurs in East Asia and Pacific countries face lots of barriers that are very difficult to overcome. The main issue starts early on, in education, as shown by a research paper written by the United Nations Economic and Social Commission for Asia and the Pacific (UNESCAP), which points out that the region is "losing $42 to 47 billion per year because of restrictions on women's access to employment opportunities, and another $16 to 30 billion per year because of gender gaps in education" (UNESCAP, 2007). There have been improvements in the gender gap in labor employment in recent years – for example North and Central Asia have more than90 females employed for every 100 males – but when it comes to entrepreneurship, the gender gap is still very noticeable. However, differences exist among countries: Malaysia shows indeed a high percentage of women entrepreneurs while China and Korea do not (GEM, 2010).

Research trends and topics in East Asia and the Pacific

Research into this area is mainly focused on the religious aspects affecting female entrepreneurs, atopic that has not been examined very closely before now. Results show that religion has a massive impact on entrepreneurship, particularly in countries such as Malaysia or Cambodia, and this may be in a positive or negative way (Audretsch et al., 2007).

Research has have shown that the behaviors associated with certain religions, such as ethic and social responsibility, can factor greatly towards success. For example, entrepreneurial women in Islamic cultures – who comply with religious rules – result to be very confident, smart, and capable of overcoming any barriers (Faud and Bohari, 2011). Obviously, this positive view is not the same everywhere. Female entrepreneurs who adhere to Confucian principles are often perceived as shameful, and in some cases, even disrespectful.

Specifically focusing on Malaysia and its culture (Ahmad and Seet, 2010), it emerges that women have played a massive role during the country's financial hardship (Alam et al., 2011), and that the Islamic influence on the economy is worth of noting (Faud and Bohari, 2011). The high number of female firms can be explained by considering the family support, social ties, and a culture that motivate women to go for what they want (Alam et al., 2011).

There *are* barriers, but Malaysian women seem to have overcome them or even have used them to boost their success. They work ethically and in a socially responsible way, actually enhancing tolerance in the country (Ahmad and Seet, 2010). This is very similar to what happens in Indonesia (Singh et al.,2001), although women's success there can be attributed to the total number of family workers in the industry sector.

For what concerns the Chinese economy, room for research still exists above all considering the economic relevance of the country as well as its socio-cultural context that, in the past, led women away from entrepreneurship. Worth mentioning is the fact that private firms have only been legal since 1988. Thus, it would be surely relevant to deepen the gendered consequences of China's transition from socialism to capitalism (Berik et al., 2007).

For example, a study conducted by Enhai in 2011 found, by looking at 3,012 private firms, that companies run by females were smaller in staffing and revenue. However, another study conducted by Tan in 2008 discovered that Chinese female entrepreneurs were more likely to "take more risks and make bolder moves in pursuit of greater returns and future competitive advantage" (p. 547). This information does not really give us a lot of information to go on, a lot more needs to be done for more conclusive evidence.

Korea provides another interesting case to be examined, one with a massive gender gap where women make up only 2.1 percent of the a total early-stage entrepreneurial activity rate (TEA). A research paper written by Lee, Sohn, and Ju in 2011 found that women felt like they needed more support from the government to be truly happy and successful in entrepreneurship.

In Cambodia, Laos, and Vietnam (Ardrey et al., 2006; Gerrard et al., 2003; Inmyxai and Takahashi, 2010; Rand and Tarp, 2011) special training programs for women entrepreneurs are highlighted, but the role of the Confucianism religion is stressed, as able to affect how people work.

Transition economies of Eastern Europe and Central Asia

When the global economic crisis hit, affecting crucial transmission channels, reducing wages, and causing job losses, the transition countries of Eastern Europe and Central Asia were among the hardest hit (LiTS, 2011). The consequences of the economic crisis affected many areas of the economy, among which we can remember the opportunity for female entrepreneurship.

Data, indeed, suggest that the number of women entrepreneurs is growing in transitioning countries; however, its overall number is still much lower than their male counterparts (GEM, 2010),

The only exception to the rule is Russia, where women represent 44 percent of all entrepreneurs. However, this can be put down to the fact that it is a post-communist country allowing a large increase of new firms to arise, giving women much more opportunity to get into the workplace.

Despite this trend seen in Russia, the area as whole gives women a lot of barriers to overcome, providing them with an extra layer of vulnerability that men do not have. Lacks of Government support, little access to business networks, and no financial assistance, have put women off entrepreneurship.

Research trends and topics in transition economies

Without access to start-up capital (i.e., Manolova et al., 2006), basic skill training, and support (i.e., Salmenniemi et al., 2011), even the companies that are started by women have very little room to grow in this area (i.e., Manolova et al., 2007; Yordanova, 2011).

Among the different issues investigated in this cluster, that of networking seems particularly relevant. Aidis, Smallbone, and Isakova (2007) in particular, found women's networking to be much weaker than business ties established by men.

Turkey presents an interesting case in this cluster. Among mature firms, only one woman to every five men is a registered business owner (GEM, 2010), which is easy to understand when the specific patriarchal socio-cultural context is considered (Ufuk and Özgen, 2001). One study, in particular, found this constraint to be even more difficult to overcome for women living in rural areas (Yetim, 2008).

Latin America and the Caribbean

There has been progress in the Latin America and Caribbean region for women in recent years; for example, new gender equality rules have been included in many countries belonging to this cluster (The World Bank, 2016): Jamaica repealed the 1942 restriction for night work for women, Mexico has made child care payments tax deductible, and Uruguay has increased the length of maternity and paternity leave. On top of this, Nicaragua has brought in paternity leave to give both sexes equal rights in the household, and has also raised the minimum age of marriage for girls and boys, while improving women's property rights in divorce cases.

However, even as strides are being made in the gender equality area, women are not allowed to hold the same jobs as men in 16 economies in this region. For example, women in Belize are not allowed to do night work in factories, or handle goods at a dock, and Honduras and Colombia restrict women from undertaking jobs that are considered to be hazardous.

Turning to female entrepreneurship, a recent World Bank–IFC (International Finance Corporation) Enterprise survey found that more than 40 percent of companies registered in Latin America and the Caribbean are owned by women. When it comes to laws helping women into business, Colombia, Costa Rica, Trinidad, and Tobago have helped women with companies in small claims court by raising the maximum threshold of a claim, and Jamaica has opened a new credit bureau that offers smaller loans and gives more access to credit, but there is still a long way to go.

Research trends and topics in Latin America and the Caribbean

Financing for business is a massive roadblock for women in this area of the world. Even in areas where women are proved to be the higher educated sex, they still have difficulties finding the resources for their own start-up business (Smith-Hunter and Leone, 2010a,2010b).

Many studies have looked into this, most notably in Guatemala (Kevane and Wydick, 2001), Paraguay (Fletschner and Carter, 2008), and Trinidad and Tobago (Storey, 2004). Specifically, Kevane and Wydick (2001) look at the impact that the childbearing years has on the woman's ability to get credit; Fletschner and Carter (2008) examine social norms and expectations that are put upon females, and Storey (2004) analyzes the difference in successful loan applications and bank rates between men and women.

The clearest picture of female entrepreneurship in this region is surely provided by Terjesen and Amoros (2010). The authors consider 13 different Latin American and Caribbean countries and examine how best the female entrepreneurs could be (and in some cases, are being) supported.

South Asia

South Asia is currently among the lowest region in terms of the number of women participating in the workforce. The potential for female entrepreneurs is seemingly ignored, thus preventing social and economic growth. Only 8 percent to 9 percent of micro, small, or medium enterprises are owned by women, with Bangladesh and Pakistan rating the lowest score among all of the countries examined in the GEM report. Discriminatory laws can be blamed for this as it is incredibly difficult in this region for women to get any kind of recognition. This unfortunately does not seem to be changing any time soon. Only three reforms have been made to the restrictive laws in two economies in the past couple of years. Without any major changes, there no chance of things improving.

India is an example of this problem: In the region's biggest economy, including a population of 612 million women, job restrictions make it very difficult for women to get by. They cannot work in the mining industry, or with heavy lifting over a certain threshold, nor can they work with glass. Anything that is "involving danger to life, health or morals" is off limits for women. On top of this, there is no protection against sexual harassment in public places (The World Bank, 2015).

Education can also form a massive barrier in South Asia (Salze-Lozac'h, 2011). Limited access to a formal education, combined with lack of training, and credit that is almost impossible to get, makes it impossible to close the gender gap.

Research trends and topics in South Asia

Studies into this geographical region often examine how women could boost the economy thanks to entrepreneurship. Researchers who study this area examine the lack of social acceptance that comes with a woman desiring to run her own business, or even doing so but with little to no room for growth. They also discuss how microcredit and training opportunities could reform this dramatically. If women were given the skills, education, and support they needed, plus access to start-up money, the economy would see a big upturn (Ayadurai and Sohail, 2006; Bhatti et al., 2010).

India is the most widely analyzed country, and the findings in this area demonstrate how its social caste system still strongly affects women and their chance to start their own business. To date, businesses being run successfully by female entrepreneurs are often non-profit and very small (Handy et al., 2007; Menon and van der Meulen, 2011; Nagadevara, 2009).

Indian women are also restricted by the social expectations put upon them. Indeed, they cannot consider growing their enterprises at the expense of their first and most important job: i.e., supporting family and social relationships (Mitra, 2002). For this to change, and for more women to become entrepreneurs, society as a whole and the individual families will need to be much more supportive (Pandian et al., 2011). Other scholars (such as Kantor, 2005), agree with this, suggesting that if women were given more power at home, then this will help them to translate this power into entrepreneurial success.

However, as shown by studies grounded on Bangladesh, this is not always enough. Women may be more aware of their possibilities and capabilities (Afrin et al., 2010; Kabir and Huo, 2011), but the economic and cultural restrictions still marginalize their opportunities, thus highlighting the need for more microcredit support programs to be set up.

Sub-Saharan Africa

Data that have been collected on gender equality and the empowerment of women in Sub-Saharan Africa suggest that women face a very difficult environment. They face a much higher gender gap than other geographical areas when it comes to education and property rights. Moreover, the economic rights are tailored much more towards men.

The legal system is extremely complex, with countries overlapping their laws and practices leaving the economic rights of the women very insecure. While this does not actively prevent women from starting up their own enterprise, it does impact tremendously on their chances for success and growth. If anything is accomplished, the business will be small with very little profits.

Access to financial support and credit is an issue that is faced by both genders in Sub-Saharan Africa, with companies finding themselves 40 percent less likely to get any access to credits than anywhere else. While this *does* impact men, it has a much higher effect on women trying to get start-up capital.

However, despite this, half the entrepreneurs in Sub-Saharan Africa are women (GEM, 2010). However, they generally work in the informal sector, creating crafts or offering personal services. Moreover, by investigating the firm's dimension, the number of female entrepreneurs running companies with five or more employees is significantly lower than men.

Research trends and topics in Sub-Saharan Africa

There are many elements affecting women's ability to go into business in this area; among them, the main reason is definitely related to women's family responsibilities. Women have on average five or six children, all of whom need looking after, and it is the social norm for women to take charge of this (Amine and Staub, 2009; Belwal et al., 2012; Singh et al., 2010). On top of this, there is not much social recognition for female entrepreneurs. In fact, women who run their own companies are viewed negatively, not considered chaste or respectable at all. Any females who find success in business are seen as unsuitable mothers and wives (Singh et al., 2010).

These cultural norms are extremely restrictive, and cause a big roadblock for women who are trying to find customers and other business owners to network with (Singh et al., 2010).

Then there is the problem with training and education. Without the correct knowledge and skills at their disposal, it is very challenging for women to compete in such a male-dominated area (Chirwa, 2008). Furthermore, if they cannot add value, then their firms quickly become overlooked (Belwal et al., 2012).

However, research papers *have* noticed some important changes in progress. Access to credit is becoming more readily available for women; now at 14.9 percent, compared to 7.7 percent of men (Belwal et al., 2012). This is allowing women to gain access to business in urban, peri-urban, and rural regions (Chirwa, 2008).

This change has begun to lead to new, broader attitudes too. Money lenders are becoming happier to lend to women as they are perceived as more community-oriented than men (as shown by the numbers). They are also considered as motivated, particularly when educated and free from family ties (Aterido and Hallward-Driemeier, 2011; Garba, 2011;Mahadea, 2001; Singh et al., 2010).

These changes affect the socio-cultural acceptance of female entrepreneurs as a whole. People are starting to evaluate positively rather negatively the way in which women network within their own community (Rutashobya et al., 2009). Women tend to use the role of the Church in their interactions too, with positive outcomes for the economy (Kuada, 2009).

Middle East and North Africa

The situation in the Middle East provides some unusual data when examining female entrepreneurs. GEM and the World Bank have discovered in their research that compared to other developing countries, this region has the lowest participation of female labor force employees in the world. This leaves entrepreneurship as a great way for women to generate their own income (see Figure 10.1, Figure 10.2 and Figure 10.3).

The region shows a big gap between entrepreneurial intentions and actual start-ups, which suggests that there are a lot of potential entrepreneurs who are not actually doing anything. This is particularly relevant to women. For every one female entrepreneur, six more have declared their desire to start a business. When you consider that for every male entrepreneur, there are two and half who have only declared their intentions, the gender gap is obvious.

This simply highlights the impact that women *could* be having on the economy. They could be making positive development in all kinds of areas. Thus, it is very important to understand why this is not happening, and what barriers are in the way.

It is among the cultural norms for women in the Middle East to wholly engage in household activities. They are not often involved in external activities, so travel and dealing with markets does not come as naturally to them. Women who do wish to get into entrepreneurship have to juggle their business with ensuring that the family is well looked after, which can be very challenging to manage.

In some countries, women are also deprived of a good education, and they are kept away from family businesses too, which leaves them without the necessary skills to run things for themselves. It can be extremely challenging to write a business plan, negotiate finance, and do market research without any experience with it at all. The mindset of the society is very male oriented, which obviously impacts on women's desire to take that brave step. Despite the many steps some countries are making towards empowering women, the situation is still unsatisfactory in many others. Governments in the Middle East need to take steps towards building better education and training programs to make these positive reforms (Mathew, 2010). As women often need the permission of their husbands or fathers to apply for anything, they are often discouraged before they even get started. In fact, by closely examining the current female-run businesses in this

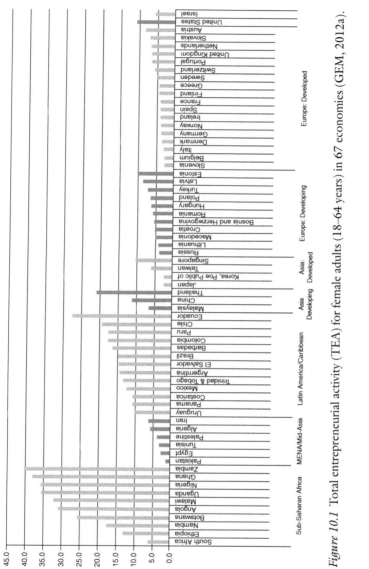

Figure 10.1 Total entrepreneurial activity (TEA) for female adults (18–64 years) in 67 economies (GEM, 2012a).

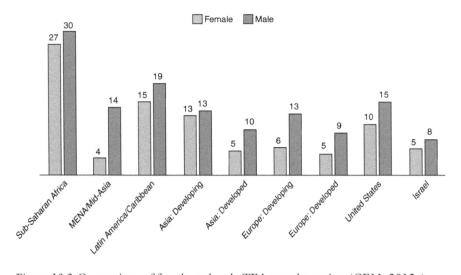

Figure 10.2 Comparison of female and male TEA rates by region (GEM, 2012a).

	Nascent Prevalence Rate			New Business Owner Prevalence Rate			Established Business Owner Prevalence Rate		
	Male	Female	Male to Female Ratio	Male	Female	Male to Female Ratio	Male	Female	Male to Female Ratio
	%	%		%	%		%	%	
Palestine	4.7	1.2	3.9:1	9.4	2.2	4.3:1	11.1	2.5	4.4:1
Jordan	9.2	2.4	3.8:1	7.5	2.3	3.3:1	9.1	1.3	7:1
Syria	4.9	1.8	2.7:1	8.7	1.4	6.2:1	11.9	1.3	9.2:1
Lebanon	8.8	4.8	1.8:1	12.4	5.5	2.3:1	25.3	7.5	3.4:1
Yemen	27.9	17.6	1.6:1	1.1	1.2	0.9:1	3.1	2.7	1.1:1
Algeria	12.8	9.7	1.3:1	7.4	3.7	2:1	6.4	2.9	2.2:1
Morocco	7.9	6.0	1.3:1	13.1	5.7	2.3:1	23.6	6.7	3.5:1

Figure 10.3 Gender gap in entrepreneurial activity rates in seven GEM–MENA countries (GEM, 2012a)

Table 10.1 Narrowing gender gap in entrepreneurial activity rates

	Nascent prevalence rate			New business owner prevalence rate			Established business owner prevalence rate		
	Male	*Female*	*Male to Female Ratio*	*Male*	*Female*	*Male to Female Ratio*	*Male*	*Female*	*Male to Female Ratio*
	percent	*percent*		*percent*	*percent*		*percent*	*percent*	
Palestine	4.7	1.2	3.9:1	9.4	2.2	4.3:1	11.1	2.5	4.4:1
Jordan	9.2	2.4	3.8:1	7.5	2.3	3.3:1	9.1	1.3	7:1
Syria	4.9	1.8	2.7:1	8.7	1.4	6.2:1	11.9	1.3	9.2:1
Lebanon	8.8	4.8	1.8:1	12.4	5.5	2.3:1	25.3	7.5	3.4:1
Yemen	27.9	17.6	1.6:1	1.1	1.2	0.9:1	3.1	2.7	1.1:1
Algeria	12.8	9.7	1.3:1	7.4	3.7	2:1	6.4	2.9	2.2:1
Morocco	7.9	6.0	1.3:1	13.1	5.7	2.3:1	23.6	6.7	3.5:1

area, they are normally family owned, and the females run businesses what are considered to be women's areas, such as wedding planning or family advice.

Research trends and topics in the Middle East and North Africa (MENA)

Research into the role of women in the MENA region focuses mainly on social segregation and the barriers females are faced with in Middle Eastern countries. The fact that the region has the lowest level of female participation in the work-force in the world despite the high levels of literacy (GEM, 2009) is always a focal point of any study. It seems to be that male domination impacts on the fact that women are unable to gain employment (Itani et al., 2011). This results in low levels of confidence and the reinforcement of the belief that their lack of skills and knowledge in terms of business will hold them back (De Bruin et al., 2006, 2007; Ettl and Welter, 2010).

The World Bank and Verme (2014) have suggested that these countries are actually turning towards something positive, and that the

> jobless growth and the lack of growth in employment sectors such as manu-facturing and services, which proved critical for female employment in other countries, weaken labor demand and strengthen the role of institutions that may discourage female participation, such as marriage, legislation, and gen-der norms.

What this tells us is that the average age women leave employment is 25 years old, which is also the average age of marriage (GEM, 2009; The World Bank, 2005; Verme, 2014). This is the perfect time to transform these women into entrepreneurs, giving them the independence of their own income and helping them to boost the lifestyle of their family.

The Arab world is noticing female entrepreneurship with growing attention, given the growing numbers. The more it becomes the cultural norm, the easier a path will be (Itani et al., 2011). There have been many studies, attempting to profile the typical female entrepreneur, in the United Arab Emirates (Goby and Erogul, 2011; Itani et al., 2011; Naser et al., 2009), Saudi Arabia (Ahmad, 2011; Welsh et al., 2014), Jordan (Al-Dajani and Marlow, 2010; Mehtap, 2014), Bahrain and Oman (Dechant and Lamky, 2005; Khan, 2013; McElwee and Al-Riyami, 2003), Yemen (Ahmad and Xavier, 2011), Iran (Hosseini and McElwee, 2011; Movahedi and Yaghoubi-Farani, 2012), Morocco (Gray and Finley-Hervey, 2005), and Lebanon (Jamali, 2009). There have also been papers written about the whole country (Hattab, 2012) and industry-specific studies (Mathew, 2010; Welsh and Raven, 2006). These studies, plus a comparative one of women entrepreneurs in Algeria, Egypt, Lebanon, Morocco, Syria, West Bank, and the Gaza Strip and Yemen, showed that female entrepreneurs in this region are between the ages of 25 and 44, well educated, usually married and living mostly in urban areas (Hattab, 2012).

The women in business in this geographical area have a lot of social barriers to overcome. The MENA region is very challenging for access to funding, support, and family involvement. It is hard for female entrepreneurs to get start-up help from their relatives when the Government and society does not.

The difficulties in gaining access to start-up capital is a general problem for both male and female entrepreneur (e.g., Smith-Hunter and Boyd, 2004) although it is much more challenging for women. As previously stated, they often need permission and a co-signature from a male family member. This can discourage them from even trying, or can be a barrier before they even try. If their husband or father says "no", there is not much that they can do (Welsh et al., 2014). A study conducted by Itani et al. (2011), which is supported by another research paper by Ahmad (2011), discovered that the female entrepreneurs in the area actually ended up using their own capital as start-up, to overcome this barrier.

This is another reason why women use the entrepreneurial path of opting into the family business, rather than starting up alone (De Vita et al., 2014). It also helps them to feel more protected and legitimate, and this social acceptance gives them confidence to work more effectively. Male business owners usually tend to respond better when their business counterpart is a male. Indeed, if a woman works as a sole owner of a business, this generally sparks the assumption that her male family members cannot provide for her and for the family (Zeidan and Bahrami, 2011), which is embarrassing and the reason that most men do not agree to co-sign anything (Al-Alak and Al-Haddad, 2010; Al-Dajani and Marlow, 2010). Without this consent, the patriarchal society in the Middle East will not help female entrepreneurs at all (Al-Alak and Al-Haddad, 2010; Goby and Erogul, 2011; Itani et al., 2011; McElwee and Al-Riyami, 2003).

This is even more unfair when you consider the fact that despite the essential need for permission from a male relative, female entrepreneurs are expected to pursue their careers without affecting their ability to look after the home, support their husbands, and care for their children. These responsibilities as a wife and mother cannot be compromised (Al-Dajani and Marlow, 2010). A research paper focused on Jordan, in particular, found that women entrepreneurs were necessary to running the home with a critical financial contribution, but that they also needed to run the home. To make this work, they construct their entrepreneurial activities around the preservation of the family home, limiting the challenges that face them. They have discovered a way to make the patriarchal system work for them (Al-Dajani and Marlow, 2010).

This certainly is not the case everywhere, though: Higher-income environments, such as the United Arab Emirates, report a different attitude from female entrepreneurs entirely. They do not feel like there is a conflict between their home and business life at all (Itani et al., 2011; Naser et al., 2009). Without this frustration, they find it a lot easier to focus. A lot of the female entrepreneurs in this area have full-time domestic help, saving them the worry of running the household, allowing them to concentrate on their work (Ahmad, 2011; Goby and Erogul, 2011; McElwee and Al-Riyami, 2003; Naser et al., 2009). This work and family life balance is much more of an obstacle to running a business in areas with lower reported incomes, such as Lebanon (Jamali, 2009).

When surveying female business students in Jordan, Mehtap (2014) discovered that the majority of them were not aware that there were local and national initiatives designed to encourage and finance new companies. These opportunities for start-ups are one of the most under-utilized sources of funding in Jordan, which was clearly down to the lack of successful communication about it (GEM, 2009). The next section will delve into Jordan much deeper, examining the society as a whole and its impact on entrepreneurship.

Female entrepreneurship in Jordan

Despite the fact that the Hashemite Kingdom of Jordan is situated in an area suffering a lot of widely reported turmoil, this developing country is also very stable and it is encouraging female entrepreneurship (Caputo, Mehtap et al., 2016). Aside from the Gulf region, Jordan is one of the few countries in the Middle East that fosters a safe, vibrant business environment. The fact that there are a number of multinational, successful companies running there is evidence of this.

There is an estimated population of around 8 million people in Jordan, over half of these people are under the age of 24, which makes Jordan a very interesting case to study. Half the population has Palestinian origins, and more than six hundred thousand people living there are registered refugees from Syria and Iraq, making for a heterogeneous population. The Shiite Muslim religion dominates, with a whopping 92 percent of the population, with various Christian denominations, Shi'a Muslims, and Druze taking up the final 8 percent. Ethnically, Jordan consists of mostly Arabs, with some Circassians and Chechens.

The society as a whole is collectivist, paternalistic, patriarchal, and tribal, and all of this plays a huge role in the way the country is governed. The religion of Jordan is hugely important to social norms, gender expectations, and restrictions people face. Sharia law forms the legal system of the country. The Islamic religion might be practiced differently from country to country, but the impact is still great.

The population level of Jordan is very high, but the country as a whole suffers from lack of natural resources. The services sector makes up more than 70 percent of the economy (The World Bank, 2015). Because of this, Jordan is forced to rely heavily on foreign aid.

While women make up the majority of the population of Jordan, a variety of economic, social, and cultural factors make it harder for them to seek business success. The predominant view of women's role is that they need to be committed only to their homes and families (Abdalla, 1996; El-Rahmony, 2002). This leaves men as the primary breadwinners, so if their women work that is regarded as somehow a failure on the men's ability to provide for the family. This mindset explains why on 25 percent of the labor workforce are female. They have the literacy levels, but no available (Barcucci and Mryyan, 2014; ILO, 2014).

There is a belief among some that Islam is to blame for the limited rights of women. It is suggested to actively encourage gender discrimination (Ahmad and Xavier, 2011; Al-Sadi et al., 2013; Itani et al., 2011). Of course, this is not the reality; when interpreted correctly Islam actually provides women with a lot of legal and economic freedoms including the ability to manage their own businesses and money.

This is clearly demonstrated in the case of Khadija, the wife of the prophet Mohammed (peace be upon him). She was a successful businesswoman who employed the prophet on a commission basis. If Islam were such a constraining religion, this wouldn't be considered a suitable part of the sacred text. Despite this, even though women have high levels of literacy (Barcucci and Mryyan, 2014; Majcher-Teleon and Slimène, 2009), it is still considered the norm to look for a husband and start a family, rather than looking for a career (Hakki and Somach, 2012).

Moving to a more political and economical context, the Government of Jordan have had aims to increase access to higher education, helping the society as a whole to become much more knowledge based. This has been successful to date, with school enrollment at a much higher level than the previous century. Research shows that the literacy rates in 1952 were only 33 percent, whereas they rose to 85 percent in 1996, and again to 94 percent in 2009. Being the highest spender on education in the region has had a big impact. Around 230,000 students are currently enrolled in public and private universities, and community colleges (TEMPUS, 2012). Yet, the high literacy rates have not impacted as positively on the unemployment figures as hoped. For the 15- to 24-yearold age range, the unemployment rate still stands at almost 30 percent (Central Intelligence Agency, 2014).

The possibilities for entrepreneurship in Jordan, with the high population and good education, are very high. This has been seen with the boom in the Information Communication Technology sector in Jordan, which is slowly spreading into other areas in the region. The hope is that this will continue, fueling prosperity. In fact, the region is so keen for this to happen that fostering entrepreneurship is actually set out as a priority in the Jordan national agenda (Caputo, Lombardi et al., 2016), and the new educational agendas are significantly helping with these brand new business ventures (Galloway and Brown, 2002; Lüthje and Franke, 2002).

This is helping women get into business themselves, and female entrepreneurship is increasing and becoming a growing market. Over the last decade, a steady and noticeable number of women have declared themselves as entrepreneurs, and more are doing so all the time (Hattab, 2010). Studies have discovered that women are doing this for a source of their own income, and as a way to prove themselves. Now that they *can* achieve more things, this is what they want to do. Of course, even with all of this success Jordanian women are expected not to compromise their role in the home. Their job as a wife and mother must still come first (Al-Dajani and Marlow, 2010).

A research paper written by Caputo, Mehtap, and colleagues (2016) discovered the importance of institutions that provide support for female entrepreneurs in Jordan. The study analyzed 28 of these and concluded that the curve towards a more female-friendly economy is having positive results, but that more is needed to be done to nurture these opportunities. This is also shown in the study conducted by Mehtap (2014), which found that better education and training is key. The author used the case of the European Union to highlight this, by discussing how the European university partnerships under the EU-TEMPUS framework developed very successful graduate and undergraduate entrepreneurship courses.

Participation in this type of entrepreneurial education and associated events has led to higher motivational levels in Jordan business students for creating their own start-up company (Caputo, Lombardi et al., 2016). Two focuses on Jordan's activities in fostering female entrepreneurs follow.

Jordan focus 1 – supporting opportunities for female entrepreneurs

Caputo, Mehtap, Pellegrini, and Al-Refai conducted a study in 2016 to examine the real-world opportunities for these highly educated women in Jordan in terms of support for their start-up. The authors examined 22 institutions set up to offer support for entrepreneurs in a hope of discovering how women truly found it.

A large log of case studies were examined (Yin, 2014), with a closer look on the context of environment that ever before (Dana, 1995; Dana and Dana, 2008; Light and Dana, 2013). Although similar studies have been carried out (Dana, 1995; Dana and Dana, 2008; Light and Dana, 2013; Ramadani et al., 2013) this study was not as specific and examined all the support areas for female entrepreneurs in Jordan.

They faced a lot of challenges in collecting a comprehensive set of data for the support resources available in the region, because they found it to be very different everywhere. In the less-developed regions, it was difficult to discover anything at all (Ramadani, 2015; Ramadani et al., 2013). Without an existing database with all of this information already registered, as can be found in other areas, the authors were limited in what they could examine.

The 22 entrepreneurial support organizations examined for this study in Jordan have been categorized by the background of the business, the services offered (financial support, training services, mentoring, etc.), and also any support specifically tailored towards female entrepreneurs. Out of the 22 places looked at, 14 of them classified themselves at non-profit organizations, 4 private companies, and the final 4 were registered as public organizations – either for the Jordanian government (such as *JEDCO*) or a foreign government (such as *MEPI*).

All of the businesses were based in Amman, but claim to operate throughout the whole of Jordan, and offered a variety of services: seven of them incubation (32 percent), 12 offered training (59 percent), consulting services made up seven of them (32 percent), seven of them offered direct funding (32 percent), four offered microcredit (18 percent), and six offered networking (27 percent). Of course, a lot of these services were offered by more than one institution. Only 6 offered only the one service.

The support centers that offered female-specific support for entrepreneurship include the King Hussein and Queen Noor Foundations. Here, they cater to women who have companies in the north and south of Jordan under their WAGE

(Women and Girls Empowerment) program. This has helped women, particularly those from rural areas, to recognize the potential entrepreneurship offers. They then have access to varying levels of training to assist them with their start-up.

As a partner to the WAGE program, the Jordanian Micro Credit Company (Tamweelcom) helps out female entrepreneurs with finances. They offer start-up capital and micro financing to get people up and running. Tamweelcom actually started out in 1999 as a non-profit organization, funded by *USAID*, but is now financially independent and has 21 branches all across the country. The aim is to reach out to low-income entrepreneurs and micro enterprises, and up until 2016, Tamweelcom had loaned out US$154 million, with women making up 94 percent of their clients. It is important to note that their repayment rate is the very high 99.7 percent.

As well as finances, Tamweelcom also offers marketing services, offering women a platform the begin showcasing and selling their products nationwide (Noor Al Hussein Foundation, 2015).

However, this support for female entrepreneurs is not restricted to only local initiatives. The Government is also helping internationally with programs such as Middle East Partnership Initiative (MEPI) and USAID. The MEPI is run by the US Government and focuses on women in the geographical region. They have created the Women in Technology (WIT) initiative, which aims to empower women by bringing them into the workforce, and is supported and implemented in Jordan using Shabakat Al Urdon as the lead partner. WIT works by providing the necessary IT and professional development training, including the 'Business Planning for Sustainability' program for managerial staff. On top of this, there is also the Professional Development Networks (PDN) program to assist women in career advancement (MEPI, 2015). This has become an essential program, because of companies such as Oasis 500, which is an important seed investment company in both Jordan and the region, surprisingly with male only board members. These networking opportunities opens doors to women that would otherwise be closed, offering females a voice to challenge the gender and society norms and expectations. Support can also be found for their own start-ups, with the chance to be mentored by female entrepreneurs with a lot of experience under their belts.

Jordan focus 2 – encouraging female entrepreneurship

In a 2016 study, published in the book *Entrepreneurship and management in an Islamic context*, Mehtap, Caputo, and Pellegrini investigated environmental factors, obstacles and challenges that affect the decision of females to become entrepreneurs.

Using a starting point of the seeming lack of desire to get started into business, in both young and adult females alike (Díaz-García and Jiménez-Moreno, 2010; Mueller and Dato-on, 2010; Wilson et al., 2007), the study aims to work out why this is the case, and what can be done about it. Ajzen's (1991) research suggested that there are three main factors that come into play, preventing the idea of female entrepreneurship before it can become a reality. These are social norms, attitudes, and perceived control. Namely, the way other people will react to a woman in business. The perceived attitudes are in line with the social norms that have been in place for a very long time, and allow women to believe that the outcome will be negative (Shapero and Sokol, 1982). Of course, this belief is perpetuated by entrepreneurship being a very male-dominated field (Díaz-García and Jiménez-Moreno, 2010; Sweida and Reichard, 2013).

This perception leads to a lack of self-belief, and without that confidence it can be virtually impossible to find any motivation (Bandura, 1997). The masculine stereotype, combined with the lack of motivation may, however subconsciously, make entrepreneurship very undesirable at a very young age. Activities that are more in line with what is expected may appeal more, simply because it is a much easier path to follow.

To study how entrepreneurial education impacts on the decision to follow that path – along with other environmental and societal factors – the authors surveyed 254 female business students from both public and private universities. They wanted to discover exactly how they felt about the potential barriers to entrepreneurship they might face, and what impact their education has had to prepare them for this future.

More than80 percent of the people surveyed were between the ages of 17 and 21, had attended private schools. A whopping 83 percent of them had graduated from the Tawjihi stream (the national high school system), and a further 8 percent of them graduated from a school that follows the British IGCSE system. Most of the students actually heard about the support systems set up for female entrepreneurs (either the Queen Rania Center for Entrepreneurship, a non-profit; or the INJAZ Al Arabi, non-profit youth empowerment program) through their education – 43 percent at university, and 21 percent in high school. However, two thirds of the respondents did not know anything about them at all.

To add more context to the students included in the survey, 38 percent of them were in their third year of study, 27 percent of them were working and studying at the same time, and 28 percent of them had actually attended a similar course before. But the most notable statistic was that nearly 60 percent of the women asked came from a family of entrepreneurs, *all* of them male members of the family.

Some major perceived issues that women feel they might face came out of the study; the weak Jordanian economy, lack of finances, fear of the potential risk, and gender issues (the male dominance of entrepreneurship, the challenges to balancing home and work life).

When thinking about education in Jordan, it is vital to remember that most of the business schools contain an entrepreneurship course in their curriculum. As well as what is offered in universities, lots of public and private organizations provide varying levels of entrepreneurship training. In the study discussed above, the students all attended universities that offered this sort of training, and when asked if they would ever take up these courses or workshop *outside* of their education establishment, nearly a third of them answered "yes". Despite this, only 38 percent suggested that they would like to open up their own business. Most of the students were studying to work in the companies already owned by their families.

Concluding remarks

Although six different regions in the world have been analyzed in this chapter, some recurring themes seem to emerge: the influence of religion, the lack of training, the obstacles in networking and in accessing to finances, the social segregation and the lack of legitimation to be an entrepreneur are the most frequently cited issues in the literature and they seem to mostly influence women in participating in entrepreneurship and in growing in their own businesses. Turning to the MENA region, for example, results from this review show that restrictions that face women in the Arab world are still very strong. Despite the new reforms the area has introduced, political, economic, and social expectations can still be problematic (Hakki and Somach, 2012; Mostafa, 2005).

Women in Jordan have more opportunities and rights than those in other areas of the Middle East, with better literacy rates than the rest of the area, but they still struggle to overcome the expectations and traditional gender roles. This leaves them under-represented in the labor workplace, which stands at less than 15 percent (The World Bank, 2015). With the current conflict and lack of stability in the area, this is not set to change any time soon. The younger generation does not have a positive outlook for themselves.

There *have* been attempts to help with this over the last decade. Thousands of people have benefited from an improved education system, better training programs, and higher levels of funding, but this is not enough. A lot more steps need to be taken by the government before Jordan can really consider its improvements truly successful. Despite the high levels of education and female graduates, the number of women contributing towards the labor force is still very low (The World Bank, 2015). This has been blamed on a number of socio-cultural and economic reasons, but the truth of it is that women *still* see themselves falling into the traditional, expected role of a wife, mother, and housekeeper, regardless of how well educated they are.

There has been a positive trend of women trying to use their knowledge and skills, without compromising their family life, by turning to entrepreneurship. These Jordanian women are starting and operating businesses from their home, using technology to help them get there (Al-Dajani and Marlow, 2010). This allows them to overcome the work and family life balance issues in a way that is more socially acceptable too.

Our literature review and the case study of Jordan led us to point in one major direction, that can be applied to all developing countries: Governments need to work with various stakeholders to actively encourage and empower women entrepreneurship. If they actively work towards fostering a suitable support system for all female entrepreneurs, then they will help to break taboos and gender stereotypes. This will help build the economy and also work through the outdated expected role of the women, leading towards a much better future.

References

Abdalla, I. A. (1996). Attitudes towards women in the Arabian Gulf region. *Women in Management Review*, 11(1), 29–39.

Afrin, S., Islam, N., and Ahmed, S. U. (2010). Microcredit and rural women entrepreneurship development in Bangladesh: A multivariate model. *Journal of Business Management*, 16, 9–36.

Ahmad, N. H., and Seet, P. S. (2010). Gender variations in ethical and socially responsible considerations among SME entrepreneurs in Malaysia. *International Journal of Business and Society*, 11, 77–88.

Ahmad, S. Z. (2011). Evidence of the characteristics of women entrepreneurs in the Kingdom of Saudi Arabia. *International Journal of Gender and Entrepreneurship*, 3(2), 123–143.

Ahmad, S. Z., and Xavier, S. R. (2011). Preliminary investigation of Yemeni women entrepreneurs: Some challenges for development and barriers to success. *International Journal of Entrepreneurship and Small Business*, 13(4), 518–534.

Aidis, R. W., Smallbone, D., and Isakova, N. (2007). Female entrepreneurship in transition economies: The case of Lithuania and Ukraine. *Feminist Economics*, 13, 157–183.

Ajzen, I. (1991). The theory of planned behavior. *Organizational Behavior and Human Decision Processes*, 50(2), 179–211.

Al-Alak, B., and Al-Haddad, F. (2010). Effect of gender on the success of women entrepreneurs in Jordan. *Interdisciplinary Journal of Contemporary Research in Business*, 1, 42–62.

Alam, S. S., Jani, M., and Omar, N. A. (2011). An empirical study of success factors of women entrepreneurs in Southern Region in Malaysia. *International Journal of Economics and Finance*, 3, 166–175.

Al-Dajani, H., and Marlow, S. (2010). Impact of women's home-based enterprise on family dynamics: Evidence from Jordan. *International Small Business Journal*, 28, 470–486.

Al-Sadi, R., Belwal, R., and Al-Badi, R. (2013). Woman entrepreneurship in the Al-Batinah region of Oman: An identification of the barriers. *Journal of International Women's Studies*, 12(3), 58–75.

Amine, L., and Staub, K. (2009). Women entrepreneurs in sub-Saharan Africa: An institutional theory analysis from a social marketing point of view. *Entrepreneurship and Regional Development*, 21, 183–211.

Ardrey, W., Pecotich, A., and Shultz, C. (2006). Entrepreneurial women as catalysts for socioeconomic development in transitioning Cambodia, Laos, and Vietnam. *Consumption, Markets & Culture*, 9, 277–300.

Aterido, R., and Hallward-Driemeier, M. (2011). Whose business is it anyway? *Small Business Economics*, 37, 443–464.

Audretsch, D., Boente, W., and Jagannadha, P. (2007). *Religion and entrepreneurship*. Jena Economic Research Papers, 075.

Ayadurai, S., and Sohail, M. (2006). Profile of women entrepreneurs in a war-torn area: Case study of North East Sri Lanka. *Journal of Developmental Entrepreneurship*, 11, 3–17.

Bandura, A. (1997). Self-efficacy: The exercise of control. *New York Freeman*, 604.

Barcucci, V., and Mryyan, N. (2014). *Labour market transitions of young women and men in Jordan.* Geneva, Switzerland: Youth Employment Programme Employment Policy Department, International Labour Organisation (ILO).

Belwal, R., Tamiru, M., and Singh, G. (2012). Microfinance and sustained economic improvement: Women small scale entrepreneurs in Ethiopia. *Journal of International Development*, 24, 84–99.

Berik, G., Dong, X. Y., and Summerfield, G. (2007). China's transition and feminist economics. *Feminist Economics*, 13, 1–33.

Bhatti, N., Shar, A. H., and Shaikh, F. M. (2010). Entrepreneur business development in Sindh: The case of Jacobabad district. *International Business Research*, 3, 132–138.

Bland, J. (2005). *About gender: Definitions.*www.gender.org.uk/about/00_defin.htm

Caputo, A., Lombardi, R., Akeel, F., Almallah, H., Dakkak, B., and Qubbaj, N. (2016). Youth employment in start up ventures in Jordan: An exploratory study. *International Journal of Entrepreneurship and Small Business*, 28(4), 468–491.

Caputo, A., Mehtap, S., Pellegrini, M. M., and Al-Refai, R. (2016). Supporting opportunities for female entrepreneurs in Jordan. *International Journal of Entrepreneurship and Small Business*, 27(2/3), 384–409.

Central Intelligence Agency. (2014). *The world factbook 2013–14.* www.cia.gov/library/publications/the-world-factbook/index.html

Chirwa, E. (2008). Effects of gender on the performance of micro and small enterprises in Malawi. *Development Southern Africa*, 25, 347–362.

Dana, L. P. (1992). Entrepreneurship, innovation and change in developing countries. *Entrepreneurship, Innovation, and Change*, 1(2), 231–242.

Dana, L. P. (1995). Entrepreneurship in a remote sub-Arctic community. *Entrepreneurship Theory and Practice*, 20, 57–72.

Dana, L. P., and Dana, T. E. (2008). Ethnicity and entrepreneurship in Morocco: A photo-ethnographic study. *International Journal of Business and Globalisation*, 2(3), 209–226.

De Bruin, A., Brush, C. G., and Welter, F. (2006). Introduction to the special issue: Towards building cumulative knowledge on women's entrepreneurship. *Entrepreneurship Theory and Practice*, 30(5), 585–593.

De Bruin, A., Brush, C. G., and Welter, F. (2007). Advancing a framework for coherent research on women's entrepreneurship. *Entrepreneurship Theory and Practice*, 31(3), 323–339.

De Vita, L., Mari, M., and Poggesi, S. (2014). Women entrepreneurs in and from developing countries: Evidences from the literature. *European Management Journal*, 32(3), 451–460.

Dechant, K., and Lamky, A. A. L. (2005). Toward an understanding of Arab women entrepreneurs in Bahrain and Oman. *Journal of Developmental Entrepreneurship*, 10(2), 123–140.

Díaz-García, M. C., and Jiménez-Moreno, J. (2010). Entrepreneurial intention: The role of gender. *International Entrepreneurship and Management Journal*, 6(3), 261–283.

El-Rahmony, S. (2002). Women in the Arab world: From role conflict to effective participation. *Al-Mustaqbal Al-Arabi (Arab Future)*, 1, 93–107.

Enhai, Y. (2011). Are women entrepreneurs more likely to share power than men entrepreneurs in decision-making? *International Journal of Business and Management*,6, 111–119.

Ettl, K., and Welter, F. (2010). How female entrepreneurs learn and acquire (business-relevant) knowledge. *International Journal of Entrepreneurship and Small Business,* 10(1), 65–82.

Faud, N., and Bohari, A. (2011). Malay women entrepreneurs in the small and medium sized ICT related business: A study on need for achievement. *International Journal of Business and Social Science,* 2, 272–278.

Fletschner, D., and Carter, M. (2008). Constructing and reconstructing gender: Reference group effects and women's demand for entrepreneurial capital. *The Journal of Socio-Economics,* 37, 672–693.

Galloway, L., and Brown, W. (2002). Entrepreneurship education at university: A driver in the creation of high growth firms? *Education+ Training,* 44(8/9), 398–405.

Garba, A. (2011). Stumbling block for women entrepreneurship in Nigeria: How risk attitude and lack of capital mitigates their need for business expansion. *European Journal of Economics, Finance & Administrative Sciences,*36, 38–49.

GEM. (2009). *Global entrepreneurship monitor, GEM-MENA regional report 2009 (Middle East & North Africa).*

GEM. (2010).*2010 women's report.*

GEM. (2012a). *2011 Extended report: Entrepreneurs and entrepreneurial employees across the globe.*

GEM. (2012b). *Global entrepreneurship monitor, 2012 women's report.*

GEM. (2014). *Global entrepreneurship monitor, 2014 global report.*

Gerrard, P., Schoch, H., and Cunningham, J. (2003). Values and skills of female entrepreneurs in Vietnam: An exploratory study. *Asia Pacific Business Review,* 10, 139–159.

Goby, V. P., and Erogul, M. S. (2011). Female entrepreneurship in the United Arab Emirates: Legislative encouragements and cultural constraints. *Women's Studies International Forum,* 34(4), 329–334.

Gray, K., and Finley-Hervey, J. (2005). Women and Entrepreneurship in Morocco: Debunking stereotypes and discerning strategies. *The International Entrepreneurship and Management Journal,* 1(2), 203–217.

Hakki, H., and Somach, S. (2012). *Gender analysis and assessment.* Report No. 11-01-595, US AID.

Handy, F., Ranade, B., and Kassam, M. (2007). To profit or not to profit: Women entrepreneurs in India. *Non Profit Management and Leadership,*17, 383–401.

Hattab, H. (2012). Towards understanding female entrepreneurship in Middle Eastern and North African countries. *Education, Business and Society: Contemporary Middle Eastern Issues,* 5(3), 171–186.

Hattab, H. W. (2010). The effect of environments' dimensions on the growth of female entrepreneurial projects in Jordan. *Journal of Small Business & Entrepreneurship,* 23(2), 211–223.

Hosseini, S. J. F., and McElwee, G. (2011). Improving the entrepreneurial potential of rural women entrepreneurs in Northern Iran. *International Journal of Entrepreneurship and Small Business,* 12(1), 15–27.

ILO. (2014). *Labour inspection, gender equality and non-discrimination in the Arab states: Guide book.* Geneva, Switzerland: International Labour Organisation.

Inmyxai, S., and Takahashi, Y. (2010). Performance contrast and its determinants between male and female headed firms in Lao MSMES. *International Journal of Business Management,* 5, 37–52.

Itani, H., Sidani, Y. M., and Baalbaki, I. (2011). United Arab Emirates female entrepreneurs: Motivations and frustrations. *Equality, Diversity and Inclusion: An International Journal*, 30(5), 409–424.

Jamali, D. (2009). Constraints and opportunities facing women entrepreneurs in developing countries. *Gender in Management: An International Journal*, 24(4), 232–251.

Kabir, M. S., and Huo, X. (2011). Advancement of rural poor women through small entrepreneurship development: The case of Bangladesh. *International Journal of Business and Management*,6, 134–140.

Kantor, P. (2005). Determinants of women's microenterprise success in Ahmedabad. India: Empowerment and economics. *Feminist Economics*,11, 63–83.

Kevane, M., and Wydick, B. (2001). Microenterprise lending to female entrepreneurs: Sacrificing economic growth for poverty alleviation? *World Development*, 29,1225–1236.

Khan, G. M. (2013). Sidab women's Sewing Group: An example of social entrepreneurship in the Arabian Gulf. *International Journal of Entrepreneurship and Small Business*, 18(1), 47–56.

Kuada, J. (2009). Gender, social networks, and entrepreneurship in Ghana. *Journal of African Business*,10, 85–103.

Lee, J., Sohn, S., and Ju, Y.(2011). How effective is government support for Korean women entrepreneurs in small and medium enterprises? *Journal of Small Business Management*, 49, 599–616.

Light, I., and Dana, L. P. (2013). Boundaries of social capital in entrepreneurship. *Entrepreneurship Theory and Practice*, 37(3), 603–624.

LiTS (Life in Transition Survey). (2011). *Life in transition survey report*. The European Bank for Reconstruction and Development.

Lüthje, C., and Franke, N. (2002). Fostering entrepreneurship through university education and training: Lessons from Massachusetts Institute of Technology. In *European Academy of Management 2nd Annual Conference on Innovative Research in Management*, Stockholm (pp. 9–11).

Mahadea, D. (2001). Similarities and differences between male and female entrepreneurial attributes in manufacturing firms in the informal sector in the Transkei. *Development Southern Africa*,18, 189–199.

Majcher-Teleon, A. M., and Slimène, O. B. (2009). *Women and work in Jordan: A case study of tourism and ICT sectors*. European Training Foundation, Turin, Italy: European Training Foundation.

Manolova, T. S., Carter, N. M., and Gyoshev, B. S. (2006). Breaking the family and friends' circle: Predictors of external financing usage among men and women entrepreneurs in a transitional economy. *Venture Capital*, 8, 109–132.

Manolova, T. S., Carter, N. M., Manev, I. M., and Gyoshev, B. S. (2007). The differential effect of men and women entrepreneurs' human capital and networking on growth expectancies in Bulgaria. *Entrepreneurship: Theory and Practice*, 31, 407–426.

Mathew, V. (2010). Women entrepreneurship in Middle East: Understanding barriers and use of ICT for entrepreneurship development. *International Entrepreneurship and Management Journal*, 6(2), 163–181.

McElwee, G., and Al-Riyami, R. (2003). Women entrepreneurs in Oman: Some barriers to success. *Career Development International*, 8(7), 339–346.

Mehtap, S. (2014). Barriers to entrepreneurship in Jordan: What do female business students think? In *3rd Multidisciplinary Academic Conference on Economics, Management, Marketing and Toursim (MAC-EMMT)*, Prague, Czech Republic.

Menon, N. R., and Van Der Meulen, Y. (2011). How access to credit affects self-employment: Differences by gender during India's rural banking reform. *Journal of Development Studies*, 47, 48–69.

MEPI. (2015). *MEPI in Jordan.* http://mepi.state.gov/med-region/jordan/ (accessed March 25, 2015)

Mitra, R. (2002). The growth pattern of women-run enterprises: An empirical study in India. *Journal of Developmental Entrepreneurship*,7, 217–237.

Mostafa, M. M. (2005). Attitudes towards women managers in the United Arab Emirates: The effects of patriarchy, age, and sex differences. *Journal of Managerial Psychology*, 20(6), 522–540.

Movahedi, R., and Yaghoubi-Farani, A. (2012). Analysis of the barriers and limitations for the development of rural women's entrepreneurship. *International Journal of Entrepreneurship and Small Business*, 15(4), 469–487.

Mueller, S. L., and Dato-on, M. C. (2010). A cross cultural study of gender-role orientation and entrepreneurial self-efficacy. *Entrepreneurship and Management Journal*, 1, 198–208.

Nagadevara, V. (2009). Impact of gender in small scale enterprises: A study of women enterprises in India. *International Journal of Business and Economics*,9, 111–117.

Naser, K., Mohammed, W. R., and Nuseibeh, R. (2009). Factors that affect women entrepreneurs: Evidence from an emerging economy. *International Journal of Organizational Analysis*, 17(3), 225–247.

Noor Al Hussein Foundation. (2015). *Jordan Micro Credit Company* (Tamweelcom). www.nooralhusseinfoundation.org/index.php?pager=end&task=view&type=content&pageid=34 (accessed March 23, 2015)

Pandian, K., Jesurajan, V., and College, X. (2011). An empirical investigation on the factors determining the success and problems faced by women entrepreneurs in Tiruchirapalli district – Tamilnadu. *Interdisciplinary Journal of Contemporary Research in Business*,3, 914–922.

Poggesi, S., Mari, M., and De Vita, L. (2015). Family and work–life balance mechanisms: what is their impact on the performance of Italian female service firms? *The International Journal of Entrepreneurship and Innovation*, 16(1), 43–53.

Ramadani, V. (2015). The woman entrepreneur in Albania: An exploratory study on motivation, problems and success factors. *Journal of Balkan and Near Eastern Studies*, 17(2), 204–221.

Ramadani, V., Gërguri, S., Dana, L.-P., and Tašaminova, T. (2013). Women entrepreneurs in the Republic of Macedonia: Waiting for directions. *International Journal of Entrepreneurship and Small Business*, 19(1), 95–121.

Ramadani, V., Gërguri-Rashiti, S., and Fayolle, A. (2015). *Female entrepreneurship in transition economies: Trends and challenges.* London: Palgrave Macmillan.

Ramadani, V., Hisrich, R. D., and Gërguri-Rashiti, S. (2015). Female entrepreneurs in transition economies: Insights from Albania, Macedonia and Kosovo. *World Review of Entrepreneurship, Management and Sustainable Development*, 11(4), 391–413.

Rand, J., and Tarp, F. (2011). Does gender influence the provision of fringe benefits? Evidence from Vietnamese SMEs. *Feminist Economics*, 17, 59–87.

Rutashobya, L., Allan, I., and Nilsson, K. (2009). Gender, social networks, and entrepreneurial outcomes in Tanzania. *Journal of African Business*,10, 67–83.

Salmenniemi, S., Karhunen, P., and Kosonen, R. (2011). Between business and byt: Experiences of women entrepreneurs in contemporary Russia. *Europe-Asia Studies*, 63, 77–98.

Salze-Lozac'h, V. (2011). *APEC 2011: Unleashing women entrepreneurship in Asia.* The Asian Foundation. http://asiafoundation.org.

Shapero, A., and Sokol, L. (1982). Social dimensions of entrepreneurship. In C. A. Kent, D. L. Sexton and K. H. Vesper (eds.), *Encyclopedia of entrepreneurship* (pp. 72–90). Englewood Cliffs, NJ: Prentice Hall.

Singh, S., Mordi, C., Okafor, C., and Simpson, R. (2010). Challenges in female entrepreneurial development – a case analysis of Nigerian entrepreneurs. *Journal of Enterprising Culture*, 18, 435–460.

Singh, S., Reynolds, R., and Muhammad, S. (2001). A gender-based performance analysis of micro and small enterprises in Java, Indonesia. *Journal of Small Business Management*, 39, 174–182.

Smith-Hunter, A. E., and Boyd, R. L. (2004). Applying theories of entrepreneurship to a comparative analysis of white and minority women business owners. *Women in Management Review.* 19(1), 18–28.

Smith-Hunter, A. E., and Leone, J. (2010a). Afro-Brazilian women entrepreneurs: Characteristics, critical issues and current comments. *Research in Business and Economics Journal*, 2, 1–15.

Smith-Hunter, A. E., and Leone, J. (2010b). Evidence on the characteristics of women entrepreneurs in Brazil: An empirical analysis. *International Journal of Management and Marketing Research*, 3, 85–102.

Storey, D. (2004). Racial and gender discrimination in the micro firms' credit market. *Small Business Economics*, 23, 401–422.

Sweida, G. L., and Reichard, R. J. (2013). Gender stereotyping effects on entrepreneurial self-efficacy and high-growth entrepreneurial intention. *Journal of Small Business and Enterprise Development*, 20(2), 296–313.

TEMPUS. (2012). *Higher education in Jordan.* Brussels, Belgium: European Union.

Terjesen, S., and Amoros, J. E. (2010). Female entrepreneurship in Latin America and the Caribbean: Characteristics, drivers and relationship to economic development. *European Journal of Development Research*, 22, 313–330.

U.S. Department of Commerce. (2014). *Doing business in Jordan: 2014 Country commercial guide for U.S. Companies.* http://photos.state.gov/libraries/jordan/444376/pdf/2014CCGFinal.pdf

Ufuk, H., and Özgen, O. (2001). Interaction between the business and family lives of women entrepreneurs in Turkey. *Journal of Business Ethics*, 31, 95–106.

UNESCAP. (2012). *Economic and social survey of Asia and the Pacific 2007.* Bangkok: UNESCAP. www.unescap.org/survey2007.

Verme, P. (2014). *Economic development and female labor participation in the Middle East and North Africa: A test of the u-shape hypothesis.* World Bank Policy Research Working Paper (6927).

Welsh, D. H. B., Memili, E., Kaciak, E., and Al Sadoon, A. (2014). Saudi women entrepreneurs: A growing economic segment. *Journal of Business Research*, 67(5), 758–762.

Welsh, D. H. B., and Raven, P. (2006). Family business in the Middle East: An exploratory study of retail management in Kuwait and Lebanon. *Family Business Review*, 19, 29–48. https://doi.org/10.1111/j.1741-6248.2006.00058.x

Wilson, F., Kickul, J., and Marlino, D. (2007). Gender, entrepreneurial self-efficacy, and entrepreneurial career intentions: Implications for entrepreneurship education. *Entrepreneurship Theory and Practice*, 31(3), 387–406.

The World Bank. (2005). *The economic advancement of women in Jordan: A country gender assessment.*

The World Bank. (2015). *Jordan overview.* www.worldbank.org/en/country/jordan/overview (accessed March 27, 2015)

The World Bank. (2016). *Women, business and the law 2016: Getting to equal.* World Bank Group. ISBN:978-1-4648-0678-0 (electronic).

Yetim, N. (2008). Social capital in female entrepreneurship. *International Sociology,*23, 864–885.

Yin, R. K. (2014). Case study research: Design and methods. In L. Bickman and D. J. Rog (eds.), *Essential guide to qualitative methods in organizational research* (Vol. 5). Sage Publications.

Yordanova, D. (2011). The effects of gender on entrepreneurship in Bulgaria: An empirical study. *International Journal of Management,*28, 289–305.

Zeidan, S., and Bahrami, S. (2011). Women entrepreneurship in GCC: A framework to address challenges and promote participation in a regional context. *International Journal of Business and Social Science,* 2, 100–107.

11 Gender entrepreneurial leadership in family businesses

A case study from Bosnia and Herzegovina

Ramo Palalić, Veland Ramadani,
Leo-Paul Dana, and Vanessa Ratten

Introduction

Many types of research are done regarding the relationship between gender and business. Some work claims that men are more interested in entrepreneurship activities (Díaz-Garcia and Moreno, 2010), and entrepreneurial intention (EI) is more observed in men than women (Goktan and Gupta, 2013). However, speculations exist. The old-fashionable stereotype, even in the Marxist approach, is that it is better for women to stay at home and take care of the family. A common fact that some men are not capable of taking care of their dependents show that men sometimes are not capable of taking part in contributing to societal values.

Naturally, men and women are very different. Nevertheless, their differences do not play an important role when it comes to understanding, observing, initiating, leading, and perform in organizations. Many examples could be found where women take care of family business and lead it for a long time very successfully. Male are more masculine than females, and the difference in strength has made a difference between men and women in their biological and physical appearance. Perhaps this is one of the reasons why some earlier research (Rosa et al., 1996) shows that women's performance is behind men's. However, nowadays it is different and women take part in an organization's business activities. There should be empirical, in-depth, research undertaken to examine these issues thoroughly (Chell and Baines, 1998).

Carter and Cannon (1992) found that family was a cause or motivational factor for why women establish new businesses on their own – and although family was a strong motivator for starting a business, some participants in the study did not think that being a mother and being a company leader were compatible goals. Such views discredit women's competence. A very interesting finding was argued by Watkins and Watkins (1986), where male business owners always had supportive wives, while the opposite happened to women, in which cases their husbands tended to create trouble for them. It seems that many men cannot accept that women, – their wives and mothers – can be very successful and that they should support them. That is why "behind a successful man stands a strong woman," which, according to Watkins and Watkins (1986), for a successful woman is not the case. This anecdote can be justified differently as it is an old quote and the role of women in the workforce has significantly changed. One of them could be that as much as men are successful, they still need someone who will stand beside them to "successfully" take care of the whole family so that men will be isolated from family issues that might distract them from business. Only in this way they can be successful. Now, the question is, why are such opportunities not given to women? Perhaps this question can open a pro-con debate.

The family business is considered as least contributing to overall economic growth since they do not grow quickly in regard to employees and profit. Due to the structure of family businesses, they usually do not expand, and thus literature suggests that a country's economic growth comes from different sources (Fitzgerald and Muske, 2016). Others claim that family businesses are one of the most important sources of job creation (Kellermanns et al., 2008; Hoy and Sharma, 2010; Hacker and Dowling, 2012; Welsh et al., 2013; Ramadani, 2015; Ramadani and Hoy, 2015). However, we should not neglect family businesses – even if they are small – because at the least they enrich the community at the local level. Moreover, several family businesses can create eventually a joint venture that could, through the time, evolve into a multinational company (MNC).

In family business, both parents (male and female) transmit their entrepreneurial mindset to their children (Hoffmann et al., 2015). Hoffman et al. shows that children, regardless of gender, can be successors of a family business. There is no exclusive privilege for sons to take over the business. Anecdotally, in the Balkan region, the role of the son is emphasized over the role of the daughter.

The main objective of this research is to find motivational factors of male and female business owners, as well as their performance regarding entrepreneurial leadership (EI and transformational leadership). Moreover, being aware of country-specific factors in Bosnia and Herzegovina (Palalić, 2017), the networking and business environment is taken into consideration (Taatila and Down, 2012; Palalić et al., 2017). These might be supporting or demotivating/discouraging factors for both males and females in creating new start-ups in this region.

Study background and models

Study model 1

This study model is intended to find the difference between male business owners and female business owners and their affinity regarding innovativeness (INN), proactiveness (PRO), and risk-taking (RiT). This is important due to the EO dimensions' importance as the growth of firms is concerned (Miller, 1983; Covin and Slevin, 1988, 1989; Lee et al., 2001; Wiklund and Shepherd, 2005; Covin et al., 2006; Runyan and Swinney, 2008; Lee and Lim, 2009; Kraus et al., 2012; Palalić and Busatlic, 2015; Palalić, 2017). Nonetheless, this growth and development include family businesses too.

Small and medium enterprises in most of the research are studied under the entrepreneurial orientation loop, which consists of *innovativeness, proactiveness,* and *risk-taking.* These dimensions are included in the factors that caused firms' growth (Brown et al., 2001; Stevenson and Jarillo, 1990). Small and medium enterprises try to be first movers in the market (Lumpkin and Dess, 1996; Trevis et al., 2009) and to make their decision on anticipated *risk* and *innovations*. Earlier works stress the importance of these dimensions (Miller, 1983; Covin and Slevin, 1988, 1989; Lee et al., 2001; Wiklund and Shepherd, 2005; Covin et al., 2006; Runyan and Swinney, 2008; Lee and Lim, 2009; Kraus et al., 2012, Palalić and Busatlic, 2015; Palalić, 2017). Although small business and family businesses are considered to be leaders in innovation, when it comes to transition economies, it is evident that large firms (corporations) take advantage of innovation (Gërguri-Rashiti et al., 2015).

It is not unusual for development and growth of firms to be influenced by the managerial leadership. Moreover, transformational leadership is a motivational tool: Transformational leaders lead employees towards goals and objectives that are in accordance with firm's strategic vision. Generally, transformational leadership's objective is to transform followers into leaders (Bass and Riggio, 2006) in the long term. Similarly, transformational leadership's role in an organization is to make the organization from an undeveloped one into a developed organization with constant growth over a period of years (Palalić, 2017). Transformational leadership constitutes of *idealized influence (II), inspirational motivation (IM), intellectual stimulation (IS),* and *individualized consideration (IC).*

Some researchers argue that men are better managers and thus lead companies to long-term prosperity (Tominc and Rebernik, 2006, 2007). Others, like Palalić, Ramadani, and Dana (2017) argue that women can perform better regarding entrepreneurial (managerial) leadership. In this diverse world, both extremes are not good. The stereotypes' strength depend on cultural values in a particular society. Some societies differentiate jobs that are for men and women (Shinnar et al., 2012; Sánchez and Licciardello, 2012). Such traits are more amplified in undeveloped societies, where women's work and men's work are strictly assigned to these categories (Ahl, 2006; Gupta et al., 2009). In this context, men supposed to provide family's life necessities, while women's role is emotional and is take care of issues in the family (Watson and Newby, 2005). There should be a balanced approach when it comes to recruitment of company, and there should be an equal chance of getting financing for new businesses by prospective male and female entrepreneurs.

Based on the discussion above, study model 1 covers entrepreneurial dimensions and transformational leadership. The model is described in Figure 11.1 and expressed in the following research questions (RQs):

RQ1: Is there any difference observed regarding EI dimensions between men and women in managing the family business?

Based on the qualitative data, the study tries to observe differences of EI's scores for men and women. The results will suggest an answer to this research question.

RQ2: Is there any difference observed regarding transformational leadership between men and women in managing the family business?

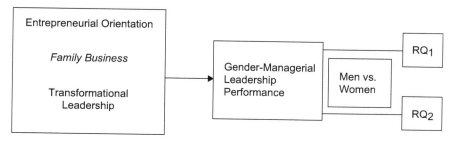

Figure 11.1 Study model 1: author's compilation

RQ$_2$ explores whether men and women perceive leadership roles differently. As the EI dimensions are important, nonetheless, transformational leadership is important as well. Its role is to lead all pioneering reflected in innovation, pro-activity, and risk-taking. Having said this, transformational leadership cannot be separated from performance in organizations, as argued by earlier works (Michie and Zumitzavan, 2012; Wang et al., 2011; Matzler et al., 2008; Podsakoff et al., 1990; Palalić, 2017). It should be noted that transformational leadership styles (idealized influence, inspirational motivation, intellectual stimulation, and individual consideration) overlap with EI dimensions. These styles lead to inno-vativeness, which is based on employees' free and creative thinking (intellectual stimulation), supported by a leader who inspires them (inspirational motiva-tion). Proactiveness requires a role model (idealized influence or charisma) who will be a real example of it. Moreover, this "charisma" allows employees to see, evaluate, and try new things from different perspectives, as their leader does (intellectual stimulation and inspirational motivation). Additionally, risk-taking is related to *anticipated* risk. Leaders with a vision (charismatic leaders) are likely to take anticipated risks. So, employees in such an environment, have a chance to transform themselves into prospective leaders in organizations, and so into entrepreneurs.

Study model 2

Motivational factors differ from one entrepreneur to another. As an outcome of too much work for others, financial difficulties, or no career possibilities in firms, many employees become employers. Others have been led by their vision from an early age. In the Western Balkan region, motives are different. For instance, in early 2000 motives were mostly based on opportunity circumstances at a par-ticular time (Tominc and Rebernik, 2004). Some of the entrepreneurs, in the early 1990s, started their own business by circumstances of a high unemployment rate and non-existent infrastructure after the war (Dana, 1999;Dana and Rama-dani,2015), which happened in Bosnia and Herzegovina. The men's motives were mainly existential – they needed to support themselves and their families. However, some of them observed a need for the country to be rebuilt; for these

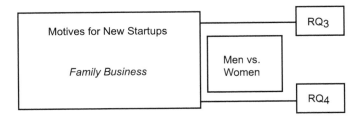

Figure 11.2 Study model 2: author's compilation

men, their motives were more related to the development of the whole society (Dana, 1999).

In the case of Bosnia and Herzegovina, some women were without husbands, and they started to think about how to survive. Women's entrepreneurial lives in Bosnia (in the late 1990s) started from scratch, with a little amount of cash and a very simple transaction. Some of these initial efforts later evolved into a businesses lasting for decades. These existential motives of women entrepreneurs in the late 1990s opposes Frank's (2012, 65) argument, which says that women's motives are "to earn an income, interest in doing business, increased flexibility, and autonomy, possibility to combine with family obligations, and re-negotiating spatial practices". More than two decades after the war, this study aims to investigate male and female entrepreneurs' motives.

The discussion in this study model (Figure 11.2) provides two additional research questions, which are:

RQ3: What were motives for male business owners that they started their own business, and what would be their motives if they would open an additional business?

RQ4: What are motives for female business owners that they started their own business, and what would be their motives if they would open an additional business?

Study model 3

The literature suggests that networking in society, locally and globally, is an important factor in starting new ventures (Karra and Phillips, 2004; Sullivan Mort and Weerawardena, 2006; Johanson and Kao, 2010). Even people who migrate from their home country to a foreign one work to build relationships in the new society, which can help them in their life and in their entrepreneurial activities (Fatoki and Oni, 2014). Women, however, rarely use the benefits of networking for entrepreneurial opportunity. Though, some argue that they do (Teo, 1996). In one of ex-Yugoslavia republics, Croatia and Slovenia, male entrepreneurs used networking opportunities to start businesses more frequently than female entrepreneurs (Kedmenec et al., 2014). Nonetheless, networking should be considered as one of the main constraints of new ventures. In addition to vision and a good financial background, it is necessary to have a strong entrepreneurial network that will help a business to grow in its early stages. Moreover, entrepreneurial people (locals, foreigners, or immigrants) need to have a good network in society (Karra and Phillips, 2004; Sullivan Mort and Weerawardena, 2006; Johanson and Kao, 2010; Fatoki and Oni, 2014), in which they can establish the starting basis of their business. However, the best basis for entrepreneurship development can create the state (Charoensukmongkol, 2016). It is so because the state controls and distributes resources (financial funds for business develpments) to the society (Volchek, Jantunen, and Saarenketo, 2013).

Entrepreneurial or business networking can be advanced using "mobile social networks" (Ratten, 2013: 143), which extend and explores new business opportunities and ideas. Using mobile technology such as smartphones, smart people establish informal networks that eventually can be used as business networks. Family businesses have to establish a mindset where they will exploit an opportunity of establishing the entrepreneurial network with global firms existing in a business environment, in a symbiotic way of doing business (Dana et al., 2000; Etemad et al., 2001, Wright and Dana, 2003). In other words, a presence of multinational companies and large corporations should be used as an opportunity to develop family businesses at local levels, while slowly approaching global markets and reducing the costs of doing so (Harrison,1997). Moreover, the outcome of this symbiotic relationship is worthwhile for both local (small and family) businesses as well as large (global/ multinational) firms (Dana, 2001).

A competitive business environment sometimes becomes friendly in which a partnership between large and small businesses can be established with common benefits (Dana, 2001). So small and family businesses can somehow deal with competition, which can evolve either into rivalry or a partnership. However, a business environment where the state creates a business atmosphere can be sometimes very demotivating, such as when the state imposes discouraging rules like huge taxes. Such state moves may create (unintentionally) an unfriendly *pond with a lot of crocodiles*. Such an environment creates an unfriendly relationship between business regardless of its size, where any relationship, which should be symbiotic (Dana et al., 2000; Etemad et al., 2001; Wright and Dana, 2003) in its nature, is almost impossible to create. As an outcome of such state attitudes, the business environment creates a business policy involving a barter system that is called "improvisation" (very well known in Bosnia). In these transactions, all businesses along the same chain are involved in this improvisation. This improvisation is a one-shot strategy that can be useful for a very short time. Thus, the firm's sustainability might be in danger. As suggested by Wagner and Svensson (2014), firms should use "transformative business sustainability" (TBS), which suggests undertaking due diligence of the current business state and the plans, so that all stakeholders will have a win-win position. Conducting business in a specific business environment (Palalić et al., 2017) is challenging, and visionary (charismatic leaders) business owners or leaders need to have a "broader vision,

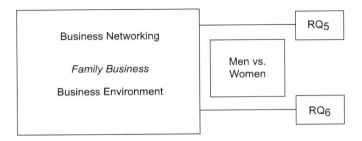

Figure 11.3 Study model 3: author's compilation

how and where to play" (White, 2009, 393). The discussion for this study model leads to the following research questions (Figure 11.3).

RQ5: Do male business owners work more on strengthening business (entrepreneurial) networking compared with their female counterparts?

RQ6: Does the current business environment motivates, supports both male and female business owners in developing their current (family) business and establishing a new business?

Methodology

One of the aims of qualitative research is to obtain from participants knowledge on an issue in depth, its outcomes and what caused these outcomes (Cooper and Schindler, 2014). Following Cooper and Schindler (2014) in this work, the researchers will examine issues related to key motivational factors of success while observing the level of entrepreneurial leadership among female and male business owners in family businesses, across Bosnia and Herzegovina.

Selected sampling method

For this empirical research, the qualitative approach is applied. Purposive stratified sampling is used due to a small sample, which can be generalized or statistically representative (Patton, 1990: 174). Additionally, this method fits the research circumstances (Van Manen, 1990: 177). Moreover, this research is based on homogeneous participants (family business owners) as suggested by Patton (1990: 174).

Data collection

Qualitative data were collected through interviews using semi-structured questions. The researcher selected 30 family businesses to interview respective business owners. All of them were contacted by phone, and out of 30 business owners, 22 of them agreed to participate in the interview. The interviews were located at the businesses' premises. One to two interview sessions were done per week. Data were collected over 14 weeks.

Interview types and questions

Interviews could be carried out on individual or group basis (Cooper and Schindler, 2014: 152). In this research, the interviews were conducted individually. The authors used questions from questionnaires used in previous works and adapted them to this research agenda. *Entrepreneurship* questions are adopted from Covin and Slevin (1989), and *leadership* questions from Bass and Avolio (1992). *Networking* questions were adapted from Taatila and Down (2012), while *business environment* questions are followed from Palalić et al. (2017).

The questionnaire constructed of five main sections. *Section 1* describes general information about the business owner and his/her family business performance. These questions (1–10) are position; gender; age; educational degree; marital status; firm size; firm type; sales in last three years; number of employees in last three years; the firm's value compared with competitors in the same industry, in the last three years. The changes in the family business performance described in percent, by increase/decrease/no change. In *Section 2*, the entrepreneurial orientation of the business owners is presented. It is split up into three subsections – innovativeness, proactiveness and risk-taking – each with three respective questions (11–19). Each of these dimensions is measured by the scale from one to seven (7-point Likert scale). *Section 3* follows the transformational leadership questions (20–23) (Bass Avolio, 1992). The 4-point Likert scale is applied. Each question represents one dimension: idealized influence (Q20); inspirational motivation (Q21); intellectual stimulation (Q22); individualized consideration (Q23). *Section 4*, the motivational factors section, is made of seven questions (24–30), whose results are not on the scale, but recorded as participants' answers. *Section 5* comprises *networking* questions (31–32).

Empirical results

Descriptives

The educational background of participants is diverse, 15 of them with a bachelor's degree, four of them have a master's degree, while three of them have a high-school diploma only. The industries are split into services (eight firms), sales (seven firms), and production (seven firms). The performance of the firms is noticed in the percentage of *sales, some employees, and performance versus competitors. The firm's performances* are expressed in percentage of increase, decrease, or no changes. Family firms' performances in *sales*, led by male-owned firms, are the following: two firms noticed a decrease in sales from 0–20 percent, six of them recorded increase (no percentages are given), and three of them observed no changes in sales for the last three years. When it comes to *employees*, male owners noticed an increase (three of them), none of the firm's observed decrease while no change, three companies observed so. When it comes to *performance against competitors*, 13 family businesses, led by males, noticed increase (one firm by 15 percent, one firm by 20 percent, one by 40), decrease four businesses (one of them firm by 50 percent), no change versus competitors, one firm has observed, while four of them were anonymous. Family businesses led by males were mostly production oriented (five firms), then sales (four firms), and lastly services (two firms).

Marital status of male family business owners was, one single, one divorced, nine married. Their educational background is that six of them hold a bachelor's degree, three of them are with master's degree, and two of them have a high-school diploma. The average age of males is 43. The male-owned firms' average age is 27 years (minimum is five years, and maximum is 61 years) of existence in the market.

Family businesses led by females are mostly in services (six firms), sales (two of them), and production (three firms). Regarding family businesses' performance in terms of *sales*, led by females, six of them recorded increase (no percent given), decrease two of them (no percentage given), and no change three firms (no percentage given). Regarding the number of employees, the firms observed increase (three of them), decrease (two of them), and no change (six of them). When it comes to family firms' performance *versus competitors*, six of them observed increase (no percentage given), two of them noticed decrease (no percentage given), and three of them recorded no change (no percentage given). The female family business owners' average age is 42. Their educational background compared with male business owners is slightly different. One possesses a master's degree, eight of them hold a bachelor's degree, and two of them have a high-school diploma only. Women-owned firms' average age is 16 years old whilst the youngest is four years old and the oldest is 50 years old.

Entrepreneurial leadership dimensions scores

Scores of EI dimensions and entrepreneurial leadership for males and females were examined. The following scores were observed.

Male family business owners Innovativeness is 4.2; Proactiveness 4.2; Risk-taking 4.8. The EI average is 4.4, and entrepreneurial leadership's (EL) score is 3.0. The Business environment (BE) is 3.5, and entrepreneurial or business networking (NW) is 3.7.

Female family business owners' scores in EI dimensions are Innovativeness 4.2; Proactiveness 4.3; Risk-taking 4.3. The average of EI is 3.3, while the EL score is 3. The BE is 2.2, and entrepreneurial or business NW is 3.5.

Motivational factors of males and females

Empirical results for *motivational factors* were expressed in the following questions.

1. *What was the reason to start your own business?* This question seeks to give us insight into how they started their business and what was the main reason or motive to be self-employed.
2. *What is your key to success?* Business owners were supposed to reveal the main factors in their long-term success.
3. *What is your personal favorite thing about being a successful business owner/ CEO?* Entrepreneurs were supposed to answer with their feeling about their life–business achievement. What is their personal satisfaction of being a leader-owner of their business?
4. *What motivates you to be a successful business owner/CEO?* These are the key motives of their success. Business owners are expected to highlight the main drivers for their long-term success.
5. *Are you planning to leave the entrepreneurial life?* Why would/not you do that? This question aims to test their willingness to leave the business and start a "normal" life like every other man or woman in the country. Additionally, they are supposed to say the key reasons if they would or would not change the current lifestyle.
6. *Are you motivated by the current business environment to start a new business venture?* This question pertains to the motivation set by the current environment in which they operate. The business environment is supposed to be motivational, not discouraging, so we wanted to get firsthand insights from family business owners.

Table 11.1 includes the results from these interviews, recorded as the most frequent responses.

Table 11.1 Entrepreneurial motives of male and female business owners

No	Question	Male Motives	Female Motives
1	What was the reason to start your own business?	Money own boss; social status	Being own boss
2	What is your key to success?	Hard work and dedication. A good player.	Energy
3	What is your personal favorite thing about being successful business owner/CEO	Money and power, own boss; prestige; passion for business	Social status; money
4	What motivates you to be a successful business owner/CEO?	Money; family employment; own boss	Money

(Continued)

Table 11.1 (Continued)

No	Question	Male Motives	Female Motives
5	Are you planning to leave the entrepreneurial life? Why would/not you do that?	No; when retired but be present; no, want to be more successful; no reason for that	No
6	Are you motivated by the current business environment to start a new business venture?	No	Very bad environment

Note: the motives are taken as the majority of answers on each question of both male and female business owners.

Discussion

The study has proposed several research questions. The first RQ (*RQ₁: Is there any difference observed regarding EI dimensions between men and women in managing the family business?*) addresses the EI dimensions (innovativeness, proactiveness, and risk-taking) among male and female business owners. The empirical results show that there is no difference in their scores (M: INN=4.2, PRO=4.2, RiT=4.8; F: INN=4.2, PRO=4.3, RiT=4.3).

The second RQ, (*RQ₂: Is there any difference observed regarding transformational leadership between men and women in managing the family business?*) explores the entrepreneurial (transformational) leadership (EL) scores (M: EL=3; F: EL=3) are the same for male and female business owners. No difference was found in leadership competence between male and female business owners. The traditional perception of men's superiority over women regarding leadership (Eagly, 2007) is contradicted in this research. No difference was found in leadership competence between male and female business owners, which confirms an earlier study by Vinkenburg, van Engen, Eagly, and Johannesen-Schmidt (2011).

The third RQ (*RQ₃: What were motives for male business owners that they started their own business, and what would be their motives if they would open an additional business?*) examines male owners' motives for being an entrepreneurial leader. It is observed no difference between men's and women's motives to be a successful entrepreneurial leader. Men are more toward being and independent from other employers, ("own boss"), personal source of finance ("money") and they would like to be seen in the society as good ones ("social status, prestige, employment contributors") while women have similar desires, as argued by Franck (2012).

The fourth RQ (*RQ₄: What are motives for female business owners to start their own business, and what would be their motives if they would open an additional business?*) seeks answers of what motivates female business owners to be a successful and entrepreneurial leader. Women's motives are very similar to men's motives ("own boss", "money", and "social status"). Earlier works by Buttner (1993) and Caputo and Dolinsky (1998), and McKay (2001) argued this similarity.

However, women tend more to have life and work, business and family balance (Lundstrom, 1999). The results confirm tendency of women's independence by "being own boss", which was explored in the earlier work of Sacirbey (1998).

The fifth RQ (*RQ₅: Do male business owners work more on strengthening business (entrepreneurial) networking compared with females counterpart?*) tries to inspect whether male business owners work more on entrepreneurial networking compared to female ones. The men's entrepreneurial or business networking's score (NW) is 3.7, and women's is 3.5. Obviously, business networking is a shortcoming for female entrepreneurs. One of the reasons might be stereotypical discrimination (Baker, 2014). Renzulli et al. (2000) argued that the business networking of men are likely to be heterogeneous, unlike women, who build their networking on close friends and families. However, although there is a difference in the networking basis, both men and women rely more on networks built on men (Aldrich, 1989). Moreover, the importance of networking for business growth is necessary (Wasserman and Faust, 1994; Zhao and Aram, 1995; Renzulli et al., 2000) and should not be neglected, regardless of gender.

The sixth RQ (*RQ₆: Does the current business environment motivates, supports both males and female business owners in developing their current (family) business and establishing a new start-up?*) investigates the business environment in which family businesses operate. In other words, whether both male and female business owners are being supported or discouraged by the current business landscape (Table 11.1). The average score of *male family business owners* business environment's (BE) is 3.5, and for female owners, it is 2.2. It is found that the business environment is "very harsh", and no participant finds it very supportive and encouraging. Rather, motivational factors tend to be very personal and yet similar for men and women (Buttner,1993; Caputo and Dolinsky, 1998; McKay, 2001; Lundstrom, 1999; Sacirbey, 1998). The business environment (made by the state in Bosnia and Herzegovina) should play a primary role in developing entrepreneurship development. Additionally, the state should encourage business opportunities for both, men and women.

Conclusion

Study of the family business is important for mirroring the facts of its existence, future position, and relationship with society. Some see family businesses differently, like not contributing to the economy (Fitzgerald and Muske, 2016), while others support the fact that family businesses are job creators (Kellermanns et al., 2008; Hoy and Sharma, 2010; Hacker and Dowling, 2012; Welsh et al., 2013; Ramadani, 2015; Ramadani and Hoy, 2015). This study did not examine the volume of job creation, but the entrepreneurial leadership, motivational factors, business environment, and networking, among male and female family business owners. The research showed that there is no difference between men and women business owners in entrepreneurial leadership scores (entrepreneurial orientation and transformational leadership).

Moreover, similarities have been identified when it comes to motivational factors and aspirations for the entrepreneurial life, which supports earlier works (Buttner, 1993; Caputo and Dolinsky, 1998; McKay, 2001). Being and independent psychologically and financially is one of the most reasons why both men and women are engaged in private family businesses. Being their own boss gives them the opportunity to test their ideas, employ appropriate experts, and to engage family members in the business, while creating a good status and image in the society. For them is just a pleasure to be someone who will contribute to society's development.

In addition, this study has investigated networking as a very important pillar in business growth and development (Wasserman and Faust, 1994; Zhao and Aram, 1995; Renzulli et al., 2000). Empirical results showed stronger networking with men than women. Reasons vary. One of them may be the old-fashioned stereotypes of femininity and masculinity in which men are seen as dominant. Another reason could be that women are more cautious and tend to build a network with trusted people, like family and friends, while men show more bravery in building a network. This could be justified by the natural male attitude towards friends and business networks. Men are naturally more willing to take risks when establishing a business network, compared to women.

The business environment under study proved to be very "unfriendly" for all participants. As family business owners, they do not feel that the current business environment encourages them to grow and further develop their businesses.

Study implications

The study derives several implications. Firstly, this pioneer study (in this region) in the field of entrepreneurial leadership, in family businesses, showed that gender issues do not matter when it comes to the competence of business owners. Women are inspired and eager to have their own business. However, previous research suggests that women often become entrepreneurs because of job creation and lifestyle reasons (Kellermanns et al., 2008; Hoy and Sharma, 2010; Hacker and Dowling, 2012; Welsh et al., 2013; Ramadani, 2015; Ramadani and Hoy, 2015). It should be noted that potentials for female entrepreneurship exist in which women can contribute to the whole economy while denying the status quo (Fitzgerald and Muske, 2016).

Secondly, it has been identified that businesswomen are not as strong in establishing business networking as men. Women should be more open to creating business networks: business growth, from one perspective, depends on networking (Wasserman and Faust, 1994; Zhao and Aram, 1995; Renzulli et al., 2000). It is evident that male business owners do not have this as the barrier in growing their businesses. Both genders should acknowledge the importance of business networking. Current technology, including social networks, can pave the way for establishing strong ties with prospective customers, suppliers, or partners.

Thirdly, the current business environment favors neither male nor female business owners. It does not help them in developing their current business growth or develop new business. At this point, the state policy makers should listen to the experience of private business owners as to what can be done to create an incubator for business as the lever for the future development of the country. Moreover, entrepreneurs should raise their voices regarding state policies that shackle the business environment and entrepreneurship development in this country.

Limitations

In addition to benefits that this work brings, however, there are limitations too. The study could be based on the quantitative approach to generalize similar findings to the population. Recording interviews could bring more insights, because just taking notes may omit some beneficial thoughts.

Future work

The study's scope could be expanded to more specific groups of people, such as different age ranges of males and females so different perspectives could be explored and examined. Different perspectives can then be explored and examined. Such comparisons can bring unexpected results. Additionally, it would be interesting if inherited family businesses were studied, because property acquired by heredity is different from being earned, and owners of such businesses have different perspectives from those who developed their businesses. Such a study could examine male- and female-inherited family business. Last, but not least, networking and business environment could be studied in the whole region and differences in perception and implementation of business networking establishment compared.

References

Ahl, H. (2006). Why research on women entrepreneurs needs new directions. *Entrepreneurship: Theory and Practice, 30*(5), 595–621.

Aldrich, H. E. (1989), Networking among women entrepreneurs. In O. Hagan, C. Rivchun, and D. Sexton, (eds.). *Women-owned businesses* (pp. 103–132). New York: Praeger.

Baker, C. (2014). Stereotyping and women's roles in leadership positions. *Industrial and Commercial Training, 46*(6), 332–337.

Bass, B. M., and Avolio, B. J. (1992). *Manual for the Organizational Description Questionnaire (ODQ)*. Palo Alto, CA: Consulting Psychologists Press.

Bass, B. M., and Riggio, R. E. (2006). *Transformational leadership* (2nd ed.). Mahwah, NJ: Center for Leadership Studies Binghamton University, Kravis Leadership Institute Claremont McKenna College, Lawrence Erlbaum Associates, Publishers.

Bogren, M., Friedrichs, Y. v., Rennemo, Ø., and Widding, Ø. (2013). Networking women entrepreneurs: Fruitful for business growth? *International Journal of Gender and Entrepreneurship, 5*(1), 60–77.

Brown, T. E., Davidsson, P., and Wiklund, J. (2001). An operationalization of Stevenson's conceptualization of entrepreneurship as opportunity-based firm behavior. *Strategic Management Journal,* 22, 953–968.

Buttner, H. (1993). Female entrepreneurs: How far they have come? *Business Horizons, 36(2), 59–66.*

Caputo, R., and Dolinsky, A. (1998). Women's choice to pursue self-employment: The role f financial and human capital of household members. *Journal of Small Business Management,* 36(3), 8–17.

Carter, S., and Cannon, T. (1992). *Women as entrepreneurs.* London: Academic Press.

Charoensukmongkol, P. (2016). The interconnections between bribery, political network, government supports, and their consequences on export performance of small and medium enterprises in Thailand. *Journal of International Entrepreneurship,* 4(2), 259–276.

Chell, E., and Baines, S. (1998). Does gender affect business 'performance'? A study of microbusinesses in business services in the UK. *Entrepreneurship and Regional Development,* 10(2), 117–135.

Cooper, D. R., and Schindler, P. S. (2014). *Business research methods* (12nd ed.). New York: McGraw-Hill.

Covin, G. J., Green, K. M., and Slevin, P. D. (2006). Strategic process effects on the entrepreneurial orientation-sales growth rate relationship. *Entrepreneurship Theory and Practice,* 30(1), 57–81.

Covin, J. G., and Slevin, D. P. (1988). The influence of organization structure on the utility of an entrepreneurial top management style. *Journal of Management Studies,* 25(3), 217–234.

Covin, J. G., and Slevin, D. P. (1989). Strategic management of small firms in hostile and benign environments. *Strategic Management Journal,* 10(1), 75–87.

Dana, L. P (1994). The impact on culture on entrepreneurship, innovation, and change in the Balkans: The Yugopluralist model. *Entrepreneurship, Innovation and Change,* 3(2), 177–190.

Dana, L. P. (1999). Business and entrepreneurship in Bosnia and Herzegovina. *Journal of Business and Entrepreneurship,* 11(2), 105–117.

Dana, L. P. (2001). Introduction networks, internationalization and policy. *Small Business Economics,* 16, 57–62.

Dana, L. P., Etemad, H., and Wright, R. W. (2000). The global reach of symbiotic networks. *Journal of Euromarketing,* 9(2), 1–16.

Dana, L. P., and Ramadani, V. (eds.). (2015). *Family business in transition economies.* Switzerland: Springer International Publishing.

Díaz-García, M. C., and Jiménez-Moreno, J. (2010). Entrepreneurial intention: The role of gender. *International Entrepreneurship and Management Journal,* 6(3), 261–283.

Eagly, A. H. (2007). Female leadership advantage and disadvantage: Resolving the contradictions. *Psychology of Women Quarterly,* 31(1), 1–12.

Etemad, H., Wright, R. W., and Dana, L. P. (2001). Symbiotic international business networks: Collaboration between small and large firms. Thunderbird *International Business Review, Journal of Euromarketing,* 43(4), 481–499.

Fatoki, O., and Oni, O. (2014). The networking behaviour of immigrant entrepreneurs in South Africa. *Mediterranean Journal of Social Sciences,* 5(20), 284–290.

Fitzgerald, M. A., and Muske, G. (2016, March). Family businesses and community development: The role of small business owners and entrepreneurs. *Community Development,* 5330.

Franck, A. K. (2012). Factors motivating women's informal micro-entrepreneurship. *International Journal of Gender and Entrepreneurship,* 4(1), 65–78.

Gërguri-Rashiti, S., Ramadani, V., Abazi-Alili, H., Dana, L. P., and Ratten, V. (2015). ICT, innovation and firm performance: The transition economies context. *Thunderbird International Business Review,* 59(1), 93–102.

Goktan, A. B., and Gupta, V. K. (2013). Sex, gender, and individual entrepreneurial orientation: Evidence from four countries. *International Entrepreneurship and Management Journal,* 11(1), 95–112.

Green, E., and Cohen, L. (1995). Women's business-are women entrepreneurs breaking new ground or simply balancing the demands of women's work in a new way. *Journal of Gender Studies,* 4(3), 297–314.

Gupta, V., Turban, D. B., Wasti, S. A., and Sikdar, A. (2009). The role of gender stereotypes in perceptions of entrepreneurs and intentions to become an entrepreneur. *Entrepreneurship: Theory and Practice,* 33(2), 397–417.

Hacker, J., and Dowling, M., (2012). Succession in family firms: How to improve family satisfaction and family harmony. *International Journal of Entrepreneurship and Small Business,* 15(1), 76–99.

Harrison, B. (1997). *Lean and mean.* New York: Gilford.

Hoffmann, A., Junge, M., and Malchow-Møller, N. (2015). Running in the family: Parental role models in entrepreneurship. *Small Business Economics,* 44(1), 79–104.

Hoy, F., and Sharma, P. (2010). *Entrepreneurial family firms.* Upper Saddle River, NJ: Pearson Prentice Hall.

Johanson, M., and Kao, P. T. (2010). Networks in internationalisation. In J. Pla-Barber and J. Alegre (eds.), *Reshaping the boundaries of the firm in an era of global interdependence: Progress in International Business Research,* 5, 119–142.

Karra, N., and Phillips, N. (2004). Entrepreneurship goes global. *Ivey Business Journal,* 69(2), 1–6.

Kedmenec, I., Tominc, P., and Rebernik, M. (2014). Gender differences in the usage of resources in the entrepreneurial opportunity identification process in Slovenia and Croatia. *Economic Research-*Ekonomska Istraživanja, 27(1), 366–377.

Kellermanns, W. F., Eddleston, K. A., Barnett, T., and Pearson, A. (2008). An exploratory study of family member characteristics and involvement: Effects on entrepreneurial behavior in the family firm. *Family Business Review,* 21(1), 1–14.

Kraus, S., Rigtering, J. P. C., Hughes, M., and Hosman, V. (2012). Entrepreneurial orientation and the business performance of SMEs: A quantitative study from the Netherlands. *Review of Managerial Science,* 6(2), 161–182.

Lee, C., Lee, K., and Pennings, J. M. (2001). Internal capabilities, external networks, and performance: A study on technology-based ventures. *Strategic Management Journal,* 22, 615–640.

Lee, S. M., and Lim, S. (2009). Entrepreneurial orientation and the performance of service business. *Service Business,* 3, 1–13.

Lumpkin, G. T., and Dess, G. G. (1996). Clarifying the entrepreneurial orientation construct and linking it to performance. *Academy of Management Review,* 21(1), 135–172.

Lundstrom, M. (1999). Mommy, do you love your company more than me? *Business Week,* 3660, 175.

Matzler, K., Schwarz, E., Deutinger, N., and Harms, R. (2008). Relationship between transformational leadership, product innovation and performance in SMEs. *Journal of Small Business and Entrepreneurship,* 21(2), 139–151.

McKay, R. (2001). Women entrepreneurs: Moving beyond family and flexibility. *International Journal of Entrepreneurial Behavior and Research, 7*(4), 148–165.

Michie, J., and Zumitzavan, V. (2012). The impact of 'learning' and 'leadership' management styles on organizational outcomes: A study of tyre firms in Thailand. *Asia Pacific Business Review*, 18(4), 607–630.

Miller, D. (1983). The correlates in three types of firms. *Management Science*, 29(7), 770–791.

Palalić, R. (2017). The phenomenon of entrepreneurial leadership in gazelles and mice: A qualitative study from Bosnia and Herzegovina. *World Review of Entrepreneurship, Management and Sustainable Development*, 13(2/3), 211–236.

Palalić, R., and Busatlic, S. (2015). Exploratory research on relationship between entrepreneurial orientation dimensions and business performance and growth of fast and slow growing small and medium enterprises in Bosnia and Herzegovina. *International Journal of Business and Management*, 10(2), 15–30.

Palalić, R., Ramadani, V., and Dana, L. P. (2017) Entrepreneurship in Bosnia and Herzegovina: focus on gender. *European Business Review*, 29(4). https://doi.org/10.1108/EBR-05-2016-0071

Patton, M. Q. (1990). *Qualitative research and evaluation methods* (2nd ed.). Newbury Park, CA: Sage.

Podsakoff, P. M., MacKenzie, S., Moorman, R. H., and Fetter, R. (1990). Transformational leadership behaviors and their effects on followers' trust in leader, satisfaction and organizational citizenship behaviors. *Leadership Quarterly*, 1, 107–142.

Ramadani, V. (2015). The woman entrepreneur in Albania: An exploratory study on motivation, problems and success factors. *Journal of Balkan and Near Eastern Studies*, 17(2), 204–221.

Ramadani, V., Hisrich, R. D., and Gërguri-Rashiti, S. (2015). Female entrepreneurs in transition economies: Insights from Albania, Macedonia and Kosovo. *World Review of Entrepreneurship, Management and Sustainable Development*, 11(4), 391–413.

Ramadani, V., Hisrich, R. D., and Gërguri-Rashiti, S. (2015). Female entrepreneurs in transition economies: Insights from Albania, Macedonia and Kosovo. *World Review of Entrepreneurship, Management and Sustainable Development*, 11(4), 391–413.

Ramadani, V., and Hoy, F. (2015). Context and uniqueness of family businesses. In L.-P. Dana and V. Ramadani (eds.), *Family businesses in transition economies* (pp. 9–37). Cham: Springer.

Ratten, V. (2013). The evolution of mobile social networks through technological innovation. In Brem and Viadort (eds.), *Evolution of innovation management* (pp. 132–150). London: Palgrave Macmillan.

Ratten, V. (2014). Collaborative entrepreneurship and the fostering of entrepreneurialism in developing countries. *International Journal of Social Entrepreneurship and Innovation*, 3(2), 137–149.

Renzulli, L. A., Aldrich, H., and Moody, J. (2000). Family matters: Gender, networks, and entrepreneurial outcomes. *Social Forces*, 79(2), 523–546.

Rosa, P., Carter, S., and Hamilton, D. (1996). Gender as a determinant of small business performance: Insights from a British study. *Small Business Economics*, 8(6), 463478.

Runyan, R. and Swinney, J. (2008) Entrepreneurial orientation versus small business orientation: what are their relationships to firm performance? *Journal of Small Business Management*, 46(4), 567–588.

Sacirbey, O. (1998). German women create jobs by starting their own businesses. *Christian Science Monitor*, 90(74), 7.

Sánchez, J. C., and Licciardello, O. (2012). Gender differences and attitudes in entrepreneurial intentions: The role of career choice. *Journal of Women's Entrepreneurship and Education,* 1(2), 7–27.

Shinnar, R. S., Giacomin, O., and Janssen, F. (2012). Entrepreneurial perceptions and intentions: The role of gender and culture. *Entrepreneurship: Theory and Practice,* 36(3), 465–493.

Sullivan Mort, G., and Weerawardena, J. (2006). Networking capability and international entrepreneurship: How networks function in Australian born global firms. *International Marketing Review,* 23(5), 549–572.

Stevenson, H. H., and Jarillo, J. C. (1990). A paradigm of entrepreneurship: Entrepreneurial management. *Strategic Management Journal,* 11, 17–27.

Taatila, V., and Down, S. (2012). Measuring entrepreneurial orientation of University Students. *Education and Training,* 54(8), 744–760.

Teo, S. K. (1996). Women entrepreneurs of Singapore. In A. M. Low and L. W. Tan (eds.), *Entrepreneurs, entrepreneurship and enterprising culture* (pp. 254–289). Singapore: Addison-Wesley Publishing Company.

Tominc, P., and Rebernik, M. (2004). The scarcity of female entrepreneurship. *Društvena istraživanja,* 13, 779–802.

Tominc, P. and Rebernik, M. (2006) Female entrepreneurial growth aspirations in Slovenia: an unexploited resource, In: Brush, Candida, Carter, Nancy, Gatewood, Elizabeth, Greene, Patricia, and Hart, Myra (Eds.), *Growth-oriented women entrepreneurs and their businesses: a global research perspective, (New horizons in entrepreneurship).* Cheltenham (UK); Northampton (Mass.): E. Elgar, 330-347.

Tominc, P. and Rebernik, M. (2007), "Gender differences in early-stage entrepreneurship in three European post-socialist countries", *Društvenaistraživanja, Zagreb,* 16(3), 589-611.

Treasurer, B., Adelman, K., and Cohn, L. (2013). The power of courage for women leaders. *T + D,* 67(6), 52–70.

Trevis, S. C., Moss, T. W., and Short, J. C. (2009). Entrepreneurial orientation: An applied perspective. *Business Horizons,* 52, 319–324.

Van Manen, V. M. (1990). *Researching lived experience: Human science for an action sensitive pedagogy.* Albany: State University of New York Press.

Vinkenburg, C. J., van Engen, M. L., Eagly, A. H., and Johannesen-Schmidt, M. C. (2011). An exploration of stereotypical beliefs about leadership styles: Is transformational leadership a route to women's promotion? *The Leadership Quarterly,* 22(1), 10–21.

Volchek, D., Jantunen, A. and Saarenketo, S., 2013. The institutional environment for international entrepreneurship in Russia: Reflections on growth decisions and performance in SMEs. *Journal of International Entrepreneurship,* 11(4), 320–350.

Wagner, B., and Svensson, G. (2014). A framework to navigate sustainability in business networks. *European Business Review,* 26(4), 340–367.

Wang, G., Oh., I. S., Courtright, S. H., and Colbert, A. E. (2011). Transformational leadership and performance across criteria and levels: A meta-analytic review of 25 years of research. *Group and Organization Management,* 36(2), 223–270.

Wasserman, S., and Faust, K. (1994). *Social network analysis: Methods and applications.* New York: Cambridge University Press.

Watkins, J. M., and Watkins, D. S. (1986). The female entrepreneur: Her background and determinants of business choice. In J. Curran, J. Stanworth and D. Watkins (eds.), *The survival of the small firm* (pp. 220–232). Aldershot: Gower.

Watson, J., and Newby, R. (2005). Biological sex, stereotypical sex-roles, and SME owner characteristics. *International Journal of Entrepreneurial Behaviour and Research,* 11(2), 129–143.

Welsh, D. H. B., Memili, E., Rosplock, K., Roure, J., Seguardo, J. L. (2013). Perceptions of entrepreneurship across generations in family businesses and family offices: A stewardship theory perspective. *Journal of Family Business Strategy,* 4(3), 213–226.

White, P. (2009). Building a sustainability strategy into the business. *Corporate Governance: The International Journal of Business in Society,* 9(4), 386–394.

Wiklund, J., and Shepherd, D. (2005). Entrepreneurial orientation and small business performance: A configurational approach. *Journal of Business Venturing,* 20(1), 71–91

Wright, R. W., and Dana, L. P. (2003). Changing paradigms of international entrepreneurship strategy. *Journal of International Entrepreneurship,* 1(1), 135–152.

Zhao, L., and Aram, J. D. (1995). Networking and growth of young technology-intensive ventures in China. *Journal of Business Venturing,* 10(5), 349–370.

12 Listed Italian family firms

Corporate governance composition and effects on performance

Laura Broccardo and Elisa Truant

1. Introduction

Analyzing the literature about family firms, corporate governance is a relevant topic debated in the last 20 years especially for the relationship between family and business. A well-functioning board of directors is a critical source for family and business and this relationship emerges in particular inside the board of directors.

The *main goal* of this study is to analyze the impact of board composition in listed Italian family firms on performance. This research will also try to understand the specific features of this kind of firm and some possible changes in corporate governance. Corporate governance has a relevant impact on business performance.

The relevance of board composition is in its perceived role in enhancing the firm's performance. The primary function of boards of directors is to monitor the managers' actions and decisions, in order to protect the interests of owners from managerial opportunism (Fama and Jensen, 1983).

Some different theoretical perspectives have been used to define and explain the composition of the board of directors, but the main classification distinguishes between outside and inside boards. Pearce and Zahra (1992) considered insiders as current members of top management team and employees of the firm, while outsiders do not have such associations. But it's important to underline that in the studies about family firms another category of members could be considered: family board members, because board composition is a reflection of family characteristics and objectives (Corbetta and Salvato, 2004; Voordeckers et al., 2007). Analyzing the composition of boards of directors for a sample of listed Italian family firms, we identified the family members and the independent members.

Listed Italian family firms comprise the sample analyzed and the data used are from AIDA database and the Borsa Italiana website, which contains the official data of the listed companies.

Definitions of family businesses are various and ambiguities persist (Chua et al., 1999); indeed, the family firm constitutes a wide range of firms, from small owner-manager firms to large listed family-controlled corporations (Mustakallio, 2002). Consequently, for this study it was decided to focus on family firms with

(1) at least 50 percent of the ownership controlled by the family, and (2) family firms in which at least one family member occupies management role.

This study analyses the composition–performance relationship in the family business also because in the *organizational management* studies the *family* is a relevant *variable*, but sometimes it is forgotten. Also Dyer (2006, 253) refers to the family as "the missing variable in organizational research" and he warns that "failing to use the family as a variable in organizational research can lead to incomplete or misleading findings".

In the literature *different theories* to study the *board of directors* were used like agency theory, stewardship theory, resources dependency theory, contingent approach. Most of the studies (e.g. Bartholomeusz and Tanewski, 2006; Fiegener et al., 2000; Voordeckers et al., 2007; Anderson and Reeb, 2003) underline the relationship between the composition of the board of directors and the firm's performance.

This study contributes to the literature on family corporate governance and emphasizes that the family role has a positive effect of family performance, underlining the relevance of the family members inside the board. In particular, the structure of the board of directors influences the performance in Italian listed companies. In addition, the family board members play an important role in facilitating communication between the family firm and the board of directors.

This study is organized as follows. In Section 2, it analyses the theoretical background about family firms and corporate governance, particularly referring to the family firm. In Section 3, the research method is outlined, and a brief presentation of the analyzed sample is given. Section 4 discusses the findings and the results. Finally, in Section 5 the main conclusions are underlined, with future developments.

2. Literature analysis

About family firms

In the last years, family firms have received increased attention. Several recent studies have reported that in continental Europe, Asia and Latin America, the vast majority of publicly traded firms are family controlled (La Porta et al., 1999; Daily et al., 1993, Claessens et al., 2000; Faccio and Lang, 2002). These studies also suggest that family firms play an important role in economic activity worldwide. In fact two-thirds of private businesses in many countries are considered to be family firms (Neubauer and Lank, 1998). They contribute to wealth creation and job generation with reference to narrow and broad definitions of the family firm (Astrachan and Shanker, 2003).

Notwithstanding the significant presence of family firms worldwide, it is only over the last few decades that academia has turned its attention to the family dimension as a determinant of business phenomena, with a significant growth in interest over time (Prencipe et al., 2014).

The attention on family firms increase, but *it's not so easy to give a definition of family firm* and in the literature ambiguities persist. In fact in the first issue of *Family Business Review* in their editorial note, Lansberg et al. (1988) asked: "What is a family business?" People seem to understand what is meant by the term "family business", yet when they try to articulate a precise definition they quickly discover that it is a very complicated phenomenon (Hoy and Verser, 1994). The question continues to be asked because definitions of "family business" abound in the literature.

This research is based on the common selected criteria of ownership and management control (Chua et al., 1999), to identify family businesses.

In this study a firm is classified as a family firm if:

- at least 50 percent of the shares are owned by the family, and the family is responsible for the management of the company;
- or at least 50 percent of the shares are owned by the family, the company is not family-managed, but the CEO perceives the firm as family firm;
- or family ownership is less than 50 percent, the company is family managed, the CEO perceives the firm as a family firm, and a venture capital or investment company owns at least 50 percent of the shares (Broccardo, 2011).

Prencipe et al. (2014) state that although the field of family firms has been of interest to researchers in the area of management since the 1980s, in the early years the study of family businesses fell into the field of sociology, and at a later stage into small business management. Only during the last decade has a growing diversity of research interests led to the development of a more comprehensive and interdisciplinary body of knowledge related to family companies. In particular, our study focuses on corporate governance in family firms.

Corporate governance and family firms

In the literature of family firms, the corporate governance is a relevant topic debated in the last 20 years especially for the relationship between family and business (Neubauer and Lank, 1998). A well-functioning board of directors is a critical source for family and business; this relationship emerges in particular inside the board of directors (Miller, Le Breton-Miller, Lester, and Cannella, 2007).

When investigating this topic, the researchers use different theories like the agency theory, contingent approach, life-cycle approach, stewardship theory and social capital. In particular, attention is focused on the composition of the board of directors and its influence on business performance, but the obtained results are sometimes contradictory, and it is not clear how board composition affects firm performance.

Consequently it is important to understand the focus, the use in governance and how these theories can be applied in family firms governance, as shown in Table 12.1.

Table 12.1 Corporate governance theoretical framework

Theoretical framework	Focus	Application in governance	Application in family firm governance
Agency theory	Minimization of problems caused by the separation of ownership from control	Relationships between principal and agent, usually among owners and management	Effects of the separation of ownership from managerial control
Resource dependency theory	Political approach to manage interdependencies between organizations	Networks, interfirm, intrafirm governance	Power and resource aspects of relationships in family firms
Stewardship theory	Altruism, good stewardship Managers are trustworthy	No alignment problem stewards, relational governance	Effects of no alignment problems between owners and managers

Source: Mustakallio, 2002

Analyzing agency theory, which states that the primary function of board of directors is to monitor the actions of agents in order to protect the interests of owners (Fama and Jensen, 1983), and focusing on family firms, it is possible to underline that family firms have less agency cost. This is because most of owners, managers and board members belong to the same family. In particular, the boards of directors have to monitor the managers' actions to guard the interests of owners from managerial opportunism. Consequently, following agency theory, a high number of independent members are positively related to family performance, also if in family firms the agency problem is less intense because property rights are largely restricted to internal decision agents.

Resource dependency theory (Pfeffer, 1981, 1982, 1987) affirms that business continuity is dependent on the firm's ability to access and control environmental resources like human capital and relational resources, which can help the firm to reduce environmental uncertainty. The board can facilitate the acquisition of resources that are critical to the firm success and its role become determinant (Zahra et al., 2004).

Stewardship theory holds that fewer outside members are needed in the board of directors and its main role is to support the management (Corbetta and Tomaselli, 1996;Corbetta and Salvato, 2004). Managers are motivated by collectivistic behavior and inside directors or affiliated directors lead a firm to higher performance. This theory underlines that board structure should be characterized mainly by insiders or by affiliated outsiders who are linked to organization or to each other by family and social ties (Sundaramurthy and Lewis, 2003).

From these different theories the direct relationship between board composition and firm performance does not emerge clearly; consequently this research investigates about relationship considering two types of boards – family members and independent members – and seeks to determine what kind of theory can explain the results in the context of family business.

In addition, this study also analyzes the composition–performance relationship in the family business because in the organizational management researches, the family is a relevant variable, but sometimes it is forgotten. Also Dyer (2006, 253) refers to the family as "the missing variable in organizational research" and he warns that "failing to use the family as a variable in organizational research can lead to incomplete or misleading findings".

3. Methodology

Sample

This study is based on a random sample of listed Italian firms, including only the companies classifiable as family or non-family in a clear way. The sample includes 10 listed family firms, which represent the 11 percent of the domestic market capitalization, belonging to different sectors, avoiding the sector influence (see Table 12.2).

As stated earlier, in this study a firm is classified as a family firm, if:

1. at least 50 percent of the shares are owned by the family, and the family is responsible for the management of the company;
2. or at least 50 percent of the shares are owned by the family, the company is not family-managed, but the CEO perceives the firm as family firm;
3. or family ownership is less than 50 percent, the company is family managed, the CEO perceives the firm as a family firm and a venture capital or investment company owns at least 50 percent of the shares.

The data used were extracted from the AIDA database and the Borsa Italiana website, which contain the official data for the listed companies.

Table 12.2 The family firms sample

Listed family firms	Classification
Autogrill S.p.A.	FF
Bulgari S.p.A.	FF
Buzzi Unicem S.p.A.	FF
Campari S.p.A.	FF
Exor S.p.A.	FF
Fiat S.p.A.	FF
Luxottica S.p.A.	FF
Mediaset S.p.A.	FF
Pirelli & C. S.p.A.	FF
Tod's S.p.A.	FF

Source: own elaboration based on AIDA database

Research questions and method

The main goal of this study is to analyze the impact of the board composition in the listed Italian Family firms on performance. We analyzed board composition by distinguishing between family members and non-family members, and also independent members. The "independent member" is a board member non-executive who has not recently maintained, even indirectly, relations with the firm or persons linked to the firm that would influence their independence of opinion.

To reach the declared goals, the following main research questions were formulated.

- RQ1: If the presence of family members in the board of direction increases, does also family firm's performance increase?
- RQ2: If the presence of independent members in the board of direction of family firms increases, does also family firm's performance increase?

To answer RQ1 and RQ2, the Pearson correlation ratio was used to identify a positive or a negative relation between firm performance and board composition.

Regarding the Pearson ratio (p) it is also important to emphasize that if:

- if $p > 0$ there is a direct correlation;
- if $p = 0$ there is no correlation;
- if $p < 0$ there is a indirect correlation;
- if $0 < p < 0,3$ the correlation is weak;
- if $0,3 < p < 0,7$ the correlation is moderate; and
- if $p > 0,7$ the correlation is strong.

4. Findings and results

In answering the formulated research questions, we tested and correlated the following: return on investments (ROI), return on equity (ROE), return on sales (ROS), quick ratio and current ratio. We used the mean of the last five years (2011–2015) to determine the presence of family members and independent members inside the family firms' board of directors (using the meaning percentage of the last five years).

Answering *RQ1 "If the presence of family members in the board of direction increases, does also family firm's performance increase?"* we analyzed the data shown in the following tables.

We began by identified the percentage of family members inside each company, as shown in Table 12.3.

In the next phase, we calculate the correlation between the main ratios and the presence of family members (see Table 12.4).

It emerges that the economic and financial performance increases if the number of family members in the board increase. This is supported by a moderate correlation between each ratio and the percentage of family members inside the board of directors.

Table 12.3 Family members

Family firms	% Family members (B)
Autogrill S.p.A.	16,67%
Bulgari S.p.A.	28,57%
Buzzi Unicem S.p.A.	33,33%
Campari S.p.A.	11,11%
Exor S.p.A.	11,76%
Fiat S.p.A.	13,33%
Luxottica S.p.A.	6,67%
Mediaset S.p.A.	14,29%
Pirelli & C. S.p.A.	5,26%
Tod's S.p.A.	33,33%

Source: own elaboration

Table 12.4 Relationship between family members and performance

Ratio analyzed (mean 2011–2015)	Pearson ratio between ratio analyzed and % family members
ROI	0,43
ROE	0,15
ROS	0,44
Quick ratio	0,42
Current ratio	0,71

Source: own elaboration based on AIDA database and Borsa Italiana website

Answering the *RQ2 "If the presence of independent members in the board of direction of family firms increases, does also a family firm's performance increase?"* we analyzed the data shown in Table 12.5.

The presence of independent members varies from 28.57 percent to 57.14 percent. In the next phase, we calculate the correlation between the main ratios and the presence of family members (see Table 12.6).

It emerges that economic and financial performance increases if the number of independent members in the board decreases. This is supported by the indirect correlation between each ratio and the percentage of independent members, how the table shows.

In particular analyzing both economic and financial ratio it emerges how the family members influence positively the firm performance and how the independent members are indirectly correlated with the performance.

5. Conclusion, contribution and future developments

The purpose of this study was to scrutinize the relationship between board composition and the performance in the listed Italian family firms.

Table 12.5 Independent members

Family firms	% Independent members (C)
Autogrill S.p.A.	50,00%
Bulgari S.p.A.	57,14%
Buzzi Unicem S.p.A.	33,33%
Campari S.p.A.	33,33%
Exor S.p.A.	29,41%
Fiat S.p.A.	53,33%
Luxottica S.p.A.	46,67%
Mediaset S.p.A.	28,57%
Pirelli & C. S.p.A.	52,63%
Tod's S.p.A.	41,67%

Source: own elaboration

Table 12.6 Relationship between independent members and performance

Ratio analyzed (mean 2011–2015)	Pearson ratio between ratio analyzed and % family members
ROI	–0,28
ROE	–0,15
ROS	–0,50
Quick ratio	–0,55
Current ratio	0,05

Source: own elaboration based on AIDA database and Borsa Italiana website

The analysis underlines the relevance of the presence of family members in the board, demonstrating how the family members positively influence the performance. It also emerges that independent members have an indirect correlation with the performance. This evidence contrasts with agency theory, which affirms that a high number of independent members is positively related to family performance.

Our findings are in line with stewardship theory. Besides, the family board members have an important relation with family performance, helping the firms to open the communication between the family and the firm.

Also Gnan et al. (2015) affirm that agency theory cannot be considered a fully explanatory theory. Indeed, based on the results of the companies analyzed and as stewardship theory sustains, fewer outside members of the board of directors are needed. This is due to operative managers being motivated by more collectivistic behavior and inside directors or affiliated directors, which leads firm to achieve a higher performance. In addition, this research underlines that the companies outperform with a board structure, characterized mainly by insiders who belong to the family.

This study contributes to the literature on family corporate governance. It shows that the family involvement has a positive effect on the firm's performance, underlining the role of the family members. In particular, the research contributes empirically to a deeper understanding of governance in family firms, underlining how the structure of the board of directors influences their performance. Furthermore, the theoretical contribution focuses on the conversation about the different theories, particularly referring to the agency and stewardship theories.

To conclude, as observed by Gnan et al. (2015, 357) "Governance systems, mechanisms, and roles are relevant concepts at the family level as wells in firms, as the family has to be directed and controlled to protect both its intangible assets (unity, trust, values, and so on) and its tangible ones".

Future developments could consider a large number of companies and also compare the board composition of family firms in different countries.

References

Anderson, R. C., and Reeb, D. M. (2003). Founding-family ownership and firm performance: Evidence from the S&P 500. *Journal of Finance*, 58(3), 1301–1328.

Astrachan, J. H., and Shanker, M. C. (2003). Family businesses' contribution to the US economy: A closet look. *Family Business Review*, 16, 211–219.

Bartholomeusz, S., and Tanewski, G. A. (2006). The relationship between family firms and corporate governance. *Journal of Small Business Management*, 44, 245–267.

Broccardo, L. (2011). Family versus non family firms in the luxury yachts sector: Strategy – structure combination to manage the performance. *Electronic Journal of Family Business Studies (EJFBS)*, 5(1–2), 96–125.

Chua, J. H., Chrisman, J. J., and Sharma, P. (1999). Defining the family business by behaviour. *Entrepreneurship: Theory and Practice*, 23(4), 19–39.

Claessens, S., Djankov, S., and Lang, L. H. P. (2000). The separation of ownership and control in East Asian corporations. *Journal of Financial Economics*, 58(1), 81–112.

Corbetta, G., and Salvato, C. A. (2004). The board of directors in family firms: One size fits all? *Family Business Review*, 17(2), 119–134.

Corbetta, G., and Tomaselli, S. (1996). Boards of directors in Italian family businesses. *Family Business Review*, 9(4), 403–421.

Daily, C. M., and Dollinger, M. J. (1993). Alternative methodologies for identifying family versus non-family businesses. *Journal of Small Business Management*. 31(2), 117–136.

Dyer Gibb, W. (2006, December). Examining the "Family Effect" on firm performance. *Family Business Review*, 19(4), 253–273.

Faccio, M., and Lang, L. H. P. (2002). The ultimate ownership of Western corporations. *Journal of Financial Economics*, 65, 365–395.

Fama, E. F., and Jensen, M. C. (1983). Separation of ownership and control. *Journal of Law and Economics*, 26, 301–325.

Fiegener, M. K., Brown, B. M., Dreux IV, D. R., and Dennis Jr., W. J. (2000). The adoption of outside boards by small private US firms. *Entrepreneurship and Regional Development*, 12, 291–309.

Gnan, L., Montemerlo, D., and Huse, M. (2015). Governance systems in family SMEs: The substitution effects between family councils and corporate governance mechanisms. *Journal of Small Business Management*, 53(2), 355–381.

Hoy, F., and Verser, T. (1994). Emerging business, emerging field: Entrepreneurship and the family firm. *Entrepreneurship Theory and Practice,* 19(1), 9–24

La Porta, R., Lopez-de-Silanes, F., and Shleifer, A. (1999). Corporate ownership around the world. *The Journal of Finance,* 54(2), 471–517.

Lansberg, I., Pertow. E. L., and Rogolsky, S. (1988). Family business as an emerging field. *Family Business Review,* 1(1), 1–8.

Miller, D., Le Breton-Miller, I., Lester, R. H., and Cannella Jr., A. A. (2007). Are family firms really superior performers? *Journal of Corporate Finance,* 13, 829–858.

Mustakallio, M. A. (2002). Contractual and relational governance in firms: Effect on strategic decision-making quality and firm performance. Doctoral Dissertation, Helsinki University of Technology.

Neubauer, F. F., and Lank, A. G. (1998). *The family business: Its governance for sustainability.* New York: Routledge.

Pearce, J. A., and Zahra, S. (1992). Board composition from a strategic contingency perspective. *Journal of Management Studies,* 29, 411–438.

Pfeffer, J. (1981). *Power in organizations.* Marshfield, MA: Pitman Publishing.

Pfeffer, J. (1982). *Organizations and organization theory.* Cambridge, MA: Ballinger Publishing Company.

Pfeffer, J. (1987). A resource dependence perspective on intercorporate relations. In M. S. Mizruchi and M. Schwartz (eds.), *Intercorporate relations: The structural analysis of business.* Cambridge: Cambridge University Press.

Prencipe, A., Bar-Yosef, S., and Dekker, H. C. (2014). Accounting research in family firms: Theoretical and empirical challenges. *European Accounting Review,* 23(3), 361–385.

Sundaramurthy, C., and Lewis, M. (2003). Control and collaboration: Paradoxes of governance. *Academy of Management Review,* 28, 397–415.

Voordeckers, W., Van Gils, A., and Van den Heuvel, J. (2007). Board composition in small and medium-sized family firms. *Journal of Small Business Management,* 45, 137–156.

Zahra, S. A., Hayton, J. C., and Salvato, C. (2004). Entrepreneurship in family vs. non-family firms: A resource-based analysis of the effect of organizational culture. *Entrepreneurship Theory & Practice,* 28(4), 363–381.

13 Future research directions for women entrepreneurship in family business

Vanessa Ratten, Veland Ramadani and Leo-Paul Dana

Introduction

One of the fastest growing research areas is women's entrepreneurship, which is due to women having a greater role in economic decisions than they did in the past. Whilst there has been a growth in research about women entrepreneurship and family business, there is still a lack of understanding about how they are related. This is due to the stereotypes existing about women entrepreneurs particularly in terms of their role in family business (Ratten, 2012). This chapter aims to describe the role of women entrepreneurs in family business by suggesting future research directions. Thereby, the chapter takes into account the gender differences in family business that influence behaviour and outcomes. The practical implications from this chapter are in terms of helping attract and retain women entrepreneurs to family businesses.

Women's entrepreneurship is evident in the business management literature but is considered an underdeveloped area in family business. This is evident in Marlow et al. (2009: 139) stating "only since the mid 1990s has the female entrepreneurship project gained credibility and respect". Therefore, there is a lack of development around the concept of women's entrepreneurs in family business. This is due to there being is a tendency to study women entrepreneurs in terms of gender differences without embedding them into the context of family business.

This chapter will focus on the ways gender relations affect family business, which provides useful insights into women entrepreneurs in family business. This allows for an understanding of the way women entrepreneurs act in family business and the constructions of family businesses as a form of gendered activity. This has meant that whilst women's entrepreneurship contributes to economic growth and development, there is little understanding about the role of gender in family business. The next section will further discuss the importance of focusing on women's entrepreneurship and family business.

Women entrepreneurship and family business

Often women entrepreneurs have to reconcile work with family in order to have a career. The appropriateness of women entrepreneurs in family business depends on the cultural and religious context. This has meant that there has been a trend towards recognizing gender roles in family business rather than biological sex in determining business decisions. In family business, there are both feminine and masculine traits needed in business dealings, the feminine traits including being caring and patient with employees and customers whilst the masculine traits involve being assertive and risk taking. Both male and female entrepreneurs need to possess creative and innovative behaviours when developing new family business ventures.

Women entrepreneurs tend to view their work and personal life as being in a combined network of relationships (Brush, 1992). This is in contrast to male entrepreneurs who typically consider separately their work and private life, particularly in terms of family businesses (Ratten, 2011). This influences how women behave in family businesses as they are more likely to engage in their local community as part of their social and business interactions.

There has been less criticism that studies on family business are gender biased and do not adequately take into account the role of women in family business. Moreover, there has been a tendency to focus on developed countries in family business studies, which may influence the understandings about the role of women in entrepreneurship. The lack of integration of women's entrepreneurship into family business makes this book necessary to develop new theoretical and practical insights.

Galloway et al. (2015) suggests that the masculine paradigm of entrepreneurship is limiting and should focus more on the role of women in entrepreneurship. The adoption of a feminine perspective to family business is necessary in shifting future research. Galloway et al. (2015: 684) states "the enactment of entrepreneurship as growth-oriented behaviour is culturally masculinized". Therefore, theoretically there are parallels to the bodies of knowledge on women's entrepreneurship and family business due to their unique characteristics and place in society.

Glover (2014: 279) states "gender bias in family business can stem from the broader societal attitudes and cultural expectations of their gendered roles in society". This gender bias has affected the role of women in family businesses particularly in terms of daughters ascending to power. Chant (2014: 297) states that there is a "comparative neglect of gender in family business literature and theory". In family businesses, women are sometimes overlooked in terms of managerial and leadership capabilities.

Contributions of this book

This book contributes to the scholarship on women's entrepreneurship and family business by envisioning a connection between these two sometimes disparate streams of literature. This helps to shift our understanding about the integral role women have within family business. The key findings of this book are that women in family business are important parts of the entrepreneurial capabilities. This book highlights the role of women as partners in family business by exploring the effects of women entrepreneurs in family business as a way to understand social changes. This may assist family business practitioners realize that gender has an effect on performance.

This book has raised some important issues about the topic of women entrepreneurs in family business. In doing so, the book has considered the role of gender in family business but also in terms of changing perceptions due to there being a growing interest in research focusing on how women entrepreneurs affect family business strategy. Whilst research has explored the role of women entrepreneurs, this book contributes to the literature by exploring how women working in family business affect overall performance.

This book has sought to provide insights into women's entrepreneurship and family businesses thereby shaping intentions regarding business development. In addition, this book addresses the gap in the literature about women's entrepreneurship by focusing on family business. This book posits that an understanding of gender issues in family business is required to aid women in achieving entrepreneurial success. The conclusions from this book provide a way for women entrepreneurs to be more productive in family businesses. This is due to it being important to make more women entrepreneurs achieve leadership positions in family business, since it fuels the need for more diversity in entrepreneurial activity.

There are fruitful insights from this book in terms of understanding the way women entrepreneurs behave in family businesses. The international composition of authors in this book gives a diverse array of views about the role of women entrepreneurs in family businesses. In all chapters, there is a common prevailing view that women entrepreneurs need specific attention in terms of how they function within family businesses. As there is currently a disconnection between women's entrepreneurship and family business, this book helps to detail the integral role both play in global economic development.

This book has contributed to our knowledge of women's entrepreneurship by identifying the need for women in family business. We argue that women entrepreneurship approaches can strengthen our understanding of family business. This is reflected in the approach of this book to focus both on women's entrepreneurship and family business, which seems more appropriate given current social conditions emphasizing both areas of research. This book on women's entrepreneurship and family business has presented new perspectives that will stimulate future policy debates. The collection of chapters bring together new international perspectives about the reciprocal relationship between women's entrepreneurship and family business.

There are a number of challenges women entrepreneurs encounter in family business and this book addresses some of these issues. Each chapter in the book deals with a different topic related to women's entrepreneurship in family business. This is due to there being a number of elements within women's entrepreneurship that relate to family business including new venture creation and small business management. These themes are discussed in this book as a way of understanding how gender affects family businesses.

Implications for practice

This chapter highlights the most promising research avenues for family entrepreneurship. Most research about family business tends to focus on economic goals like performance. The psychological components of family entrepreneurship deserve more attention than it has received due to its role in the sustainability of family businesses. Family businesses permeate society and serve as the cornerstone of a good community. Women entrepreneurship and family business research can help inform practice by suggesting possible innovative changes. This could be helping family businesses incorporate more women into their organizations by learning more innovative behaviours that increase financial performance. Often family businesses are focused on the day to day running of their businesses and do not have time to research behavioural psychology. This means women can teach family businesses about new behaviours that lead to better performance. This could be by outlining positive practices to promote well-being of women entrepreneurs in the family business. As family businesses deal with balancing new and old members it may be useful for them to implement a planning process towards encouraging more female participation. This could be conducted by giving examples of successful and unsuccessful women entrepreneurship in family businesses. Finally, there needs to be more diversity in the type of studies about family entrepreneurship. Most of the existing studies still tend to focus on North American approaches whilst particularly in Asia there are rapidly developing new forms of women entrepreneurs in family business. A more focused analysis of new forms of women in family entrepreneurship based on culture are welcomed and need to be conducted. This could include more descriptive analysis about how societal trends are affecting women in family entrepreneurship in different parts of the world. More sophisticated longitudinal analysis should be conducted to see how women in family entrepreneurship is adapting based on environmental contexts.

More research about family firm researcher centres is needed to understand their role in developing women's entrepreneurship. As most family firm research centres are located at universities it would be helpful to understand their role in the entrepreneurial ecosystem. The relationship between family businesses, universities, the government and society could be a useful addition to the field. More research is needed about the role of family business research centres in the community and promoting research. There has been an increase in the number of family business centres particularly in North America that have endowed research professor chairs. The ways universities encourage women in family businesses to be more entrepreneurial is needed. This will facilitate more research into family entrepreneurship and further develop this dynamic field.

Future research suggestions

A path forward for women entrepreneurs in family business is to consider the family as a sense of people with a belonging. This will contribute to social policy about how despite more people living by themselves they are connected in other ways. The field of family entrepreneurship needs to bring in the role of societal networking particularly in an online context to see the changing role of women in families. This chapter suggests that "the family" is a fluid and changing topic that depends on the view of an individual. Future research could continue and further theorize a novel definition of a family. As women's and family entrepreneurship scholars are tackling important new topics such as parental entrepreneurship, there still needs more work done. We need to consider how changing living and working situations are informing women in family businesses. If social practices are changing family compositions then the women's entrepreneurship in family business field has abundant opportunities for further research. There is also an ethical imperative to include diversity initiatives for women's entrepreneurship in family business.

This chapter paves the way for more research on women's entrepreneurship in family business in several ways. There are a number of issues that appear to be promising for women in family business. Future research can focus more on the family/women's entrepreneurship link to address new opportunities and help encourage more understanding of this important topic area. These issues are based around their significance to extending the link between the family and entrepreneurial behaviour. First, this chapter identifies the need for scholars to take a more contemporary approach to the definition of family. The recent societal acceptance of a more wider and inclusive approach to family transcending blood relations needs to be adapted by researchers. This will help to better understand how women in family businesses may differ based on the composition of family members. Currently most research about family business has been dominated by a definition of family implying blood relations that takes the form of a nuclear family. Future research needs to connect current forms of family to extend the research about women in family business. This will be helpful to extend our understanding of what a family means based on backgrounds or interests. Second, there needs to be more international comparisons of women's entrepreneurship in family business that take into account culture and religion. This chapter has suggested that there are different factors affecting women's entrepreneurship in family business depending on the international context. In emerging economies more research about women's entrepreneurship should be conducted to see whether the stage of economic development and societal attitudes impact business performance. As the majority of women's entrepreneurship and family business research has been conducted in developed countries it is important to see whether the same theories apply in emerging economies. This chapter provides justification of the importance of counting the stream of women's entrepreneurship in family business research into previously under researched international markets.

Third, a more detailed understanding about how technological innovations such as social media are affecting women's entrepreneurship in family business is needed. Due to social networking applications such as Facebook and Instagram it is becoming easier for smaller family businesses to reach international audiences. Further efforts are need to expand family business research into new technologies to see how they are changing business models. This will encourage more scholars to focus on emerging forms of women in family business that are becoming important in the international marketplace.

Finally, by analyzing the importance of women's entrepreneurship in family business research, there has been a number of research trends that merit more attention. The changing notion of the family derives investigation due to the importance of having definitional clarity about families. The research trends about women's entrepreneurship are related to technology but also traditional businesses that are sometimes overlooked in the literature. The goal of this chapter was to stimulate more interest into women's entrepreneurship in family business to build momentum on things topical of this research theme. The potential gaps to be filled in the women's entrepreneurship in family business literature were stated that highlighted a dynamic and emerging field.

Conclusion

This chapter has given an overview of the literature on women's entrepreneurship in family business, which is recognized as a key area of family business and entrepreneurship research. The research about women's entrepreneurship in family business was summarised and the rationale for studying this area stated. The importance of having an entrepreneurial culture towards women entrepreneurs in family businesses was highlighted as being increasingly important for the practice of global business.

References

Brush, C. (1992). Research on women business owners: Past trends, a new perspective and future directions. *Entrepreneurship Theory and Practice*, 17(4), 5–30.

Chant, S. (2014). Exploring the feminization of poverty in relation to women's work and home-based enterprise in slums of the Global South. *International Journal of Gender and Entrepreneurship*, 6(3), 296–316.

Galloway, L., Kapasi, I., and Sang, K. (2015). Entrepreneurship, leadership and the value of feminist approaches to understanding them. *Journal of Small Business Management*, 54(3), 683–697.

Glover, J. C. (2014). Gender, power and succession in family farm business. *International Journal of Gender and Entrepreneurship*, 6(3), 276–295.

Marlow, S., Henry, C., and Carter, S. (2009). Exploring the impact of gender upon women's business ownership. *International Small Business Journal*, 27(2), 139–148.

Ratten, V. (2011). A social perspective of sports-based entrepreneurship. *International Journal of Entrepreneurship and Small Business*, 10(3), 310–325.

Ratten, V. (2012). Sports entrepreneurship: Towards a conceptualisation. *International Journal of Entrepreneurial Venturing*, 4(1), 1–17.

Index

For Product Safety Concerns and Information please contact our EU
representative GPSR@taylorandfrancis.com
Taylor & Francis Verlag GmbH, Kaufingerstraße 24, 80331 München, Germany

www.ingramcontent.com/pod-product-compliance
Ingram Content Group UK Ltd.
Pitfield, Milton Keynes, MK11 3LW, UK
UKHW021007180425
457613UK00019B/840